STUDYING POPULAR MUSIC CULTURE

STUDYING POPULAR MUSIC CULTURE

Studying **the Media**

TIM WALL

Hodder Arnold

A MEMBER OF THE HODDER HEADLINE GROUP

LONDON

Distributed in the United States of America by
Oxford University Press Inc., New York

First published in Great Britain in 2003 by
Arnold, a member of the Hodder Headline Group,
338 Euston Road, London NW1 3BH

http://www.hoddereducation.com

Distributed in the United States of America by
Oxford University Press Inc.,
198 Madison Avenue, New York, NY10016

British Library Cataloguing in Publication Data
A catalogue record for this book is available from the British Library

Library of Congress Cataloging-in-Publication Data
A catalog record for this book is available from the Library of Congress

ISBN-10: 0 340 74180 5
ISBN-13: 978 0 340 74180 1

3 4 5 6 7 8 9 10

Typeset by Dorchester Typesetting Group Ltd, Dorchester, Dorset
Printed and bound in India by Replika Press Pvt. Ltd

Contents

Series Editor's Preface

One of the most visible characteristics of the changing nature of social experience and cultural life in the twentieth century was the rise and development of specialised institutions and systems dealing in the industrialised provision of information, amusement and entertainment. From the 1920s onwards, these generally became known as the 'mass media'. First publishing and the press, then film and cinema, recorded music, advertising, and then broadcasting – in radio and then television – all have made their marks on the historical transformations involved in the emergence of modern society and culture.

As the modern times of the twentieth century have changed gear into those of the twenty-first, the centrality of the media in contemporary social and cultural life becomes more and more critical. If you were a visiting anthropologist from Mars you would be forced to note that social life on earth is partly carried out in face-to-face, direct forms of communication and cultural exchange; in households, neighbourhoods and localities and in their private and public spaces and variations. But, as a Martian visitor, you might also conclude that if these continue to provide both the bedrock and the dynamo for modern cultures, they are also more and more interwoven with forms and networks of *mediated* communication and culture. Those that come from 'the outside' – like the Martian – from beyond direct, unmediated, daily experience, from dispersed, national, global and virtual locations. These systems – especially radio, television, advertising and the Internet – are now absolutely fundamental to the textures of modern life, etched into experience and aspiration. More than ever, they strive to establish forms of 'intimacy – at a distance', and they *saturate* and colonise our time, culture, imagery, opinion, money and attention. We are not, however, entirely made up of what we watch, listen to, read, or log on to. And, we do not have to be visiting from Mars, to be involved in the critical project of Media Studies.

The *Studying the Media* series is designed to provide an important foundation and springboard for student work in this fast moving and dynamic field of enquiry and education. It has been developed from the experience and success of the book *Studying the Media*, now in its third edition. The series seeks to chart current developments and scholarship regarding the full range of media sectors and industries, relating this to matters of historical or cultural significance or concern. Above all, the series aims to do this in an accessible, enthusiastic and engaging style, mindful of the needs of student readers. Current contributions to the series include important studies of Radio (2000) and Film (2001). This, the third contribution to the series, examines popular music, and forthcoming titles will address advertising, television, new media, news and popular culture.

Studying Popular Music Culture, makes a very valuable addition to the series. It engages with the soundtracks of modern life – from the ambient public spaces we wander into and out of – to the many and diverse moments of private, selected musical consumption. Popular music has been an inescapable and omnipresent feature of cultural life, identity and generation from the latter part of the nineteenth century onwards, when music began to extend out from the immediate confines of the live performance or concert, as technical systems of reproduction – sheet music, cylinder, disc, tape, cassette, CD – allowed the mediation of the original. The music industry, radio broadcasting, cinema and then television have all played their part in making music an essential, ever present and taken-for-granted feature of modern life. If *Studying Popular Music Culture* enables you to begin to systematically analyse, reflect upon and understand the place and forms of music in modern mediated environments, it will have succeeded. Just listen . . . as you read!

Tim O'Sullivan
Leicester
July 2003.

Acknowledgements

I would like to thank the many people who have helped and supported me in the development, writing and production of this book. In particular to say thank you to Nadine, Carys and Matty whose forbearance counted for a lot.

I would also like to recognise the contributions of some significant individuals: Tim O'Sullivan for suggesting the idea and supporting its development; Lesley Riddle, Alexia Chan, Colin Goodlad and Lynn Brown at Hodder Arnold; Mark Duffett for reading it all and making so many thought-provoking suggestions; all my UCE colleagues present and past for their support, but especially Paul Long, Ben Calvert and Sharon Wheeler, who have made significant differences to the ideas and writing; more widely, all those people I have ever talked to about music, but especially to Dave Hesmondhalgh, Dave Swann for ideas on stars, and Michael Green who has always encouraged my work.

Those students who contributed to my modules in popular music, radio and popular culture have also made a big difference. Thank you for taking such an interest in this project, for trying out most of the activities, giving me so many interesting examples, and making me think again.

Sara Harris and the UCE Media Content Lab have been invaluable in organising the original photographs used in this book. I would like to thank Edward James Stokes and Stefan Klenke for taking my ideas and turning them into striking images, and Kay Blackwell and Pru Fiddy for allowing me to use their photographs.

INTRODUCTION

Definitions and approaches

Popular music has been called the soundtrack to our lives: we can hear it on the radio, on our CD player, on the tape in our walkman, piped into shops, and during television adverts and programmes. Like the soundtrack to a film it plays an important part in cultivating our moods and feelings. We listen to it because it is a source of pleasure, excitement and passion. Music is also a key topic of media attention. It is written, criticised and enthused about, while music-makers are photographed and their opinions sought, music videos are broadcast, and pop shows present bands playing live or miming. These experiences are not only part of our culture, they are also part of the culture of the record industry, which uses them to promote the music they have produced. This relationship between music, the industry, and consumers is what constitutes popular music culture. The purpose of this book is to introduce you to ways of studying this culture.

 Keep a diary for a weekday and a weekend day, noting down all the occasions you come into contact with popular music. Compare your popular music contact with that recorded by others.

What do we mean by popular music culture?

Before we start, though, we should get a few things straight. What do we mean by popular music culture? If you look for a literal definition, popular music is just music that is popular. However, the term popular can mean very different things. It is one of a collection of words that Raymond Williams termed 'keywords' (Williams 1976), which are at the centre of our attempt to understand our social world, but also have multiple definitions. 'Popular' simultaneously has three different senses. In one sense popular things are widely liked. In another, popular things have poor cultural value and are associated with lower levels of education (as in the popular press). In the third sense, popular things belong to ordinary people of a society and express their interests and concerns.

These three very different definitions indicate that the concept of the popular is one that is used in different ways, by different people and from different viewpoints. This is reflected in the way people discuss and argue about popular music. Popular music is associated with the music that sells the most CDs and the stars with a large fan following. To others it is the poorest type of 'dumbed-down' music that is easy to listen to and enjoyed by people who know little about, or do not appreciate, more complex music. Finally, though, popular music is seen in very positive terms as any type of music made and enjoyed by a particular scene as a way of celebrating its distinctive identity.

More often, you will find popular music is used as a wide category for a series of types of music that include pop (itself a contraction of the term popular music), and a whole range of other forms from ambient through indie and techno to world beat. In this book the term is used to cover both of these sets of ideas – part of culture that is argued about, and a broad category of music types – but it is not simply defined by these ideas. What is most striking about the attempts to define popular music is that so many different definitions have been produced (see Middleton 1990, 3–7; Shuker 1994, 6–10).

This range of definitions indicates that we are not dealing with a simple thing to be studied, but a number of processes of definition. Popular music *is what it has come to be defined as*, and, in part, our study encompasses the processes that have produced these competing definitions. These processes take place in the institutions of our culture, in the places we listen to, watch, buy and dance to music, and in the record companies and media organisations that produce and distribute it. Interestingly, 'institution' and 'culture' are two more of Williams' key words, and these too have a range of meanings. Institutions are legally constituted organisations – like Sony Music or Radio 1 – but they are also fields of custom and practice, while 'culture' signals both the artefacts of the upper classes and a more general 'way of life' (Williams 1976).

The institutions of popular music culture are to some degree all centred on the production and distribution of recorded popular music. Record companies create and distribute recorded music, and radio stations use it as the basis of their programming. It was the ability to record music that transformed the way music was produced, how it could be distributed, and ultimately how and what we could consume. Today you can listen to recorded music in a vast range of formats from older shellac and vinyl discs, through various tape-based systems, to modern digital forms like CDs and MP3 files. The term 'record' is used throughout the book to refer to these different formats of recorded music.

Popular music culture is used to mean:

- a set of ways of making, consuming and thinking about music

- the economic and technological practices ordered by those ways of doing and thinking

- the sounds and images created by those practices.

Centrally this book will be looking at music produced by a highly organised music industry and distributed by an equally structured system of media networks, constituted as a set of sounds and images, consumed by people who make it a significant part of their lives and their own identity, but derided by others. These are the qualities of popular music that make it worth studying.

Collect together current examples of statements about popular music that show different definitions being used. A range of examples from textbooks, the general media, the specialist music press and internet discussion boards would make good contrasts. How different are they? Are they easily categorised into the different ways of defining popular examined above?

How should we study popular music culture?

This book aims to develop your skills in the *scholarly* study of popular music. Most of you will be reading this book because you are already interested in and enjoy modern popular music. You will therefore already know quite a lot about certain aspects of popular music. However, fan knowledge is not the same as scholarly knowledge. One of things we want to study is this very fan knowledge: how it is produced and distributed, and how it allows fans to make music meaningful. Your existing knowledge is very important and valuable, but scholarly study is not about simply reproducing your existing likes and dislikes, or reproducing the journalistic ways of commenting on popular music and stars you are used to. Scholarly study deepens your understanding of popular music culture based upon a series of activities:

- researching facts and existing theories

- using theories to develop tools for analysing texts and cultural practices

- apply the theories to understand the facts and using the facts to test the theories

- developing ideas/theories of your own.

That will mean finding things out about music and its history, the record industry and music fans, trying to work out why one type of music sounds different from another or one star appeals to one group and not another. Building on this, it is possible to make arguments about many different parts of popular music culture. To do this it is necessary to engage with what other researchers have written. Different popular music scholars, just like different fans, have different ways of understanding popular music, and we need to identify these different ways, and test them out against our own fan knowledge and things we find out through our own research and analysis. This is not to say that fans and scholars are just the same. The best scholars reveal facets of popular music we were previously unaware of, analyse popular music culture and develop theories we can apply to help us understand in greater depth. However, both fans and scholars are active within what we can call the discourses of popular music culture.

Discourses are the kinds of language that we use to talk about popular music, the sorts of social practices of listening, watching and buying we use to consume music, and the assumptions and beliefs that lie behind our use (see Mills 1997). These practices and their underlying assumptions are often so institutionalised that they are simply taken for granted. Our job as scholars of popular music, then, is to analyse the conditions and practices of the production, textual form and consumption of music to understand how it is institutionalised, what its hidden assumptions are, and how the practices produce its meanings. The definition of discourse outlined by the poststructuralist philosopher and historian Michel Foucault (Foucault 1972, 49) can be adapted for our specific study and expressed as *the knowledges and practices of popular music that constitute it as a set of cultural objects.* The following case study demonstrates what this means.

CASE STUDY CASE STUDY **The Charts**

So central and 'obvious' are these lists (i.e. the charts) that the term used to describe them has lost most of its connection to the rank order list of the best-selling records of a specific week on which they are based. Behind this practice of listing and publishing sales of individual records is an assumption that sales of records are important. Sales are obviously important to record company workers, but these lists have been centrally important to music consumers for at least 40 years. Television and radio chart shows generate some of the largest audiences; music magazines and websites make prominent use of charts; and the chart positions of our favourite music are for some of us a key discussion point. The discursive practice at play here contains the assumption that more sales = better. Of course not everyone thinks that. Some music fans think that the higher up in the charts a record is, the worse it is. This is also a discursive practice, but one with the assumption that music is corrupted by its association with obvious commercial activity.

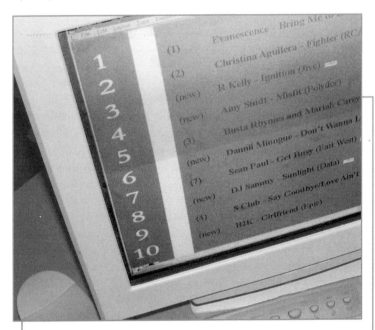

FIGURE 0.1. The chart listings of record sales have a significant place in popular music culture
Photo: Tim Wall

The discursive practices of the charts are magnified in radio chart shows, which share the assumption that more sales = better, and never give the suggestion that music is corrupted by its association with obvious commercial activity. They privilege one set of assumptions over another. The programmes' common structure reproduces the hierarchy of the chart itself, telling a story of change from those spent forces and rising hopefuls to those that have reached chart-defined success. They emphasise new-ness, and changing hierarchies. The style and tempo of the programme signifies increasing excitement.

Record a chart show, and analyse the structure and presentation between records. How are the structure and presentation devices of the show used to create the meanings identified in the case study?

But the practices of popular music culture are not only revealing of hidden assumptions and values, they also actually define what popular music is. In Foucauldian terms the charts not only constitute a practice which assumes that commercial success = cultural success, but they *define* popular music as being music that is commercially successful. Equally the style of the chart shows *defines* popular music as new and exciting.

Of course a definition of popular music as new, exciting and commercially successful music promotes the interests of the record companies. Any particular definition of 'what popular music is' gives greater power to some people than others. If popular music *is* commercially successful music, the idea gives more power to commercial interests; if popular music *is* the music of communities of people; then it makes that community more powerful.

Using ideas of discourse and cultural practice allows us to think about what we *know about*, *say about* and *do with* popular music, not simply as an exercise of individual taste or opinion, but as part of a cultural construction that produces power relationships. We need to understand that when we talk about popular music we *constitute it as a particular cultural object*. That does not mean we have to ignore what we already think about popular music, but as scholars we need to understand the cultural implications of what we think. Likewise, we should treat what others say and do in the same way. We want to understand why they think and say different things, consume in different ways, and constitute popular music as a very different cultural object.

Using this book

This book covers the main areas of the study of popular music culture. Part 1 aims to develop thinking about the histories of popular music that have been told. Part 2 focuses on the industries and institutions that organise and sell popular music. The third part explores the ways in which it is possible to analyse pieces of popular music and understand what they mean and how they create representations. Part 4 looks at popular music culture from the fans' point of view and examines how we listen, dance to and buy music. The final part offers three case studies of how to analyse an aspect of popular music culture, and some reflection on the study of popular music culture as a whole.

Each part is based on detailed approaches to studying one dimension of popular music culture. Although they each draw heavily on existing scholarship, they are written to encourage you to undertake your own research, apply theories to your own examples, and to reflect critically on your own music fandom and existing scholarship. Each time I use someone else's work, I indicate this by naming the author and giving the date of the published work; you can follow this up by using the full details listed in the Bibliography at the end of the book. There is also a list of recommended reading at the end of each chapter. You can find out a lot from studying popular music through this form of secondary research. The authors have usually spent a long time studying the topic, and by metaphorically standing on their shoulders, you can see further. However, there is no substitute for developing your own skills as a primary researcher and analyst. Each chapter therefore includes exercises linked to the ideas outlined, which encourage you to start applying theories and finding out about popular music culture for yourself. Also included in each chapter are a number of case studies, either drawn from the work of other scholars or my own research and analysis, which demonstrate how you could conduct a study of your own. The case studies in Part 5 of the book show how you could integrate the techniques developed in the whole book into a focused study of one aspect of popular music culture.

Further reading

Hesmondhalgh, David and Negus, Keith 2002: 'Popular Music Studies: Meaning, Power and Value' in D. Hesmondhalgh and K. Negus (eds) 2002: *Popular Music Studies*. Arnold.

Middleton, Richard 1990: *Studying Popular Music*. Open University Press.

Part ONE:
Histories

Popular music lends itself particularly well to historical study; different styles of music have clear paths of development, and influences can be mapped out over the years of the twentieth century. A grasp of the history of the music, its listeners and the institutions that produce it provides us with an explanation of why music is as it is today. In addition the study is interesting in itself because it can reveal how and why music-making and consumption were different in the past from how they are now. For this reason a good historical analysis of popular music will attempt to look at the processes of development and change as well as drawing out principles of analysis that can be used for any period of music history, including our own.

Studying history involves the study of both primary and secondary material. Because the music industry and much music consumption is focused on the recording of music performance there is a large amount of primary material available for study through records and videos; associated films, memorabilia and media reporting are archived and often commercially available today. The importance of the history of popular music is signalled by the large number of books (both general and academic) on the subject to be found on the library bookshelf. Because of this abundance of secondary material the aim of the next four chapters is not to provide a definitive history of popular music, but to indicate what conclusions can be drawn from analysing existing histories. This will demonstrate how to actively read existing histories and how to research neglected ones.

This part is divided into four chapters. The first will examine the ways that authors have told the story of popular music, and the differences and commonalities of these histories. The chapter then goes on to look at some of the criticisms of these existing histories, and offers a model for undertaking an historical analysis of popular music culture. Chapters 2 and 3 look in detail at two parts of this model, so that you can understand the approach in some detail. The fourth chapter presents case studies to show how this analysis can be applied in practice.

CHAPTER ONE

Constructing Histories of Popular Music

This chapter examines how histories of popular music have been constructed, along with some of the criticisms of these conventional approaches. Drawing the most useful elements from the existing secondary accounts of popular music's past, as well as responding to the critiques of these histories, the chapter ends with a model for approaching a historical analysis.

Histories construct a narrative of the past in which the significance of certain events is emphasised over others, and ideas of cause and effect are woven into an unfolding story. In histories of popular music these narratives are usually built around musical artists, genres of music and the social worlds in which they operated, and the histories are given a strong sense of chronology through the use of key dates. However, for all these similarities of style, one of the first things that strikes the reader flicking through books on popular music history is that they often cover quite different narratives, with diverse musicians and genres highlighted. Even when they are offered as general histories, they can focus on very different periods of time. A comparison of three such books reveals this clearly (see Table 1.1 on page 10).

Comparing the three lists, it is apparent that each book constructs a very different history of popular music. This is in part because the books are focused on different questions and make different arguments. Clarke's history contrasts what he considers the two golden decades of popular music, starting in 1940, with what he sees as the fall of popular music in the present day. Friedlander traces the origins and then dominance of Rock music in the 1960s and 1970s. Chambers focuses on British

	Donald Clarke (1995): *The Rise and Fall of Popular Music*	Paul Friedlander (1996): *Rock & Roll: A Social History*	Iain Chambers (1985) *Urban Rhythms: Pop Music and Popular Culture*
1840–1900	minstrelsy, vaudeville		
1910–1920	Tin Pan Alley, Ragtime	blues	
1920–1930	jazz		
1940–1950	Broadway, big band bebop and cool jazz	rhythm & blues	
1955–1960	rock & roll skiffle	doo-wop, rock & roll	blues, rock & roll,
1960–1965	folk, rock and soul	60s pop, Beatles,	blues revival, Mersey beat soul, mods
1965–1970		Rolling Stones, Dylan, soul, Motown	rock, folk
1970–1975	teenyboppers	guitar rock	singer-songwriters heavy metal, glam rock
1975–1980	disco, punk	punk rock	funk, northern soul, reggae, punk
1980 to present		MTV	electro-pop, new pop

TABLE 1.1 Schematic of three histories of popular music

popular culture and music from 1956 to the early 1980s.

It is valuable to have an overall sense of what music was being made in different periods and the schematic of the content of these three books is a good starting point. However as this simple exercise demonstrates there is not one history of popular music, but many different ones. As well as differing in their styles of scholarship or writing, each book also differs in the particular history that it constructs. It is important therefore that we ask questions about why they highlight particular people, styles and moments, and what sorts of histories they construct.

Produce an analysis of other books on the history of popular music. Select three histories of popular music from your library. Using the contents page and the chapter subheadings produce a schematic of the dates and key musicians and musics used to tell that story of popular music. What story do they tell? What periods do they emphasise? Do they see popular music as progress or decline? How important are non-musical events in the story? What role is assigned to the music industry?

For all their different emphases on different musicians, though, most histories of popular music share common features in the way they are constructed. First, they often outline their history as a series of dramatic disruptions. Second, they draw a clear distinction between a 'mainstream' musical culture and a marginalised 'alternative' one (usually they champion new alternative music cultures). Finally, they emphasise the idea of musical roots, so that each new musical form is understood in terms of earlier precedents. Understanding these characteristics will sharpen your ability to critically read and research other histories.

Significant moments in a history of disruption

Like the vast majority of other such histories, those listed in Table 1.1 are built on types of music and artists understood as being recognisably different from those forms that preceded them. That is, these are histories of change and disruption. New music is presented as revolutionary in some way, and it is the abrupt changes in popular music that each author wants to contextualise or celebrate. Of course, there are also other narrative components – in the examples in Table 1.1, for instance, Clarke uses a narrative of decline, while Friedlander in contrast uses a narrative of maturity – but the notion of abrupt and significant new musical forms is central to almost all such histories. However, we should not see each disruption as of equal significance. When dealing with a moment of disruption you need to ask questions about the particular historical significance of that moment. For instance: In what ways did particular artists change the music? Was the music of these artists widely liked, or did it in some way articulate the 'voice' of a particular group or subculture? Why are these events significant: because they show a change in music-making, or in music consumption, or in the mediation of the music?

As you investigate various representations of each historical moment you will discover that there is no consistency in the selection of music or artists that populate these histories. For instance, Clarke selects two types of music for the 1920s and 1930s: Tin Pan Alley and ragtime, but they are selected for very different reasons. While Tin Pan Alley is the name given to the mainstream of commercialised songwriting that dominated music publishing and then film soundtracks and recorded music for urban white Americans through the first half of the century, ragtime was a short-lived music with minority appeal. It remains significant because it is one of the earliest examples of a musical form rooted in African-American culture that gained popularity with a white American and European audience.

We must be aware, then, of two important points. First, each historical moment was as musically and culturally eclectic and diverse as today's popular musical culture. Second, each historical moment was not necessarily dominated by the music or artists identified with that moment by historians. A particular musical form may have significance for a particular historian not because of its role at that time, but in some future moment. For instance, the blues music of the 1940s was not particularly influential on the mainstream of American and European popular music at the time, but became hugely influential on the popular music of the 1950s and 1960s. In almost all cases the music identified with an era was not the best-selling, nor the most exposed in the wider media, but is significant in some other way that the author often assumes (even if it is not always explicit).

The mainstream and the marginalised underground

Most histories emphasise musical forms that at their moment of origin had small followings, and that were often produced on the margins of the record industry. Dave Harker has pointed out that the best-selling records of the late 1960s – a period often written about as dominated by the classic period of rock – were soundtrack albums from film and theatrical musicals like *The Sound of Music* (Harker 1992). In the 1960s rock-based musical forms were named 'the underground' to distinguish them from the forms of music that dominated record releases and sales, radio plays and film and television appearances. Although the term 'underground' has moved in and out of general usage, and of course has been used to define some very different sounds, the concept remains a very useful one to understand the history of popular music.

The emphasis in histories on less prominent sounds can demonstrate this quite simply by examining the sales charts for particular years highlighted in the histories. For instance, here (in Table 1.2) for comparison are the artists in the British top 20 charts of single (45s) record sales in the same week of 1957, 1967, 1977 and 1987.

	1957	1967	1977	1987
1	Tommy Steele	Tom Jones	David Soul	Jackie Wilson
2	Guy Mitchell	Monkees	Showaddywaddy	Housemartins
3	Malcolm Vaughan	Seekers	Abba	Madonna
4	Frankie Vaughan	Who	Johnny Mathis	Europe
5	Johnnie Ray	Donovan	Stevie Wonder	A-ha
6	Bing Crosby/Grace Kelly	Dave Dee	Mike Oldfield	Alison Moyet
7	Eddie Fisher	Troggs	Tina Charles	Erasure
8	Elvis Presley	Cliff Richard	Julie Covington	Communards
9	Pat Boon	Val Doonican	Smokie	Oran 'Juice' Jones
10	Bill Haley	Supremes	10cc	Gregory Abbott
11	Frankie Vaughan	Kinks	Paul Nicholas	Gap Band
12	Fats Domino	Four Tops	ELO	Bon Jovi
13	Elvis Presley	Georgie Fame	Status Quo	Dexy's Midnight Runners
14	Frankie Lane	Move	Queen	Berlin
15	Frankie Lane	Cat Stevens	Barry Biggs	Genesis
16	Garry Miller	Wayne Fontana	Yvonne Elliman	Elkie Brooks
17	Elvis Presley	Easybeats	Rose Royce	Jaki Graham
18	Jimmy Young	Cream	Kursaal Flyers	Eurythmics
19	Pat Boone	Jimmy Ruffin	Boney M	Status Quo
20	Mitchell Torok	Temptations	Steely Dan	Pretenders

TABLE 1.2 Sample singles charts for the second week in January in 1957, 1967, 1977 and 1987
Source: Rees *et al.*, 1995

In most histories these years are constructed as emblematic of rock & roll with Elvis Presley, psychedelic rock (and maybe soul) with the Beatles (and Otis Redding), punk (and maybe disco) with the Sex Pistols (and the Bee Gees) and house with DJ artists like Farley 'Jackmaster' Funk. My analysis of these charts suggests that even by the most generous interpretation there is never more than 25 per cent of each type of music to be found in the sample chart for that year. In fact, it is mainstream pop music that is dominant in each chart, covering between 50 and 75 per cent of the artists in each sample chart. Interestingly there were the same number of rock artists charting in the sample chart of 1987 as 1967, and while it is possible to identify five rock & roll singles in 1957, four rock and four soul singles in 1967, three disco singles in 1977 and five dance-based singles in 1987, the vast majority of them relied very heavily on the conventions of mainstream pop. Additionally, in January 1977 there were no punk singles at all and in January 1987 there was no house music (although both styles are apparent in the lower top 40 later in the those years).

Of course it could be countered that rock & roll, soul and house were in 1957, 1967 and 1987 respectively American phenomena, or that psychedelic rock was usually issued on LPs rather than singles, or that punk and house were issued by small independent companies not well represented in the high-street shops used to construct the charts, and so were unlikely to be prominent in a top 20 singles chart. These are all telling points, but they merely reinforce the fact that however significant these were as cultural and musical phenomena, at these times at least, these forms of music were being produced and distributed on the margins of the record industry, and purchased by a minority of music consumers.

The historians of popular music culture, then, emphasise forms of popular music and artists that were not dominant in popular music culture of the time. Rather, they emphasise new sounds and styles of artists. The historical story is that they are part of a new type of music that starts in the margins and moves into the mainstream. Its existence in the margins is seen as significant because the music was associated with other significant social or cultural movements, or because the performers introduced radically different forms of music-making. A music's adoption by the mainstream is presented as a decline in its social relevance or vigour. Rock & roll, rock, punk and house are all presented in this way in histories of popular music.

We can not read these histories, then, as accounts of what was happening in popular music culture at a particular time, but as ways of highlighting certain values (those of innovation or social significance) over others, and of processes through which new musical or social ideas move from a minority interest to have a place in the mainstream. This distinction between the underground and the mainstream is itself an oversimplification, and the processes of change in popular music culture are far more complex. Nevertheless, as will become clearer in the rest of this book, the concepts of the 'mainstream' and the 'margins' does allow us to understand that there are differences between different parts of popular music culture. Different parts of the music industry and the wider media are organised around different patterns of music production and promotion. And different social groups give significant meanings to different ways of buying, listening and dancing. In the historical dimension this mainstream/margins distinction allows us to see how the sounds and meanings of music relate to these sociological patterns, and how these elements have changed over time. As such the idea is often linked to the notion that histories explain the roots of a type of music.

Musical roots

The idea of change constitutes a central and inevitable characteristic of written histories of popular music. As I have already suggested one of the reasons that these histories examine just one particular type of music in one time period is that they can then highlight a process of musical development. Marginal musics – particularly those established before the 1950s – are examined simply because they are seen as constituting the roots of a later style. This idea of musical roots is the final characteristic of popular music histories. The titles of many histories cannot help but belie this approach. *From Soul to Blues in Black America* (Haralambos 1974), *From Blues to Rock* (Hatch and Millward 1987), *Roots of the Blues* (Charters 1982), *Origins of Popular Style* (van der Merwe 1989) are all good examples.

Simon Frith opened his influential book on popular music, *Sound Effects* (Frith 1983), with such a study of 'rock roots'. In it he examines rock music as 'the result of an ever changing combination of independently developed musical elements, each of which carries its own cultural message' (Frith 1983, 15; see also van der Merwe 1989). The key roots Frith identifies are black music, country music, folk music and pop music. However, we should not just understand this approach to mean that the sound of one form of popular music becomes the basis for another, later, form. As Frith and van der Merwe point out, while historians of popular music often neglect the importance of the form and sound of music, the meaning of popular music is not found in a strict study of musical form, but in an understanding of each music's 'cultural message' (Frith 1983). This is a message that is not simply to be found in the music's notes or structure, nor simply in the sounds inherited from its root musics, but in the way that these forms and sounds are produced and utilised in the social practices of music-making and music consumption, and in the way that musicians, listeners and dancers actively create the music's meanings. These issues are discussed further in Chapter 13.

The concept of musical roots is a useful idea as long as we extend the concept of influence beyond that of the sounds produced by different musical forms. Frith's list of black, country, folk and pop musics refers to more than just different types of popular music sounds, and their influence on other forms of popular music at different times involves far more than a new generation copying the sound of the music produced in an earlier age.

X 1.2 Using the books you selected for Exercise 1.1 identify why the author selected the particular style of music or artist for his/her history. Can you ascertain whether these forms were widely popular at the time, or constituted a marginal taste among consumers? Are they presented as a musical form that became the roots of a later style? How does the author explain the processes of development and influence? Is the author concerned with non-musical factors? If so, what are they?

FIGURE 1.1 Behind every popular music performance is a history of influences
Photo: Stefan Klenke

Criticisms of existing histories of popular music

Thinking through the issues already raised highlights the point that pop history is authored. There is no single history, or definitive description or analysis of music-making and consumption. Rather there are acts of interpretation, and arguments constructed about each music's meaning, causes and effects. However, as Keith Negus (1996) has pointed out, there has been a dominant perspective in popular music histories. This is the idea of the 'rock era' as a process of development in popular music from the mid-1950s to the late 1970s.

It is certainly the case that within academic and journalistic accounts the terms 'rock & roll' and 'rock' have been used as synonyms for popular music, and as ways of making value distinctions between forms of popular music. For Negus this 'rock imperialism' (1996, 162) has meant that many popular music scholars have interpreted musical history as a set of significant moments that first created, then sustained and developed, and finally led to the decline of the rock era. In these consensus descriptions of the 'rock era', popular musical culture has been seen to be reinvigorated by new sounds and ideas from the marginalised underground. This of course assumes that all musics other than rock are simply raw material for rock's development, or musics which by their existence serve to define the superiority of rock. It is for that reason that, within these histories, rock is widely contrasted with pop – a 'watered down, blander' music (Shuker 1998, 226).

Motti Regev has attempted to rethink these ideas, rejecting the idea of a rock era, musical decline and a rock/pop division. Instead, he argues, all the prominent genres of contemporary popular music share a 'rock aesthetic' that guides the creative production of popular music. He suggests that this aesthetic not only produces a canon of great recordings, but two distinct processes of musical change – commercialism and avant-gardism – which can be used to understand the history of popular music (Regev 2002). However, this approach still seeks to find a central story to explain how music changes, and how it relates to the culture in which it is produced.

Histories based upon the idea of a 'rock era' or a 'rock aesthetic' fall neatly into a mode of historical explanation known as 'totalising'. The most sustained criticism of this sort of approach has come from the French philosopher and historian Michel Foucault. Madan Sarup has contrasted the 'totalising history' with Foucault's approach thus:

> Whereas traditional or 'total' history inserts events into grand explanatory systems and linear processes, celebrates great moments and individuals and seeks to document a point of origin [Foucault's] analysis attempts to analyse and preserve the singularity of events, turns away from the spectacular in favour of the discredited, the neglected and a whole range of phenomena which have been denied a history.

> (Sarup 1993, 59)

Although neither Foucault nor Sarup specifically had histories of popular music in mind these comments seem very telling for our study. It is not surprising that writers who grew up in the 1960s and 1970s, and whose own lives were transformed by their love of rock music should have carried these views over into their scholarship and writing. At its best, this writing is informed and interesting (see for instance Marcus 1975; Garofalo 1992; Grossberg 1992b). However, while such approaches are valuable for us in appreciating a particular, historically located, way of understanding popular music, they have also produced a 'grand explanatory system' for understanding popular music. As Negus has pointed out:

> For many music fans across the world, there are numerous sounds that cannot be rock and there is much music being listened to by the 'youth market' which would be described using a label other than rock, such as rap, merengue, soul, reggae, cumbia, country, techno, and so on.

> (Negus 1996, 161)

Sarah Thornton (1990) has argued that historical importance has been assigned to music or music-makers on the basis of four criteria: sales figures, biographical interest, critical acclaim and media coverage. Each, she proposes, has led to a particular strategy of writing history. So sales figures are used as the basis for lists of pop's past, biographical studies tend to personalise complex cultural processes, critical judgements are used to produce canons of 'the best' music, and historical media sources have been treated as 'windows' on the past, rather than texts that construct and mediate the events and values they record. Not only is each of these strategies prominent in the 'rock era' histories, they also produce an emphasis on history as a simple timeline, full of key moments and personalities who drive change. These are the very qualities of the totalising history.

There are some important lessons to learn here about how we read the histories of other writers and how to write histories of our own. While 'rock era' histories subordinate all information to the story of 'roots, rise, maturity and then decline' a more fruitful approach is to try and understand points in popular music's past in their own terms. That involves using the sources that tell us about this past not simply to give us information but also to interpret the significance of that moment and the values it represents. It is encouraging to see that more recent studies of popular music, often by younger writers, have tended to understand popular music in different ways. Totalising histories of popular music are far less common from the 1990s onwards, and analyses of practices of particular types of (usually contemporary) music are more prevalent. In part this could be understood as an attempt by a new generation of music culture theorists to investigate areas neglected by the rock era theorists, particularly to study the 'singularity' of contemporary practices (see for instance Gilbert and Pearson 1999).

However, these analyses of specific contemporary music cultures produce their own limitations, especially in terms of the way we make sense of the present in relation to the past. In particular it represents a view – often only implicit – that contemporary popular music is more fragmented than it was in the 'rock era'. This view is obviously in part based upon reading the histories produced in previous totalising approaches, and contrasting the perception that each period of the past is dominated by one style of music, while today we have many different styles.

The 'rock era' theorists often share this idea of fragmentation themselves. Brian Longhurst, for instance, has characterised the last two decades of the twentieth-century music culture as separated from earlier periods by punk rock:

> [Punk] represented an attempt first to regain the spirit of the early days of rock 'n' roll in its desire for independence and the short three minute song; and second to reintegrate the rock and pop forms which had been increasingly split during the 1970s. It also marks the beginning of the fragmentation that was rapidly to develop in the 1980s and 90s.

> (Longhurst 1995, 111)

However, as the next three chapters will show, historical analysis does not support the idea that popular music is now more fragmented whereas, in the past, it was much more homogeneous. This view is the product of totalising histories in which the domination of rock music from the late 1960s to the early 1980s is seen to provide a homogeneous popular music culture, and its decline as leading to fragmentation. It is far more productive to interrogate the ideas that shape historical accounts to ask why moments in popular music history are presented as part of a coherent pattern of progress (or decline). We can then engage more directly with moments of popular music's past as at all times fragmented, complex and distinctive.

X 1.3

To understand these criticisms of existing histories of popular music it is helpful to again analyse two or three that are available to you in the library. First, can you identify the degree to which they build that history around the idea of the 'rock era'? This can be done by examining chapter headings and subheadings. My outline of three books at the start of this chapter (Table 1.1) reveals that Friedlander's (1996) approach is a classic of this kind. Second, can you see how the history constructs the birth, development and decline of the rock era? This requires greater attention to different sections, but it will increase your ability to critically read other authors' arguments. You will find that some writers create totalising histories even if they do not play so centrally on the idea of the rock era – Clarke's (1995) book is representative of this kind – and it is productive to analyse why and how they periodise and characterise popular music's history.

A model for analysing popular music history

The central argument of this chapter is that we should not use existing histories of popular music as defining stories of popular music's development, but as resources that we can utilise together with other forms of research to understand particular historical moments – including the present – as diverse musical cultures. When we are dealing with histories of popular music, then, we need to identify the discourse of the author of the history, as well as tease out the discourses of those involved in the historical moment itself. As Dick Bradley has argued:

> the very constituting of rock as a body of musical practices is largely the work of writers, of talkers, of listeners reflecting discursively on the music and setting a context for their own and other people's listening and making processes.
>
> (Bradley 1992, 31)

We are therefore not just seeking to understand a history of events, but a history of thinking about popular music, its interpretation and evaluation.

To do so we need to recast the characteristics of existing histories in a manner that takes account of the criticisms outlined above. This approach has three aspects. First, we should aim to examine moments in the history of music culture, but rather than choosing just those seen as significant through a totalising theory, we should start with single moments and then seek to understand their significance. Second, we should keep a sense of the mainstream and the margins, but we should seek to examine how they interact as discourses of musical culture and how they make each other meaningful at any particular moment. Finally, we should be interested in the cultural material out of which a particular practice is built, but we should see this as more than a simple idea of musical roots, and instead as the musical and cultural repertoire that is available for particular music culture practices.

These three aspects of historical analysis can be developed into an analytical model that can be used to guide an analysis of moments of musical history. The model emphasises the relationships between four key musical and cultural repertoires, and their interaction with three important social, economic and technical factors that allow us to understand the immediate society in which music-making, distribution and consumption take place. Diagrammatically the model could be represented as shown in Figure 1.2.

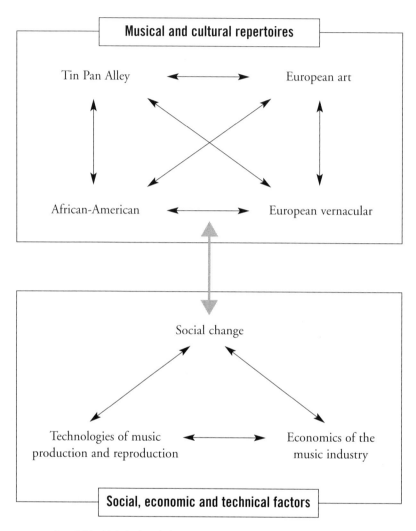

FIGURE 1.2 A model for historical analysis

The idea of musical and cultural repertoires is examined in detail in Chapter 2. The other dimension of the model, looking at the social, economic and technological factors involved in moments of popular music history, is developed in Chapter 3. The fourth chapter will demonstrate in three case studies how this model can be applied.

⭐ SUMMARY ●●●●●●●●●●●●●

This chapter has focused on the way we can conduct a historical analysis of popular music culture. Histories have tended to emphasise significant moments, give more prominence to marginal, rather than mainstream forms, and see one music as the root of another. Although these approaches provide us with valuable insights, when combined with the idea of the 'rock era' they have tended to privilege some forms of music and practice over others, and have narrowed our understanding of history, often into a totalising theory of the development of music culture. Instead it is more productive to try to unearth the plurality of voices within popular music culture, and to recognise that our knowledge, and that of the writers we read, is constructed through the discourses we utilise.

Recognising this presents us with a significant challenge. It is just not possible to individually examine all the single events in the history of popular music. So particularly when starting this study we need a set of analytical tools with which to make sense of it all. We need an approach that avoids reducing all the diverse meanings of popular music culture to that of a totalising story – and that includes avoiding both the story of rock's coherence and progress, and the story of its fragmentation – but also one that allows us to start making sense of each single moment and its whole history.

Further reading

Chambers, Iain 1985: *Urban Rhythms: Pop Music and Popular Culture.* **St Martin's Press.**

Clarke, Donald 1995: *The Rise and Fall of Popular Music.* **Penguin.**

Friedlander, Paul 1996: *Rock and Roll: A Social History.* **Westview Press.**

Frith, Simon 1983: *Sound Effects: Youth, Leisure and the Politics of Rock.* **Constable.**

Longhurst, Brian 1995: *Popular Music and Society.* **Polity Press.**

Negus, Keith 1996: *Popular Music in Theory: An Introduction.* **Polity Press.**

Regev, Motti 2002: 'The "Pop-Rockization" of Popular Music', in **D. Hesmondhalgh and K. Negus,** *Popular Music Studies.* **Arnold.**

Thornton, Sarah 1990: 'Strategies for Reconstructing the Popular Past', *Popular Music* 9(1).

CHAPTER TWO

Musical and Cultural Repertoires

This chapter explores the cultural resources that are available to music-makers when they compose and perform music. When musicians or singers produce innovation in music they have to do so by modifying and adapting forms with which they are already familiar. When they perform their material they do so by drawing on styles that interest them. However, the traditions that music-makers draw on, and that are seen as the roots of popular music, are not just traditions of musical form or style. They are also traditions of practices in music-making, listening and evaluation. These practices are produced by the ways that musicians, record company executives, radio station programmers, journalists and listeners think and talk about the music.

From this perspective, I want to recast the idea of musical roots into the idea of 'music culture discourses'. Musical sounds are part of the wider cultural practices, which collectively constitute our knowledge of popular music, so it is not simply that musicians have 'musical influences', but rather 'musical cultural influences'. These influences/discourses constitute whole ways of playing, listening and moving to, talking and thinking about music, and in turn ways of 'knowing' other aspects of our social world. To clarify this approach, it is useful to think about the four areas most commonly seen as musical roots and convert them into four music culture discourses: Tin Pan Alley, African-American, European vernacular, European art.

Each of these discourses constitutes a distinct set of ways of understanding music and its cultural role. As such each is a set of knowledge about what music is, how it should be produced, what it does, and why it is 'good' or 'bad'. They constitute traditions, and people involved in musical cultures can draw from the past to justify or explain the values of their distinctive musical culture. However, it is important to emphasise that these discourses have never existed separately from each other, that their availability varies to different cultural groups at particular moments, and that different styles of popular music draw upon these discourses to different degrees and often in contradictory ways. They therefore constitute the repertoires out of which a distinctive (and new) musical culture can be built. Which aspects of the repertoire will be drawn upon, and in what way, will depend upon how these practices are made meaningful by the particular cultural group.

To help you to be clearer about the idea of a set of discursive practices, take two musical cultures with which you are already familiar – a historical one and a contemporary one makes the exercise more effective – and list characteristic ways in which the music is made, consumed and thought about. For instance: What instruments are used? How are pieces of music composed and structured? Who composed the music and words? How do musicians make the music? (Individually or in groups? By jamming or by rehearsing pre-composed pieces?) Where and how do listeners mostly hear the music? (At home on a record, in a club, at a live concert, or on the radio?) Do listeners just listen or do they tap their feet, use it as a background to other activities, or dance to it? How do they value it? (As entertainment, as produced by great musicians, as good to dance to, as produced by an adored star, or as a statement of their identity?) How do these characteristics differ from those of other music cultures? These are the distinctive discursive practices of that music culture.

Under the next four sections I will outline each of the four key music culture discourses, giving some sense of their history and of their dynamic relationships.

Tin Pan Alley

The phrase 'Tin Pan Alley' is an American term for the professional songwriting industry that dominated mainstream popular music from the late nineteenth century until well into the second half of the twentieth century. Specifically it referred to the area in New York where the cluster of music publishing firms and songwriters who created new popular songs were based. The area was so called because of the cacophony of sound that could be heard on a summer's day emanating from the badly tuned pianos of the tens of tunesmiths working at their open office windows (Shepherd 1982). There was an equivalent area around Denmark Street in London, and in most European capital cities. The songwriters produced songs, which were then published as musical scores with lyrics for professional musicians to be able to reproduce the music in public venues, and increasingly to enable amateur singers and musicians to reproduce the song at home. The publishers made their money through the sales of these scores and the songwriters of the nineteenth century were paid a flat fee, while those working in the twentieth century usually (but not always) gained a royalty on each copy of the sheet music that was sold.

Sheet music publishing had expanded dramatically in the nineteenth century to meet demand from a number of diverse sources. The patriotic songs of the American Civil War, and political satire after, as well as the Christian revival movements in North America and Europe were an important basis for mass music publishing (Clarke 1995). The development of community singing and playing (particularly brass bands) as part of Victorian social philanthropy or working-class solidarity and the associated new styles of musical teaching aimed at amateur musicians and singers expanded commercial songwriting further (Hamm 1983; Russell 1997).

As the central aim of these songwriters was to produce a quick succession of songs and accompanying melodies that would be accepted by a publishing company and sold to North Americans and Europeans as sheet music, the writers utilised a set of conventional techniques they hoped would quickly allow their new song to be recognised, played and sung by the people who bought the sheet music. John Shepherd has suggested that these conventions ordered the production of songs around fashionable musical styles, topical events or appeals to the public's emotions (Shepherd 1982, 2). In the late nineteenth and early twentieth centuries the dominant form was the sentimental ballad, a musical structure based on songs in which the lyrics were centrally important to creating emotional responses in the listener, and where the music aimed to underscore the telling of the story of the song and reinforce the emotions its writer was attempting to articulate.

The establishment of commercial songwriting was tied very closely to the development of public musical entertainment. Both the older travelling musical shows and 'free and easy' drinking and singing clubs aimed at the working class, and the pleasure gardens and opera houses aimed at the new middle class, were increasingly being overshadowed by city-based establishments that became the foundation of musical theatre in the twentieth century (Hamm 1983; Clarke 1995; Russell 1997). Generically called vaudeville in North America and music hall in Britain, these increasingly grand palaces of musical entertainment began to censor many of the more bawdy songs that had been the mainstay of the working-class, male-dominated, 'free and easies'. Music halls attracted far larger and more widely drawn audiences, generated a far higher turnover of songs, and established a sophisticated system of promoting and selling published songs (Bailey 1986; Bratton 1986; Sanjek 1988). That sales and promotion imperative became very important in Tin Pan Alley discourse.

In response to this commercial impetus, song form became even more standardised during the first years of the twentieth century. Songwriters were altering the form of popular song to increase its appeal to the music hall audience. Charles Hamm (1983, 290–7) identifies a number of important characteristics that became typical of the Tin Pan Alley-style song. The verses, which before had told complex stories, reduced steadily in number. The short repeated refrains, which had followed the verses, became longer, increasingly carrying the most memorable melodic lines. They shifted to become parts for the solo star rather than the supporting chorus singers. The 'catchy' repeated sections of the songs were still called the 'chorus', and once they were established in the audience's memories they became the focus for what was left of communal singing. Meanwhile the melodies themselves became organised around fixed lengths of musical time, and built upon simple forms of three chords in major keys. At the same time, though, songs that displayed novel subject matter or musical devices were often the most popular with audiences. For this reason, popular songwriters focused on combining a durable, limited form with quickly exhausted novelty devices. That approach became the staple of mainstream popular music for over 50 years. Many of the songs produced became known as 'standards' of the musical repertoire.

Standardised forms were often widely criticised by musicians and self-appointed guardians of the public good. A classic example of such a critical position is Theodor Adorno's famous article *On Popular Music* (1941/1990). The critics argued that the process of creating music was heavily industrialised and commercialised, that the musical form itself was heavily formulaic, and that the emotions evoked were unreal and idealised. (This argument is discussed in some detail in both Parts 3 and 4). Such views are still common today, both from critics of all popular music and supporters of more marginal popular forms.

The Tin Pan Alley tradition, then, provides a basic pattern for a song-based musical composition that remained characteristically strong as the pop mainstream throughout the twentieth century. In totalising histories of popular music this mainstream is constructed as a bland mechanistic set of conventions challenged by pre-war folk and black musics, and finally disrupted by rock & roll in the mid-1950s at the beginning of the rock era. However, the basic structure of Tin Pan Alley underlay much of this alternative popular music, while professional songwriters utilised many aspects of alternative forms as novelty devices in their own compositions.

As I emphasised earlier in this chapter, the Tin Pan Alley tradition represents more than a form of music. It is also a set of values and associated practices. The emphasis within the Tin Pan Alley discourse on the division of labour between professional songwriters, musicians and star singers is characteristic of the industrialised music industry that we will examine in Part 3. The idea that music should aim to entertain large audiences is judged by sales figures in lists of best-selling recordings, and requires a polished presentation based upon practice; the skill of background professionals has been the staple of the music business for the whole of the last century. For audiences it represents vital, always renewed, 'alive for the minute' experience, mixed with a communal will to sing the chorus of a song, as well as adoration for a star and the excitement of the show. These ideas and practices of making and listening to music are to be found in moments of popular music history as diverse as the ones defined by the girl group sound of the late 1950s (exemplified by the Shangri-Las), the soundtrack LPs of the mid-60s (such as *The Sound of Music*), the glam pop of the early 1970s (including bands like Sweet), the new pop of the early 1980s, or the boy and girl bands of the turn of the twenty-first century.

 2.2 Make a list of points defining the Tin Pan Alley tradition, and then identify a contemporary group or artist who seems to personify the tradition. What evidence can you find that the artist fits with each aspect of this tradition? Then considerer each point in detail. Can you identify their music with the traditional song form? Are their songs produced using professional songwriters? How do their fans think about the music and the performers? Can you find examples of others denigrating the performers? What sorts of criticism do they make?

African-American

'African-American' is the widely used term to describe the culture and music of the black communities in North America. It would be mistaken to think that there is a set of musical forms and practices that is uniquely 'black', and like the other three repertoires of music culture we will examine here, the African-American tradition of music-making has constantly interacted with other traditions. However, the formation of a distinctive African-American tradition out of a continuing relationship of black Americans with white Americans and Europeans has produced musical cultures that are at the same time both troubled and validatory: troubled because an African-American culture only exists because the African peoples who became the first black Americans were forcibly transported to a different continent to work and live as slaves, and their descendants were compelled to make their lives in a society riddled with racism and racial discrimination; validatory because in the face of such inhumane treatment black American musicians constantly attempted to transcend racist white society and find pride in cultural achievements.

Philip Tagg has gone as far as challenging the notion that there is something we can describe in any essentialist way as black music (Tagg 1987). I too have been careful not to suggest that there is an essential form of music that is solely belonging to, or somehow reducible to, the people of the African diaspora. However, the term is meaningful as it points to an important connection between music and identity. It is worth quoting Stuart Hall here. In his view, black popular culture, including music, has

> come to signify the black community, where these traditions are kept, and
> whose struggles survive in the persistence of the black experience (the historical
> experience of black people in the diaspora), of the black aesthetic (the
> distinctive cultural repertoires out of which popular representations are made),
> and of the black counter narratives we struggle to voice.

(Hall 1992, 28)

Hall points to the vital role that music has played in the development of African-American and Caribbean identity in the 350 years of its development in North and Central America and its islands. This music has been the primary way that the changing experience, aesthetic and counter-narratives of the sons and daughters of African slaves in America have been expressed (see Jones 1966). The African peoples who were enslaved were caught in the tension of diverse backgrounds and a common oppression in which the almost complete annihilation of any African culture – language, personal names, religious practices, music and dance – was a parallel to their physical domination. Music was allowed some outlet: to regulate work, to celebrate Christian festivals, and to provide music for slave owners and their guests. Some slaves provided music for their white 'masters' as a service like any other of their servitude, and carried out this technical service to the requirements of European conventions. However, remnants of African music were kept and developed as a means to keep some semblance of identity under slavery, and articulate the shared solidarity against oppression. Some of this distinctive black music was performed for the white oppressors, and seen by them as exotic entertainment (Southern 1983).

The development of black American music, therefore, was caught in another set of tensions, this time between being an articulation of an oppressed black identity, and as entertainment for the white oppressors. This paradox is a central dynamic of the history of black music. The changing roles of African-American music, and the shifts of identity in relation to the political and cultural history of America have been built around the contradictory tugs of two alternative cultural and political stances: separatism/self-sufficiency from mainstream white America, and the possibility of assimilation into and success in that culture (George 1988). The development of music in the Caribbean shared many of the same cultural factors, but the annihilation of African-originated customs and music seems to have been less complete, and the scale of island life, the different history of colonial rule and the lower level of professional exploitation of black musical forms led to a different and distinct history of music and identity (see Clarke 1980; Davis and Simon 1983; Bradley 2000).

The changing musical genres of black America – hot jazz, swing, blues, jump blues, R&B, soul, hip-hop and house – and of its near neighbours in the Caribbean – ska, rock steady, reggae (in all its forms), calypso, dance hall and ragga – all reflect the pulls of an economic and cultural self-sufficiency on the one hand, and the promises of success in a wider, fully integrated North American society on the other. In this history the roles of musicians and music entrepreneurs – like Louis Armstrong, Duke Ellington, Louis Jordan, Don Robey, Charlie Parker, Miles Davis, Chuck Berry, Duke Reid, Lee Perry, Berry Gordy, Kenny Gamble and Leon Huff, Bob Marley, Michael Jackson, Russell Simmons, and Derick May – are as important as political leaders like Booker T. Washington, Marcus Garvey, Martin Luther King, Malcolm X, Jessie Jackson and Elijah Muhammad. Equally, the notions of black power, Afro-centricism, black nationalism, Rastafarianism and civil rights have been central to musical production and consumption in black America (for excellent discussions of these issues see Jones 1966; Clarke 1980; Davis and Simon 1983; George 1988; Lipsitz 1994; Kofsky 1998).

However, as I have indicated, the repertoire of African-American music culture has been produced as much by the practices of white Americans and Europeans as it has by black Americans themselves. There are many historical examples of both a fear of, and a fascination with, African-American music among whites. Southern (1983) catalogues the way that the dancing and music of black slaves was seen as exotic to white observers, and how this led to the development of minstrel shows in which whites blackened their faces and reproduced simplistic versions of African-American dance and music for white, mainstream audiences. Equally, though, Southern's history (1983) contains many examples of white Americans expressing disquiet about the same activities, fearful of their perceived moral corruption. This range of responses from fear to fascination, often both in the same individual, is not just characteristic of the eighteenth century, but also found throughout the nineteenth and twentieth centuries. Whether it was the so called 'Jim Crow' statutes (named after a minstrel show character) that forbade blacks and whites meeting in public entertainment, right through to the 1960s, or the orchestrated attack on first jazz and then rock & roll as 'nigger music', or the 'Disco Sucks' campaign waged against black music in the late

1970s, or the Housewives Alliance's vilification of rap in the 1990s, African-American music has been at the centre of many 'moral panics' in American and European society (Southern 1983; Lott 1993; Ward 1998; Werner 1999, 117–211).

For another constituency of whites, black music and culture was highly prized. Andrew Ross has traced a connection between 'hipness' and black culture, and the perceived dangers of 'cross-over' and 'commerciality' (Ross 1989, 65–101). These same themes are addressed by a number of writers, but with a different emphasis. Nelson George has attacked the cross-over of African-American music into white culture as 'the death of Rhythm and Blues' (George 1988). Others have explored those black musical forms that, it is argued, are attempts to repudiate this appropriation. Included in the list are 1940s bebop and the free jazz of the 1960s (see Jones 1966; Kofsky 1970; Litweiler 1990). In Britain the veneration of soul music and reggae among whites in the 1960s and 1970s prefigures the wiggers' (white niggers') fascination with hip-hop and black culture of the 1980s and 1990s (see Chambers 1985, 139–64; Jones 1988; George 1998, 60–8).

FIGURE 2.1 The individual and impressionistic styles of performance usually draw heavily on the African-American tradition

It is also important to note that a high proportion of books that examine the African-American tradition are written by white Americans and Europeans who share many of the values of this wider white constituency (see for instance Broven 1974; Haralambos 1974; Oliver 1978; Charters 1982; Frith 1983; Gillett 1983; Keil and Feld 1994; Lomax 1998). We can identify in these books' subtexts a passion for black musical forms, and the feeling that because of continuing racism among white

Americans and Europeans the contributions of black musicians to the shifting history of popular music had not been widely understood or respected. The fascination and veneration of black musical forms and often their associated African-American or African-Caribbean cultures, by white Americans and Europeans is so strong that it is possible to identify a major part of the origins of the majority of mainstream popular musics in black forms. Table 2.1 lists just some of them.

Date	Mainstream form	Black music source
1930s to 1940s	Big band swing	Jazz
1950s	Rock & roll	Rhythm & blues
1960s	Beat	Rhythm & blues
1960s to 1970s	Rock	Blues
1970s	Punk	Rhythm & blues, reggae
1970s	Disco	Soul, funk
1980s	Two-Tone	Ska
1980s	New pop	Soul, reggae
1980s	Acid house	Chicago house
1990s	Techno	Detroit techno
1990s	Boy/girl bands	Soul, new jack swing

TABLE 2.1 Mainstream popular musics and their black music origins, 1930 to 2000

Simon Frith has characterised the music of the African-American tradition by highlighting its emphasis on performance, its immediate emotional impact on the listener, its spontaneous, often improvised, qualities, and its dual expressiveness through vocal sounds and its rhythmic properties (Frith 1983, 15–23). Other writers have noted the greater emphasis on certain musical qualities like call and response, syncopation, and the use of blue notes. As indicated earlier, such claims have been criticised as essentialist (see Negus 1996, 100–7 and Longhurst 1995, 127–33 for a summary). It is also difficult for modern listeners to hear any of these qualities as distinctive to black musicians because the African-American tradition has been so influential on the general development of popular musics.

For these reasons Craig Werner's ideas of the gospel, jazz and blues impulses are perhaps a more productive way forward (Werner 1999). While it may lack the precision of the discussions of the musicological debates, and is somewhat poetic, it gets closer to the idea that the African-American tradition – like the other three traditions examined here – is not a narrowly musical one, but one of values and approaches to ways of making and consuming music. For Werner, the gospel impulse emphasises interdependence, communality and connectedness, by recognising and bearing witness to the burden of oppression, but also by seeking redemption from it; the blues impulse emphasises reaffirmation in the face of adversity or 'fingering the jagged grain of your brutal experience' (Werner 1999, 69); while the jazz impulse is seen as a continuous process of redefinition, examining what does not fit, challenging us to rethink our assumptions.

X
2.3

The African-American tradition has been influential on a range of artists and musics, including many outside African-American culture. What influences can you identify in the reggae of the late 1970s, the new romantics of the early 1980s, rap in the late 1980s and early 1990s, and UK garage in the late 1990s? How many of these musics also articulate the strong fight for equality apparent in this tradition?

European vernacular

'Vernacular' refers to qualities of ordinary people, so this tradition relates to music culture repertoires originating with the ordinary people of Europe. The term most often used here is 'folk music'. Popular music is often distinguished from folk music, with folk being seen as an organic, communally produced music, and popular as industrialised and professionalised music production for mass consumption. This distinction between the different ways that making and consuming music is organised is worth noting. However, it is equally important to investigate how popular music has drawn upon the musical forms and practices produced outside the industrialised and commercialised modern media and which became repertoires of sounds, practices and values for new musical styles.

The European vernacular tradition has mainly found its way into popular music production in two, paradoxically, opposed ways. Either it has been the raw material for professional songwriters, or at the opposite pole it has been celebrated as an alternative to the values perceived to be present in the Tin Pan Alley tradition itself. In both cases, though, the music and its practices have been utilised and 'remade' by people other than those who originally produced the music. The song writers of Tin Pan Alley remade vernacular music as the sentimental ballad, while the European and North American middle class recast working-class vernacular music as a set of symbols of 'authenticity', which are set against the slickness and formula of music made for commercial ends.

Charles Hamm has shown how traditional – though modified – Irish melodies were utilised with new words and the innovation of first-person narration by professional songwriters in the nineteenth century. These songs emphasised nostalgia and loss, and their music was often seen as 'novel, wild, irregular, even barbaric' (Hamm 1983, 50) when compared with popular music produced from other musical traditions. Nevertheless, as Hamm points out, such songs 'were taken by common people in ... America as examples of the force and beauty of folk culture and expression, as opposed to the learned classical arts of the aristocracy' (Hamm 1983, 57).

For its listeners, the music celebrated the ideals of populism, which venerate the independence of the individual, celebrate the values of the ordinary person, and express a belief in the possibility of greatness or fame for everyone. These ideals are expressed in the twentieth century in 'the American Dream' often represented in Hollywood films (Richards 1973, 222–87) and perhaps even more strongly in country music. Country developed out of Irish, Scottish, Welsh and English folk forms, and integrated German, Mexican, Native American, African-American and even Hawaiian influences. As it developed in the early part of the twentieth century it did so as a folk form itself, as the product of community music-making and as a way of articulating a new American rural identity. But it also drew heavily on the industrialised song-publishing industry, which circulated the folk-derived melodies and new songs that constituted its primary texts (Malone 1985). Today country music is the exemplar of the paradoxical nature of popular music. It is the product of a highly organised industry that produces a standardised musical text and skilfully manipulates promotional media to sell records and associated commodities (Peterson 1997). At the same time, though, it is a musical form that its fans invest with potent individual and social meanings, and that is perceived to be an authentic expression of the people of the southern states of the USA. These signifiers of authenticity, in turn, resonate with country fans across the world. This combination of economic and cultural forces has made country music recordings among the biggest-selling commodities of the American record industry, and one of the most influential forms of global music. Yet in turn it is marginalised by mainstream media like radio, television and the press, and often publicly derided by its detractors as pure 'schmaltz'.

The idea of 'authenticity' is the central repertory concept of the European vernacular tradition. It is used as a positive reference point by those who look for an alternative to our modern, commercialised, industrialised world and culture. In the pre-industrial past, it has long been claimed, people had stronger relationships with each other, which grew out of more organic, natural ways of life, and their music, song and dance expressed these relationships. By collecting together and publishing the songs that had been widely sung by previous generations it was felt that these great traditions could be treasured. In the nineteenth century the broadsides and chapbooks – cheaply published sheets – of English and Scottish song were collected together and published with commentaries that emphasised ideas of essentialist national identity and counter-posed the supposed 'natural simplicity' of folk song with the 'artifice' of florid Italian music, which was fashionable in elite circles at the time (Harker 1985, 24). A similar approach was taken in other countries in the first half of the twentieth century. The growth of nationalism and socialist politics was often paralleled by an interest in indigenous folk forms and used to express identities for the people of new nation-states. African-American spirituals were highly regarded by intellectuals in Britain and Europe, and distinguished from the minstrel shows which were seen as vapid entertainment (Southern 1983, 221–7). This veneration of certain forms of black music was to be repeated in the twentieth century when New Orleans jazz, country blues, and rhythm & blues were taken to be folk forms by middle-class Europeans and Americans.

The collection of folk music was consolidated in the late nineteenth century by F.J. Child, an American professor of English, whose ideas became the basis of how intellectuals treated folk culture for the next hundred years. He saw his song collecting as an extension of his literary studies. Just like more recent histories of popular music he developed practices of collection, categorisation and analysis that were selective, constructing a story that expressed implicit values. His story was centrally about the way later commercial forms of songs were seen to be exploiting the purer antecedents and so corrupting their musical form (Harker 1985, 101–20).

Folk song in Britain at the beginning of the twentieth century was most strongly associated with attempts by radical intellectuals to 'improve' working people's cultural and moral life, especially through school and municipal singing, and with efforts to 'discover' previously unpublished folk songs still being sung in Britain (Harker 1985, 172–95; Russell 1997, 41–66). By the middle of the century, though, folk music became the basis for more inclusive ideas of a counter-culture. Central here was the notion that by focusing on our cultural practices, and especially our music-making and consumption, we could produce a different form of music culture that expressed different values than those of modernist, capitalist societies, and create different forms of personal relationships that would galvanise people to change the society itself.

Ron Eyerman and Andrew Jamison have argued that US social movements, including the campaigns for civil rights and those against the Vietnam War, have been built around just such an attempt to use cultural traditions to build new collective identities (Eyerman and Jamison 1998). Dave Harker's more sceptical examination of similar British developments can be deduced from the title of his book *Fakesong* (Harker 1985). He implies that a whole range of political and musical activity – from the collection of working-class songs in the 1940s, the BBC's broadcast of radio ballads in the 1950s and the folk clubs of the 1960s – can be understood as a rather crude attempt by the British Communist Party (CP) to dominate radical politics. As Porter (1998) has shown, while CP members clearly played an important role it was more the initiative of radical individuals, rather than a political conspiracy, that built the revival of folk music in the 1960s. Although for many individuals the folk music culture of the 1960s offered a life-changing experience, as the music's popularity rose it was adapted by the music industry, leading a major American label to claim 'The Revolutionaries are all on Columbia'. Simon Frith has further argued:

> By the 1960s folk songs had become rhetorical; they expressed only individual discontent with events. Conventions in lyrics became increasingly literary and the artistic distance between singer and audience was confirmed musically by the shifts from acoustic to electronic instruments, from the stage to the studio.
>
> (Frith 1983, 31)

The more politicised of singer-songwriters, like Pete Seeger, Bob Dylan and Joan Baez were eclipsed in popularity by the more personal songs of James Taylor, Paul Simon and Carole King. Simon and King had even started their careers as successful Tin Pan Alley songwriters.

However, it is probably mistaken to see the singer-songwriter with acoustic guitar as the major example of the influence of European vernacular music in popular music. Dick Bradley has argued that skiffle – that late-1950s and early-1960s British DIY music of tea-chest basses and washboard rhythms – transformed British popular music by combining the values of the European vernacular tradition with American rock & roll. He suggests that skiffle established the ideas of amateurism and group-based music-making on which the Beatles built their distinctive work, and which dominated music-making for the next 30 years (Bradley 1992). Dave Laing has also suggested that similar principles, derived from the European vernacular traditions, can be found in the British punk scene of the late 1970s. He emphasises the way that the distance between audience and performer was initially reduced and the culture encouraged everyone to form a band to make music in which participation and energy were the most important qualities (Laing 1985).

These observations emphasise that the repertoires of music culture are not always utilised by musicians and listeners in simple ways. In fact the more obvious notions of the folk form are now most often found in the way the music of other cultures is consumed in Europe and North America, and especially in the idea of 'world music'. Here the repertoire of authenticity has mixed with the exoticisation of the music of South America, Africa and Asia to recast the ideas of the European vernacular tradition on to a world stage (Taylor 1997). On the other hand Sarah Thornton has argued that new forms of authenticity have been established in contemporary western popular music cultures, built around the production and collection of records and the communality of dancing in clubs, which have negated and displaced those of the acoustic instrument and the live music event that were dominant in the folk tradition (Thornton 1995).

X 2.4 Different groups and musical forms are perceived to have different degrees of authenticity. An effective way to test this out is to produce an 'authenticity line' showing different degrees of authenticity from 'fully authentic' to 'no authenticity'. You can then mark on a range of artists to see the variation among performers you are familiar with. It is then interesting to ask what it is about them, their performances or their music that seems to project (or not project) authenticity.

European art tradition

The final tradition covers the range of musical forms and practices that are usually called 'classical music'. Although until recently the distinction between classical and popular music would have seemed obvious, like the definition of folk music, the process of defining a field of 'classical music' has been a long and complex one. It is easiest to understand what is included, and what is excluded, in this definition by its association with ideas of 'art' established in Europe over the last 200 years. It is for this reason that the music of this tradition is also often called art music. The repertoire of 'art' emphasises the idea that certain gifted individuals can produce music that transcends their historical and social location. Art is seen as requiring considerable knowledge and developed 'taste' to appreciate and understand. This definition is also the reason that many who associate themselves with this position often define themselves against the perceived values of popular music (see Hamm 1995, 1–41).

Given this definition of music as art it is interesting to note that there are a number of styles of music that, today, would be firmly placed in the art or classical category, which have in the past been understood as popular music. The category of 'light music', widely used before 1950 is such an example. In the canon of classical music composers like Bach and Beethoven were seen as superior to the light music of Strauss.

Paddy Scannell has shown how the early BBC's music policy has had a major influence on the process of defining what, in Britain at least, music was art and what was popular. This position was systematised in the way the corporation was organised in the 1920s and 1930s with a separation between the music output organised by the Music Department (symphonies, chamber music, opera and the avant-garde) and that which was the responsibility of the Variety Department (dance bands, the cinema organ, operetta and musical revues). In doing so a distinction was made between 'serious music' and what senior BBC staff saw as 'vapid entertainment' (Scannell 1981). There were two core aspects of music policy: 'the pursuit of standards of excellence in the authentic performance of great music, and an endeavour to raise the level of the general public's taste for, and appreciation of, good music' (Scannell 1981, 242). Stephen Barnard has noted that 'the prime criterion for broadcasting music outside the classical sphere was therefore its "relaxing" quality – and any music that disturbed or excited had no place on the BBC airwaves' (Barnard 1989, 8).

The competing ideas of art and commerce are still present in the very nouns we use to describe music-makers. 'Artist' obviously comes from this tradition, emphasising their creativity and artistic skills. 'Act' or 'performer' is drawn from the Tin Pan Alley/music hall tradition, and emphasises their role in performance of a theatrical event rather than as creators of a piece of music. This latter tradition even uses the term 'artiste' to bring some European cachet to the performer without making them explicitly creative individuals, although this term is less widely used in contemporary popular music outside the cabaret circuit.

In the nineteenth century, Italian opera was a major influence on American popular music and songwriting through its musical form and style of singing, and many 'upmarket' music halls were called opera houses (Hamm 1983, 62–88). Perhaps the first recording star was the operatic tenor Enrico Caruso (1873–1921) and his 'art music' style had a huge influence on many major singers of popular music before the crooning style of Bing Crosby offered a major alternative in the late 1930s (Clarke 1995, 130–2). Operatically derived composition or performance styles were still prominent through the 1930s, though, with artists like Nelson Eddie, and still identifiable into the 1950s with singers like Mario Lanza. The style still has a major hold in musical theatre, but has declined in other areas of popular music after the African-American influences from rock & roll onwards. Even so the style still echoed on in the 1970s and 1980s pomp rock of bands like Queen and in the renewed commercial success in the 1990s of popular opera singers like the so-called 'Three Tenors' (José Carreras, Placido Domingo and Luciano Pavarotti).

In addition to these more obvious influences there have been continual attempts throughout the history of popular music to separate off certain forms of popular music and make a claim for them as art rather than popular culture. Some writers make a claim for seeing certain Tin Pan Alley songsmiths as at least craftsmen, and their work as distilled art (see for instance Clarke 1995). Others point to the influence of modernist art music on some composers of popular song, with Gershwin receiving particular praise in this respect (Hamm 1983, 551).

The most significant example of reformulating a popular music practice as an art one, however, is the attempts by white intellectuals to canonise jazz (Ross 1989, 65–89). Histories of popular music tend to marginalise jazz, and in studies of post-1950 music they tend to ignore it completely. Histories of jazz, on the other hand, argues Peter Townsend, have

> tended to describe Jazz as some sort of musical creed that has somehow kept itself intact in hostile environments, sometimes being forced to compromise with commerce and show business, but passing the flame from hand to hand in a permanent detachment from the rest of the world. ... This appears to be a retrospective projection of the post-war autonomy of the form on to a very different set of circumstances.
>
> (Townsend 2000, 38)

His analysis is fruitful as he recognises the post-war shift in the discursive position of jazz in popular music, but emphasises how this later discursive positioning of the music is used to produce a unified story of its development. In fact, while musical styles designated as jazz have always related strongly to the African-American tradition, the place of jazz in popular music is complex, and provides an excellent case study in the role of the art discourse at work.

Jazz is normally presented as a new style of music originating in the multicultural milieu of New Orleans at the turn of the twentieth century, and then spreading to the rest of America and then the world. The characteristic combination of ensemble instrumental improvisation and a rhythmically charged style was celebrated as 'hot playing'. However, it is equally possible to tell the story from a different perspective. This narrative emphasises the importance of commercial entertainment and the uneasy relationship between white and black Americans and Europeans. Jazz enters mainstream popular culture in the early 1920s at the height of the so-called 'dance craze'. Nightclubs, with their animal dances like the foxtrot and bear hug, were a spectacular part of the life of the American city in a period of rising prosperity. The New Orleans approach to collective music-making was not widely copied, but the sounds of the hot style were carried by soloists whose performances were integrated into the approach of the dance orchestras.

An interest in primitivism among the white bohemian middle class exoticised anything perceived to be 'African', nightclubs featured jungle themes in their decor and acts, and whites sized upon the new sound. Black band leaders like Duke Ellington were as eager to move away from this as white leaders like Paul Whiteman, and it was the concept of European art that gave them the conceptual resources to imagine a 'symphonic jazz' (Tucker 1993). This shift to an emphasis on arrangement and composition, rather than improvisation, became a principle of the swing big bands that were to dominate popular music in the 1940s (Townsend 2000, 65–91).

It was in the post-war years that jazz finally became marginalised from the mainstream of popular music. In the after-hours 'jam sessions' that big band musicians ran, a new aesthetic was being established. The soloist and his/her complex improvisations became the central characteristic of jazz and as the form became established in small nightclubs the mythologised smoky jazz club and the genre of bebop was born. This new form was marked more by the idea of the heroic artist who dies for his art after being met by indifference from the world of commerce; a complex musical form built around ever-expanding experiments in composition and improvisation; and the underground bohemians separated from the rest of the popular music audience by their cultural distance from the mainstream of 'square' society (Townsend 2000, 137–59).

Iain Chambers succinctly traces the continuation of this white middle-class bohemian sensibility into the birth of the hippies on the east coast of America and the diverse influence they had on a popular music that became known as rock. Those same value judgements used to understand bebop jazz were transferred to musical forms based on African-American blues guitar bands and rural folk musics as a sign of authenticity, but now developed through European concepts of art music. These ideas combined with the new recording technology of the studio and the longer playing time of the new 12-inch microgroove LP record to produce a move away from the three-minute pop song and towards more formally complex and longer musical forms (Chambers 1985). The importance in Britain of the art school education, and its associated ideas, enjoyed by many rock artists was also considerable in the development of musics as diverse as beat, progressive (prog) rock, punk, electro-pop, indie and house (Frith and Horne 1987).

Collect together some media coverage of two performers: one who seems to draw heavily on the idea of the gifted artist, and another who seems to be more squarely in the tradition of entertainer. Compare their coverage. Are ideas of the artist and of art creation more prominent in one set of coverage than the other? What other aspects of the art tradition are apparent in the coverage? How strongly is the Tin Pan Alley tradition used as a repertoire for talking about these performers? What conclusions can you draw?

SUMMARY

The European art tradition, along with the European vernacular, the African-American and the Tin Pan Alley traditions, then, are the four key ways that music cultural practices have been organised in popular music. By studying them separately we have been able to see their distinctive qualities and how each has been a major influence in popular music history. However, the overwhelming majority of musics established at different moments of popular music have been created by mixing parts of these traditions together, to produce a distinctive set of musical sounds and cultural practices of making, consuming and evaluating popular music. To understand why certain elements were mixed at particular moments in music culture history we need to move on to examine a range of social, economic and technological factors. These are outlined in detail in the next chapter.

Further reading

Bradley, Dick 1992: *Understanding Rock 'n' Roll: Popular Music in Britain, 1955–1964*. **Open University Press.**

Bratton, J.S. 1986: *Music Hall: Performance and Style*. **Open University Press.**

Brewster, Bill and Frank Broughton 1999: *Last Night a DJ Saved My Life: The History of a Disc Jockey*. **Headline.**

Guralnick, Peter 1986: *Sweet Soul Music: Rhythm and Blues and the Southern Dream of Freedom*. **Harper & Row.**

Hamm, Charles 1983: *Yesterdays: Popular Song in America*. **Norton.**

Malone, Bill C. 1985: *Country Music USA*. **University of Texas Press.**

Southern, Eileen 1983: *The Music of Black Americans: A History*. **Norton.**

Thornton, Sarah 1995: *Club Cultures: Music, Media and Subcultural Capital*. **Polity Press.**

Toop, David 2000: *Rap Attack 3: African Rap to Global Hip Hop*. **Serpent's Tail.**

Townsend, Peter 2000: *Jazz in American Culture*. **Edinburgh University Press.**

CHAPTER THREE

Social, Economic and Technical Factors

Musical and cultural repertoires are available to different groups of people in uneven ways, and serve their cultural practices in different ways. Musicians and music consumers do not arbitrarily choose to play or like one type of music over another. Nor is it just a matter of individual preference. The music we like is a significant expression of what is available to us, and what we make it mean. The history of popular music, then, is the product of the changing choices that millions of music producers and music consumers have made. And if the musical and cultural repertoires constitute the way the available choices are ordered, we can understand how and why those choices were made by examining the social, economic and technical factors in play in that historical moment.

Social factors

Nearly all histories of popular music link the changing styles of popular music to changes in the wider society. Rock & roll is seen as the product of the birth of the teenager, or the changing role of African-Americans; rock is seen as the creation of new middle-class youth audiences for popular music; punk is seen as a sign of the disenchantment with Britain's social decline; rave as the hedonism of post-feminist, postmodern youth. As long as we avoid the danger of being over-deterministic – that is, seeing the social change as causing the musical shift – then this linkage of social to musical changes can produce important insights.

Society changed significantly from the turn of the twentieth century to the turn of the twenty-first. The demographics of western countries have been altered by migration, rising economic prosperity and changing power relationships. Understanding how individual musical preferences and styles of music-making interlink with these greater changes has been a recurring theme of much popular music scholarship. Although most popular music histories have tended to emphasise the role of individual musicians as creative *auteurs* who determine the direction of musical development, other approaches have attempted to relate styles, forms of composition and particularly performance to the organisation of society.

The starting point for this sort of analysis is that music is cultural. It is made, listened to and danced to in particular cultural contexts. When these contexts change so does the music, the music-making and the music consumption. But music is also political. It is certainly perceived as such by many writers, musicians and music fans; and when we examine the politics of popular music we are not just looking at the way that it has been used in organised political campaigns, or has been controlled by the state, although these are very important (see Street 1992). Primarily, though, the politics of popular music is linked to the relationships between individuals and groups in society. Even the argument that pop music is 'just entertainment' is a political position because it seeks to define the role for popular music in society, and possibly seeks to conceal the complex ways that the music was influenced, created and distributed. Music is never 'just there', and its style and associated practices relate to social change in substantial ways.

Popular music is significantly linked to moments in which late nineteenth- and twentieth-century society underwent profound change. Industrialisation and urbanisation in Europe from 1850 led to the development of a shift in the scale and organisation of music-making from a communal activity to a professionalised and commercialised one (Earl 1986). The shifting and unevenly distributed prosperity in Europe and the USA before the Second World War plays an important part in the development of distinct ethnic and class social groups, which formed the basis of the American distinction between the pop, race and hillbilly markets for popular music (Sanjek and Sanjek 1996, 117–46), and the ideas of light entertainment that were to dominate British popular music for 30 years (Frith 1988e). The post-war boom in the West created the conditions for the link between youth culture and popular music (Frith 1983, 181–234).

The struggle from slavery and towards equality made by African-Americans is articulated through the development of a distinct African-American musical tradition (Jones 1966; Southern 1983). The modernism and hedonism of the 1920s was tied as much to jazz as it was to painting and literature (Shaw 1987). Brian Ward even goes so far as to argue that there is a mirror image between the level of support for integrationist or separatist politics in African-American society and tastes for white pop, or more self-styled Africanised forms of black American music (Ward 1998). The later civil rights movement of the 1960s was entwined in the identity and music of freedom songs and soul (Eyerman and Jamison 1998). More recent black musical forms of funk, reggae, rap and house through the 1970s, 1980s and 1990s have been born out of attempts to define African American and African Caribbean identity in racist societies (Potter 1995; Ward 1998; George 1999 and Bradley 2000). Equally, white Americans and Europeans have often seen black musical forms and black identity as a way to express their own feelings of marginalisation (Jones 1988; Ross 1989 65–101).

During the last century popular music was often associated with a fear of anarchy, and perceived as a challenge to social norms and cultural status quo. There are numerous attempts by the state or authoritarian groups to control popular musical forms and practices. From the Victorian policing of the music hall and the attempt to develop what they saw as more edifying music in choral societies, community orchestras and brass bands (Russell 1997), through the regulation of black music forms in America (George 1988; Ward 1998), and the attempt to control post-war rock music (Martin and Segrave 1993), to more recent attempts to control raves in Europe (Collin 1997; Gilbert and Pearson 1999, 150–2). In Europe there has been a prominent fear of the influence of American culture in which popular music has been crucial (Strinati 1995, 31–8).

Economics, too, is significant. British beat music and the origins of groups like the Beatles are located in a particular moment of post-war prosperity (Bradley 1992), just as punk made sense of the late 1970s industrial decline for its fans (Laing 1985). Late 1960s rock, and its association with an American counter-culture, indicates how music can be seen to articulate the feelings of a particular group in society and the importance of ideas of generational differences in defining the development and meanings of popular music (Grossberg 1992b).

In the last 50 years, music has been publicly connected with a series of youth subcultures. The idea that subgroups of society are important for academic study is a central part of sociology. Initially established in the 1920s and developed over the next 40 years by founders of 'modern sociology' at Chicago University, these studies saw subcultures as urban, deviant groups who rejected the norms and values of mainstream society (see Cohen 1956). Such work was later developed, and stronger links made to popular music, in the analysis of a series of theorists and researchers based at Birmingham University in the 1970s (see Cohen 1972; Hall and Jefferson 1975/1991; Hebdige 1979). In these studies a much more productive slant is given to the role of these subcultures, whose cultural practices are seen as attempts to resolve the contradictory pulls of class and generational identity for young people marginalised by the powerful in society. In these analyses music is seen to be part of a homology, that is the cultural process bringing diverse parts of life – including everything from clothing, through ways of talking, modes of transport, ways of dancing or listening, to shared attitudes and values – into a coherent set of cultural meanings of opposition (see Hebdige 1979 for one of the most developed examples of this approach).

However, as a number of critiques of the subcultural approach have noted, this emphasis on class and generation tended to, first, focus on the most publicly spectacular groups and ignore mainstream generational consumption of popular music (Clarke 1981) and, second, to downplay the importance of women in such cultural politics (McRobbie 1980). The emphasis on gender has also been the prominent part of understanding histories of particular musics in a number of studies. Lucy O'Brien has produced a history of women in popular music in the twentieth century (O'Brien 1995), while Amy Raphael has argued that women consciously challenged the gender conventions of rock music during in the 1980s and early 1990s (Raphael 1995). Most such studies examine the way in which women's contribution to popular music has been marginalised at the time of production and then further marginalised in the way that musical histories are written. A major line of enquiry, then, has been to bring women's contributions to the fore (see for instance Stewart and Garratt 1984). Particular forms of popular music have also developed upon this same critique, and the wider arguments of feminism, the most prominent being the riot grrrl movement of the early 1990s (see Leonard 1997).

Finally, the analysis of feminist theorists and researchers has raised the significance of gender and sexuality in the development of popular music. Masculinity has been central to several analytical approaches (see for instance Hawkins 1997; Palmer 1997; Whiteley 1997a). Sexuality and representation of gender and sexual preference have also played significant roles in the music and image of individual artists (Wise 1984; Schwichenberg 1993) as well as styles of music (Frith and McRobbie 1978; Reynolds 1985) and ways of consuming it (Garratt 1984). The role of gays in the development of dance music is particularly important in this respect (see Dyer 1979/1990; Lee 1995).

Any study of the history of popular music culture has to take account of these social factors. The role of economic prosperity, generational differences, the power relationships of ethnicity, gender and sexuality, and the general perception of new musical forms as undermining the status quo have all been prominent forces in forming different popular music cultures. Examining the social background, then, has to be a prominent part of analysing any one moment of history.

X 3.1 Choose a particular moment of popular music history and then research some of the social history of that place and time. Looking outside histories of popular music to more general historical analyses can be particularly informative. Can you identify factors in the economic, cultural or political environment that seem to link with choices made by musicians and music fans at that moment? Do any of the musics of that moment seem to articulate or comment on the social situation?

Technology

It is no coincidence that the history of popular music unfolded over the same period that the communication technologies of the twentieth century developed. One of the defining qualities of popular music is that it is the product of the mass media technologies and production processes of film, recording, radio, and television and video. These technologies made it possible to record or relay music performance beyond the geography and culture of its original production. The technology also made it possible to communicate to an audience many millions times larger than the audience for live music, and so in turn changed the economics of music production, making it financially worthwhile to invest massive amounts of capital in making and distributing music.

The most obvious technology of popular music is the record. However, as the current growth of the internet and the possibilities of new ways to listen and store music show, the record's dominance of music distribution is a historically specific one. The other communication technologies are equally important in the history of popular music, and it is only in the latter half of the twentieth century that the record became the primary means of listening to music. Even then formats other than vinyl records – like eight-track cartridges, music cassettes and CDs – have been as significant.

As with the histories of popular music sounds there is a narrative of technological development that structures most histories of recording and broadcasting. The stories of the early days of communication technologies are often built around individual inventors who changed the world through their new machines (Winston 1998). Later technologies are constructed as movements towards perfection in sound and visual reproduction, often built around the idea of high fidelity (see for instance Gelatt 1977; Morton 2000). As Joli Jensen has pointed out, we also have to be careful about seeing this history as about how technological 'things' changed musical 'styles'. Rather we should think about the technologies as 'processes manifested as products' (Jensen 1990, 7) and see beyond single inventions to explore how musical processes interact with technological ones.

Of course there is a chronology to this technological development and a basic timeline is reproduced as Table 3.1 on page 42. However, for our analysis it is important to be able to differentiate between the functions of the various technologies and to understand how these developments relate to the cultural world in which they were made, and so to interrogate how they were established in and changed culture.

You will see from the details of the timeline that technological innovation has taken place in four different areas of the process of producing popular music:

1. the production of musical sound itself

2. the recording of music

3. the distribution of music to consumers

4. the consumption of music.

It is also important to recognise that the implementation of technology at different historical moments has had a more profound effect in some areas than others. At the beginning of the twentieth century it was the recording and consumption of music that changed radically, with the establishment of the phonograph as a domestic technology. In turn these technological developments played an important part in altering both the production and consumption of music, and in recasting what it was to be a music performer and listener. As Michael Chanan has put it:

> If at first the phonograph record was little more than a novelty, ... it was also
> an entirely novel commodity: it turned the performance of music into a
> material object, something you could hold in your hand, which could be

1890	Phonograph and gramophone established as novelty entertainment
1900	Music recordings widely available and recording studios established using acoustic technology
1920	Radio established as the main medium for music distribution; record sales collapse
1930	Sound films establish music stars and electronic recording adopted by record companies; the 78rpm 10-inch disc becomes the main medium of recorded music
1935	Jukeboxes established and domestic radio/record-playing equipment now widely available leading to a revival in record sales
1940	Microgroove record technology on 12-inch long-playing records introduced, paralleled by developments in studio recording techniques
1945	The 7-inch 45rpm microgroove single introduced and studios now use tape as the main studio recording medium
1950	7-inch and 12-inch microgroove records now replacing 78rpm 10-inch discs; amplified guitar increasingly becomes the key instrument of popular music
1955	FM radio broadcasting leads to improvements in radio sound
1960	Stereo records introduced, and the compact cassette and eight-track cartridge introduced
1965	Portable transistor radios become widespread means to listen to music; sophisticated studio technology encourages new forms of composition
1970	Electronically generated sounds become key instruments in music; hi-fi equipment becomes increasingly common in domestic situations
1975	TV becomes a key medium for popular music as light entertainment; pop videos established as a promotional medium
1980	Cassette sales exceed vinyl; compact disc and digital audio tape formats established
1985	Personal computers allow sophisticated and low-cost recording, sampling and manipulation of music
1990	New digital formats like digital compact cassette and mini disc introduced
2000	MP3 established as the main means of internet distribution of music

TABLE 3.1 Timeline of technological developments
Source: *timeline derived from Chanan 1995; Morton 2000*

bought and sold. The effects of this innovation were both economic and aesthetic, and emerged in stages, revealing different aspects in the process.

(Chanan 1995, 7)

In time the record was to become the primary artefact of popular music, and not just a secondary practice of recording and preserving the primary performance.

Up until 1920 recording and playback was an acoustic and physical process, and record companies took no part in the developments in electrical microphones and speakers. The quality of reproduction was limited and companies understandably looked to record music that was least compromised by the abilities of the technology: small groups, mid-range and mid-volume instruments and songs of three to four minutes' duration (Morton 2000). Significantly, the technology allowed the combination of the profit motive of the existing music industry and the detachment of music from the social world in which it was formed, and it allowed music-makers to hear themselves and others in qualitative and quantitatively different ways. Aspiring musicians now learnt how music sounded from recordings, and the technology of recorded sound allowed access to those musical repertoires of African-Americans and the European vernacular tradition transformed in North America. Again Chanan summarises this process succinctly when he argues that '[the record industry] discovered how to transform the "raw" music of urban and ethnic popular culture into formulaic commodities of mass consumption' (Chanan 1995, 6).

Most histories of music technology give a significant place to the record, and to the development of recording and playback processes. However, even given the cultural significance of recording, the record remained a marginalised medium for music. Even after the invention of the record, music's main realm remained the live performance as part of an evening's wider entertainment. Recording music was just becoming a significant cultural force at the moment its development was arrested by two important economic and cultural realities of the 1920s. First, the new media of radio and sound cinema became the primary way that people heard music. These forms more closely

FIGURE 3.1 From the gramophone to the MP3 player: the formats of recorded music have changed significantly over time
Photo: Edward James Stokes

reproduced the mixed entertainment formats of music hall. Second, North America and Europe were plunged into economic depression, and expenditure on records collapsed, leaving radio as a far better-value domestic medium. Radio and sound film, once they had been established, transformed the distribution of musical sound, making the same musical performances available in new contexts and to massively larger audiences than had ever been realised before.

Film and radio also radically altered the processes of mediation as electronic microphones and speakers were institutionalised in the recording process, and a new profession of recording engineer pursued the possibility of ever improved sound quality and the opportunity to manipulate both the recording process and the recorded sound. When the record did become the main source of domestic music reproduction in the 1950s it did so as part of a new cultural practice where truth to the original through 'high-fidelity recordings' was the watchword. Paradoxically, though, the central practice of popular music production was built around the manipulation of recorded sound (Morton 2000) and the new practices of listening were enabled by the portability, but low fidelity, of the transistor, car and personal radio. Over the next 50 years popular music as recorded sound changed dramatically. The new rock & roll (which featured heavy reverb), the experiments in recorded sound stimulated first by Phil Spector and then the Beatles (which used multitracking and tape manipulation), the studio soul of the 1970s and dub of reggae (which utilised the studio as a composition tool), were all built upon a new aesthetic of music made possible by technological innovation (Jones 1992). New electronic instruments like the synthesiser represented a shift in musical sound that built upon similar qualitative changes that followed the amplification of acoustic instruments, most notably the electric guitar. These new electronic instruments allowed the creation of a vast new range of sounds and levels of amplification. Likewise, this music could be heard on a succession of domestic and portable machines from the hi-fi to the walkman to the ghetto-blaster.

In the latter part of the twentieth century innovations in recording and music technology transformed the relationship between composing, performing and recording music, collapsing them in upon themselves. Computers can sample, sequence and manipulate sound as music in ways that could not have been envisaged when the first steps were taken to record sound. We now sit on the edge of a further shift as the internet is being established as a technology that will play its part in transforming all four areas of music production. Some of these developments are the subject of a case study in Part 5.

Single historical moments of popular music culture, then, can be related to these ordering developments of technology, and in turn these moments produce forces that push technological development itself. Technology provides different possibilities of creating, distributing and hearing music at different times, while at the same time these technological processes are institutionalised in wider cultural practices, drawn from the available repertoires of how we can make music and understand it.

To give some idea of the importance of different kinds of technology in history you can use a subtraction analysis. Select a contemporary performer and then mentally subtract the key production, recording, distribution and consumption technologies on which the performer depends. So, what would happen if MP3 technology wasn't available? If computer-based recording and manipulation had not been invented? If multitracking had not been invented? And so on. Can you draw any general conclusions about the role of technology in popular music history from this analysis?

Economics of the music industry

The one major characteristic of the music industry that almost all writers on popular music note is the domination of a small group of very large companies over the production and distribution of popular music (see for instance Negus 1992). We will be looking at the contemporary implications of this in Part 2, but this dominance of a small number of large corporations with ownership interests across the entertainment business also has a powerful role in the history of popular music. Charlie Gillett's influential history of popular music since the mid-1950s, for instance, is constructed around a binary opposition between these major record companies and the small, localised American companies who were independent of the wider entertainment industry (Gillett 1971). He argues that the major record companies produced music dominated by the Tin Pan Alley tradition and that the small 'independents' produced exciting new musical forms by drawing first upon the African-American and European vernacular tradition, and then on the art tradition.

Oliver Read and Walter Welch's analysis of the growth of record companies into entertainment corporations suggests that their history can be understood as being built around two legal processes: the issuing of patents and the ownership of companies (Welch and Read 1959, 399–407). Certainly the early years of recording were characterised by complex struggles over who had the legal rights to manufacture certain recording and playback technologies. This emphasis on ownership of technological innovations has been a key aspect of corporate history ever since. The technical developments we mentioned in the last section – including the development of the 45 and LP disc format; the tape-based cartridge and cassette; digital formats like DAT, DCC, mini disc, and CD; and audio-visual media like video cassettes and DVD – have all been linked into the political economy of corporate patent ownership. The relative success of these recording media, and the relative failure of many more that could have been listed, have had a major influence on the prosperity and power of the various corporations. For instance, the historical commercial success of the Dutch music and electronics corporation Philips was as much a result of the agreements it struck with other companies to license its cassette and CD formats as it was the ability of the employees of its music divisions to spot musical talent.

Equally as complex as the shifts in ownership of patents, and equally important in the history of popular music, are the relationships between the ownerships of the various companies involved in record manufacture, recording and distribution (see

Kennedy 1994, 14–26). In the early years of the music industry, the manufacturers of record players were linked through ownership to the companies that recorded musicians and released records, and the legal right to manufacture records and playback equipment was secured in the hands of a small number of companies. Some of these companies formed the basis of the big record companies that still dominate today's record business and their names echo in today's record labels. However, the differences between the leading companies who produced and distributed popular music in 1900 and in 2000 are the result of some complicated changes in how their ownership is organised.

In the decade or so after 1920 most records were produced by a small number of companies – Victor, Brunswick and Columbia in the USA and EMI in Europe – whose interests were focused on domestic electrical goods, including record players and the records to play on them. By 1930, however, most music was supplied by another set of companies. Most significant were the RCA and CBS radio networks and various Hollywood film companies. As we have seen, radio and film became the primary medium for popular music from the mid-1920s to the late 1940s. The moving picture and broadcasting industries, whose ability to produce and distribute on a large scale brought massive economic benefit, were characterised by a concentration of ownership in the hands of a few companies. These large film and radio companies had far greater financial strength than the record companies, and there was an obvious economic benefit in owning the company selling records by the musicians or singers who were featured on your radio show or in one of your films.

For these reasons, in the two decades after 1925 most record companies were taken over by other companies with radio or film backgrounds. Victor records – which was founded in 1901 in celebration of a victory in one of the many patent cases and which by this period had become the leading American record company – was taken over by the Radio Corporation of America (RCA) in 1929; Brunswick, which manufactured radios, record players and records, sold out to Warner Brothers films in 1929, which then sold its combined record division to Columbia in 1938; Columbia itself, although initially a record and record player manufacturer independent of the radio corporation Columbia Broadcasting System (CBS), was acquired by CBS, again in 1938 (Welch and Read 1959, 399–407). In Europe the dominant recording and equipment manufacturer Electrical and Musical Industries (EMI) was formed in 1931 out of the acquisition of the British Gramophone Company and its main British competitors, and was in turn partly owned through a complex cross-ownership deal by the American Victor Company (Negus 1992, 3). These American and European companies quickly moved to dominate all forms of commercial music production across the world (see Burnett 1996, 8–28). The new corporations continued to expand their interests by buying up, or merging with, chains of live music venues and establishing control of the writing, performance and recording rights that would produce royalty payments each time a song was performed, recorded or broadcast; all of which would generate more profit (see Sanjek and Sanjek 1996, 47–211).

By the late 1940s, then, the companies that produced recording and playback equipment, recorded musicians, released records, and used music in their films and on their radio stations were integrated together into a small number of corporations that controlled the major markets of the world. This pattern of economic ownership was paralleled by an integration of the culture of music-making and listening so that films, radio and music on record were bound together in a holistic entertainment industry. The most valuable music-makers to these corporations were those whose sound and image would sell records and seats in the cinema, and promote listening to the radio. These entertainment stars would, in turn, make profits for the corporations by singing songs whose writing, recording and performing rights were also owned by the corporations. In 1950 in America, then, Columbia and RCA were the dominant record companies, followed by the British-American owned Decca, and then Capitol and a series of film company-owned labels led by MGM (Chapple and Garofalo 1977, 15). The music they recorded and broadcast was strongly linked to the traditions of professional songwriting and performed by artists who would appeal in the cinema, over the radio, on stage and on record. The biggest stars of this period were Bing Crosby, Judy Garland and Frank Sinatra.

The small record companies who operated independently of these 1950s major conglomerates of multimedia interests are championed in histories of popular music because they are seen to produce different and innovative music from that made in the mainstream of the entertainment industry. There are some examples of independent record companies taking this approach before 1950. For instance, Black Swann made some of the earliest recordings of African-American music in the 1920s (see Vincent 1995, 92–105), and Gennett Records recorded and released innovative jazz records in the 1920s and 1930s (see Kennedy 1994). However, these records are no more significant than equivalent recordings produced by Victor and Columbia (the latter through its Okeh subsidiary from 1926). It was not until the 1950s that independent record companies became vital engines of pop music history. With the new expansion of markets for African-American and country music, the new economic significance of the young in American society, and the establishment of the record as music's primary medium, the economics of popular music was transformed forever.

The new independent record companies and the music they produced – usually by local country or African-American performers – was helped significantly by a conflict that developed through the 1940s and 1950s between the owners of the songwriting copyright and radio broadcasters. To circumvent the control of the dominant American Association for Composers Artists and Publishers (ASCAP), the broadcasters set up their own organisation, Broadcast Music Incorporated (BMI), and signed up a massive number of songwriters and performers who up to that point had been outside the music industry mainstream. When the conflict with ASCAP came to a head the radio stations simply increased their broadcasts of BMI material, and therefore promoted the previously marginalised R&B and hillbilly music, and the independent record companies that recorded associated artists (Sanjek and Sanjek 1996, 184–211)

The emergent independents were usually owned by small-time entrepreneurs. Charlie Gillett captures their origins in the 1950 and 1960s when he states:

> Most independent record firms started through a combination of accident, coincidence, and opportunism, often by people who owned record shops or a chain of juke boxes, who saw that the audience wanted certain kinds of music that existing companies didn't know about or disdained dealing with.
>
> (Gillett 1974, 27)

Their business practices, though, were often underhand, self-serving and legally dubious (see Shaw 1978). On the other hand many were run by music lovers, who valued the personal independence that small-scale music production provided. If musicians did not always get their fair share of the profits from record sales, the company owners were often equally exploited by distributors, record shops, managers and promoters further along the chain.

By the 1960s the majors had reasserted their market power. It is often argued that the music turned away from the exciting new rock & roll, which had been forged from a mixture of musical and cultural backgrounds, towards an updated model of Tin Pan Alley. This new pop was aimed squarely at young Americans and Europeans, and exemplified by young songwriters like Neil Sedaka, Carole King and Gerry Goffin, who were based in the Brill Building on Broadway in New York. It was performed by an array of young artists in styles based on the pop tradition, but infused with some of the excitement of rock & roll (Garofalo 1997, 167–9).

There are other moments when independents have returned to prominence, each time connected to a new and distinctive form of popular music. In the late 1960s independents like Stax were associated with soul music in the States while others like Elektra and Asylum, and the longstanding Atlantic, were strongly linked to the new counter-culture and rock music. In all cases these companies were ultimately taken over by major corporations who used the independent's staff expertise in non-pop forms to update their own organisations, and to secure artists who were selling increasing numbers of records (Chapple and Garofalo 1977, 69–97). By the mid-1970s most American independents produced music for very localised markets – often single cities – although their records are now highly collectable and seen as some of the most interesting music of the decade (see Guralnick 1991; Pruter 1991). Only two independents, Motown and A&M, managed consistently high national sales during this period, but even they were both later absorbed into major corporations (Chapple and Garofalo 1977, 87–9).

The 1970s in Britain were characterised by a different music economy and culture. A number of independents grew out of specialist musics or the rock underground, and were usually led by charismatic entrepreneurs. They challenged the majors in Europe by the success of their individual artists, if never quite matching their market share. Most prominent was Virgin with its origins in the alternative rock scene in Britain, and Island, which started importing Jamaican reggae mainly for British residents originally from the West Indies, but then branched out into the UK's post-Beatles rock scene. The two labels were to have a significant role in promoting art rock, reggae and later African and world music. In the late 1970s and early 1980s Britain became home to several smaller key independents, most notably Rough Trade (Hesmondhalgh 1997a) and Stiff (Muirhead 1983), which supported the growth of punk and later of indie. By the 1990s independents still had important roles in rap in America and dance music in Britain. In the USA, Sugar Hill, Def Jam and Tommy Boy were all key labels that fostered early rap in their independent periods, contributing to its global popularity and place in mainstream popular music culture (George 1994; George 1999). European dance music culture has also been based strongly upon independently produced records, but few have established long-term success without financial and distribution help from the majors (see Lee 1995; Hesmondhalgh 1998).

It should be clear now that changes in popular music styles are strongly linked to the cultural context in which they were created. Social change, the technological process of recording, distributing and consuming music, and the organisation of the record and entertainment industries have important histories of their own. More importantly we can use knowledge about these factors to help us understand the processes that were developing within popular music culture at specific moments. None of these histories is singular or isolated and they all interact in complex ways that allow us to start to understand the history of popular music.

3.3 Using the information in Table 2.1 as a timeline, for each of the moments of popular music history identify a significant performer. Any general 'history of popular music' book will enable you to do this. Try and find out as many of the original record companies they recorded for as you can. How many of these can you identify as majors and how many as independents? Again, much of this information is available in these histories. How prominent are independent labels in your list? Given that, historically, well over 75 per cent of recorded music has come from major companies, are independents more or less prominent in the careers of historically notable groups? What implications do you think your findings have?

SUMMARY ●●●●●●●●●●●●

The last two chapters have set out a model for studying histories of popular music that can be used to produce a rich analysis. The model is based upon seeing single historical moments of popular music culture as the result of an interaction of a number of cultural, social, economic and technological factors. Music-makers draw on four musical and cultural repertoires when they innovate. They are the Tin Pan Alley, African-American, European vernacular and European art traditions. These repertoires provide a rich range of musical sounds and cultural practices that make popular music meaningful. While musical innovation changes these repertoires, they have remained distinctive traditions and establish the basis of the discursive practices of popular music culture. The model also suggests that innovation in music-making is a response to social, economic and technological changes. Combining the idea of a musical and cultural repertoire with attention to social, economic and technological factors encourages an analysis that treats the historical moment in its own terms, explores the relationships between dominant sounds and music industry institutions and their alternatives, and significantly widens the idea of musical roots to one of culture. This chapter includes many examples of the influence of these individual factors. In the next chapter, a series of case studies is used to show how they interact.

Further reading

Chanan, Michael 1995: *Repeated Takes: A Short History of Recording and its Effects on Music*. **Verso.**

Gillett, Charlie 1971: *The Sound of the City: The Rise of Rock and Roll*. **Souvenir Press.**

Hesmondhalgh, David 1999: 'Indie: The Institutional Politics and Aesthetics of a Popular Music Genre', in *Cultural Studies* **13(1).**

Jones, LeRoi 1966: *Blues People: Negro Music in White America*. **Jazz Book Club.**

Sanjek, Russell and Sanjek, David 1991: *American Popular Music Business in the 20th Century*. **Oxford University Press.**

Ward, Brian 1998: *Just My Soul Responding: Rhythm and Blues, Black Consciousness and Race Relations*. **UCL Press.**

CHAPTER FOUR

Case Studies

The best way to show how these ideas of music culture repertoires and social, industrial and technological contexts can be used to analyse music history is through three case studies. The first two studies in this chapter examine distinct moments of popular music histories, and focus on performers who are often featured in popular music histories, but hardly ever in the same ones. Through a contrast of these music-makers we can try to understand them in the terms in which they first worked, and how they are viewed today. The final study concentrates on the way that one aspect of the cultural context – in this case the organisation of charts in US popular music – both reflects and orders cultural values and practices over time. Using the sorts of secondary and primary sources that would be available for a student assignment, they demonstrate how the model developed in Chapters 2 and 3 can be applied.

1954–1959: Elvis Presley and Miles Davis

Elvis Presley's music is widely known; Miles Davis has been given a prominent place in histories of jazz, and his melancholic trumpet sound is often featured as incidental music on television and in films. These performers are particularly good subjects for a historical analysis as their music, films and TV appearances, interviews, and extensive biographic analyses are widely available. Although they made music at the same time and in the same country, they are not usually considered together in histories of the period, and although the sound of their music was noticeably different, they worked in a shared cultural context. Presley and Davis are presented in very different ways in the secondary accounts of their importance. The following two extracts are typical.

Elvis Presley was a poor white kid ... who lived the American Dream. ... He became the King of Rock and Roll. Endowed with a pleasant voice, the innate ability to select the right material, and an abundance of charisma ...

[His] moment was a brief period during which white teens were becoming increasingly exposed to rhythm and blues and the classic rockers through the medium of radio. Excited by its beat and suggestive lyrics, they were ready to recognise and embrace a rock messiah. [His] team – brilliant promotion and management ... and the big recording sound and clout of RCA records – perceived the moment, captured it, and sold it to America.

... Elvis began to mould elements from the roots of blues, R&B, gospel, and country ...

(Friedlander 1996, 43)

Miles Davis was one of the other leading innovators of the decade. He continually reshaped a trumpet style that was already highly individual, and his tone became more poignant ... Gil Evans, one of the most visionary arrangers in jazz, saw the possibilities of show casing Miles Davis's individuality in a series of recordings which presented him as a soloist accompanied by a twenty-piece orchestra. ... a mixture of standard tunes and ... specially composed [pieces] presented like miniature concertos. ... [The] collaborations were recording studio projects. Miles continued to work with his own small group [which] had what was considered to be one of the best rhythm sections of the era ... [and] one of Miles's tenor saxophonist colleagues ... John Coltrane, developed into one of the most influential of all Jazz musicians.

(Chilton 1979, 121)

Friedlander's full account is an example of the common approaches of popular music histories we identified earlier: Presley is constructed as disrupting existing popular music culture by combining a range of musical roots to move marginal musical forms to the mainstream. This story also emphasises the serendipity of 'the moment' and the professional skill of his managers and record company. In Chilton's story, Davis is a highly individual innovator who works cooperatively to achieve distinctive music, characterised by its musicological qualities. There is no sense here of an audience or a record industry, just a great artist and his playing.

Both accounts downplay a common set of historical conditions in which Presley and Davis produced their music. Their music-making was born out of an intermingling of the available musical and cultural repertoires, and relates directly to shifting demographics and the role of African-Americans in the USA, to radical changes in the media and record technology, and so to major shifts in how popular music was produced, distributed and consumed.

Listening to Presley's first record release from 1954 it is easy to recognise the origins of the single's two sides. 'That's All Right Mama' takes the form of mid-1950s black

R&B, and was a cover version of a recently successful urban blues record. 'Blue Moon of Kentucky', on the other hand, is unmistakably a country song. A cover again, this time of a ten-year-old hillbilly waltz, but here speeded up and given the same drive as its flip side. The recordings were made for the Memphis-based, white-owned, Sun Records, which had been successful in selling black R&B to African-American consumers. The material selected, and the record's sound was determined by owner-producer Sam Phillips' haphazard explorations and his experimentation with studio recording techniques (Guralnick 1994, 89–105). Davis' 1954 recordings were also for white-owned independent specialist record companies producing mainly black musical forms. Today they sound like archetypes of small-group jazz, conjuring up the romanticised images and sounds of a smoky basement jazz club. In fact they are a document of just this sort of performance transferred to the recording studio, mostly based on a series of 'standards' melodies – often Tin Pan Alley tunes – that all jazz players knew. After the band play the basic melody together each musician plays a solo based upon the chord structures and bar length of the song's verse in which they forcefully state their own musical personality. They finish by restating the melody (Carr 1999, 73–83).

While musically Presley was cross-fertilising between the African-American and European vernacular traditions – repeating a process that had been going on for 200 years – Davis was contributing to the establishment of jazz as art, drawing on Tin Pan Alley songs, but recasting them as complex improvised re-compositions emphasising individual expression. Both these discursive hybrids meshed perfectly with mid-1950s shifts in popular culture and the popular music media. This was a period of rising prosperity, but the United States remained a society in which school, work, entertainment and public services remained segregated on racial lines. This division was replicated through the separate and regionalised minority markets of black rhythm & blues and southern white country & western, and the smaller, but more socially prestigious, markets for jazz, classical music and the spoken word. Artists did 'cross over' from these minority music cultures to the pop mainstream, and that possibility was part of the integrationist philosophy that dominated black American and white liberal politics in this period (Ward 1998, 19–169).

It is hard to appreciate now, but what was remarkable about Presley and his contemporaries was that they were the first white Americans able to listen to large amounts of black music without physically crossing the segregation line of a racist society, as Memphis' WDIA was the first radio station to consistently play black music in the USA (Cantor 1992). African-Americans could believe that Presley's musical fusion was the precursor to a more integrated future (Ward 1998), but it allowed southern whites to love and imitate black music without having to know blacks. Presley spent the first years of his career fully within the separate C&W music industry of live venues, radio programmes and record companies, distributors and retailers, but his appeal was far greater than the usual demographics of this market. His first single was successful in both country and black R&B charts, and his appeal was strong among the newly affluent youth, not just locally in Memphis, but across America. This quickly rising popularity occurred just as the 78rpm, 10-inch disc was replaced by the

45rpm, 7-inch disc, giving his music a sense of modernity (Guralnick 1994; Sanjek and Sanjek 1996, 333–67).

FIGURE 4.1 Miles Davies in the mid-1950s. Copyright © David Redfern/Redferns, used with permission

Davis' experience of segregated America was very different. He came from an affluent middle-class black family in the USA's midwest and attended an integrated school. He was a trained musician, studying at music school, and he started his career playing with the musical revolutionaries of bebop jazz in the late 1940s. This was the moment when jazz left the mainstream of popular dance music it had dominated up until the early 1940s to enter the more elitist world of connoisseurship appealing to black and white American and European middle-class liberals. Davis' 1954 recordings were issued on the newly established 33rpm, 12-inch long-playing records (LPs), aimed by the record industry at this affluent Middle America. The long players were presented as replacements for the multi 10-inch disc 'albums' of music of classical composers, and the LP fitted easily with the aspirations of musicians and critics to present music like Davis' as an American art form to rival any produced in Europe.

By 1959 Presley and Davis had signed to major record companies: RCA Victor and Columbia respectively. They were both amassing personal fortunes as undisputed leaders of their genres. Presley was making films and TV appearances as well as albums of polished Tin Pan Alley music. He played glitzy nightclubs in Las Vegas, and was supported by the best professionals to be found in America's entertainment mainstream. Such career changes have usually been seen in histories as a fall into the commercial mainstream, when compared to his days playing exciting, R&B-infused music just five years before (Marcus 1975, 120–75). But it is hard to see what else Presley could have done. Elvis' dream was not to fuse country and R&B, but to be famous. Vegas and Hollywood were what he wanted. For his managers there was nothing beyond the margins of hillbilly music other than the mainstream of major entertainment. Although we can now see that Presley was part of the shift in popular culture that allowed performers to have careers as rock musicians, this was not a possibility in the late 1950s. As most histories make clear, Presley's legacy was to be found in the public collapse of the rigid barriers between black and white music, and their expanding possibilities as repertoires for music-making; but it is also found in the restatement of the values of Tin Pan Alley, which followed the disruption of rock & roll, and in the idea that popular music aimed at teenagers had enormous commercial potential.

Davis' work for Columbia was equally revealing of a series of other trends that are usually hidden in popular music history by the emphasis on the 1950s as 'the birth of rock & roll'. Through a series of albums, Davis altered what was understood to be jazz, and contributed significantly to both the possibilities of experimentation and the domination of the LP in the next decade of popular music culture. *Porgy and Bess* applied the idea of jazz improvisation to the form of the Broadway show album and, as on *Sketches of Spain* – based on a piece of art music – Davis worked with white arranger Gil Evans to produce a jazz version of an orchestral suite. In these records and the 1959 small-group *Kind of Blue*, he explored new forms of musical composition and improvisation, and exploited the idea of studio-based music-making that Sam Phillips had used with Presley, along with the newly established possibilities of high-fidelity stereo recording. Through this process, jazz histories tell us, Davis asserted himself into a world of art music as a genius musician, who seemed to transcend place and time, race and culture. To many, the music sounds as if this is true, when of course, as Davis increasingly felt, it was not. Over the next ten years Davis was going to attempt to build upon these new possibilities of extended length, modernist form and studio-based composition, but in a way that rejected the integrationist ambitions of his late 1950s work, and like most African-Americans he would demand to be taken as the equal of white Americans, but on his terms, not theirs.

1975–1979: the Bee Gees, Lee Perry and the Sex Pistols

The Bee Gees and the Sex Pistols are widely presented as icons of the late 1970s, and are featured heavily in TV programmes on the popular culture of this decade. Their very different styles of music are often presented as the 'poles of pop' of that historical moment (Garofalo 1997, 301). Perry's name is less well known, and he is less often featured in general histories of popular music. However, reggae collectors revere his music and he has been widely influential in a range of genres (Toop 1995, 161–4). The differences between these three artists are well represented in the way in which their respective histories are told. Three examples will illustrate this effectively.

By the time that [the brothers] Gibb struck disco gold they had already been through three musical incarnations: as a Beatle sound-alike act[; three] undistinguished solo careers[; and a] re-union in early 1970 (which) produced a few more hits but still no distinctive voice. ... It took Atlantic's producer Arif Mardin to help them create their disco era persona. Mardin encouraged an R&B feel [and] Barry unveiled the falsetto that would be the Bee Gees' disco trademark. The sound was perfected on 'You Should be Dancing', which rose to number one in 1976. Still while they moved steadily up the ranks of the disco artists, they did not capture the disco crown until Robert Stigwood commissioned them to write the sound track for *Saturday Night Fever*. ... The Bee Gees had been associated with Stigwood since the start of their careers... [He] was a master of what the industry was beginning to call 'crossover media' a product in one medium can sell a product in another. ... The plan was orchestrated to perfection with *Saturday Night Fever*.

(Garofalo 1997, 343–5)

[Lee 'Scratch' Perry] ... made his impact performing at Studio One in the Ska era. He had then been instrumental in Joe Gibbs' early success, and went on to produce for himself, making a radical impression with the most innovative work of the Wailers' entire career, as well as a further string of classic vocal discs ... and one of the most impressive early dub albums. In the mid–late 1970s, Scratch ... was one of the quartet of innovative Jamaican producers destined to find a larger audience after the event particularly among those coming to reggae from outside. ...

[His] sound exemplified the Jamaican approach of making maximum demands of minimal resources. Sound textures that were unique anyway were developed further through working with four-track equipment, and the necessity of dumping completed tracks onto one track so as to free them for further over dubbing. Perry's fascination with new technology and his propensity for imaginative risk taking were the other essential components in the process.

(Barrow and Dalton 1997, 164–5)

Central to the myth of the Sex Pistols is Malcolm McLaren, the group's manager. [He] enjoyed picturing himself as a Machiavellian manipulator with a master plan to use the power of the music industry against itself ...

(Garofalo 1997, 306)

By the end of 1976 the Sex Pistols had signed a record contract with ... EMI, and recorded and released their first single 'Anarchy in the UK'. It sold 50 000 copies and reached the top 40 ... Mainstream newspapers were most likely to use terms such as crazed, pathological, rancid, and savage to describe the music and its players. Pressure from a variety of sources, including other artists on the label, allowed EMI to drop the Pistols from its roster … The Pistols also signed with A&M, but three days later they were dropped … Thus in the space of three months the band had accrued $250 000 for being kicked off two record labels.

Virgin records became the third label to sign the band. They released 'God Save the Queen' in May 1977. The negative publicity surrounding punk and the Pistols caused the band to be banned from performing at most venues around the [country] …

(Friedlander 1996, 253)

Garofalo's discussion of the Bee Gees highlights the role of a music industry entrepreneur, working with the industry to exploit the 'blank page' professionalism of a group, and the rising popularity of disco. In Barrow and Dalton's account of Lee Perry, by contrast, the producer is constructed as a genius of his musical genre, making contributions to key points in the development of reggae and realising the possibilities of new studio technology, and even exceeding its perceived limits. Garofalo's and Friedlander's full accounts highlight the three factors that are central to the way the Sex Pistols have been inscribed into pop history: the self-publicising, self-consciously manipulative manager; the shock of their music and its sensationalisation by the media; and the failure of the record companies to comprehend what they were taking on board. These histories construct very different versions of popular music culture. Differences that are reflected in the way we hear the music that each artist produced.

The Bee Gees' 1975 LP *Main Course* and the hit single, 'Jive Talking', it contained are typical of the group's musical approach from this point on. They draw heavily on soul and funk styles in both performance and production, the latter the responsibility of Arif Mardin, a key black music producer at Atlantic records. As if to index this connection to the African-American tradition the title of the single rather self-consciously takes its title from the term for black vernacular speech. The music did well in the discos of New York and Los Angeles, and for that reason it should be no surprise that the group's music featured heavily in the film *Saturday Night Fever*, the storyline of which is based in the disco culture of the late 1970s. However, the music's place in the film owes more to the control of Robert Stigwood – probably the most successful independent music industry entrepreneur of the 1970s – than it does to its subcultural relevance. As well as managing the group, and controlling the label that released the Bee Gees' records, Stigwood was best known for his domination of the rock musical. He had been responsible for originating or developing a series of record, stage and film extravaganzas that updated the tradition of the Broadway and Hollywood musical. In this context *Saturday Night Fever* was merely a natural progression. So effective was Stigwood in connecting and cross-promoting his various interests that it is hard to separate the meanings of the Bee Gees' music and image from the film and its LP soundtrack.

Lee Perry started recording in the 1960s and his recorded output is massive, although very few of the records are under his own name. His own musicianship and singing talent is limited, but as a producer he created one of popular music's most distinctive bodies of recorded music. By 1975 he had established a recording studio in his own home, where he was to produce what is widely seen as his best work (see Katz 2000). His productions in the 1970s were released outside Jamaica on Island records, a key British independent. The records featured a series of artists in a variety of reggae styles from solo singers and harmony groups to instrumentals and remixed dubs. The music was rooted in the very distinctive music culture of Jamaica, which was built around outdoor, record-based 'sound systems' run by entrepreneurs who also owned record studios, record presses and music shops, and produced their own records (Bradley 2000). Perry started working for these sound system bosses before branching out on his own in pursuit of a greater share of the profits and the increased freedom to produce and release his own records (Katz 2000, 137–79). Listening to any of his releases for the UK-based independent Island label – whether fronted by pop-reggae singer Susan Cadogan, spoken-word 'toaster' Jah Lion, or Perry's dubs released as the Upsetters' *Super Ape* – it is the density of the music and the producerly qualities of the sound that are first obvious. This is not music created by simply recording the performances of musicians and singers, but by recording layer upon layer of musical sound and then manipulating it at the mixing desk. As well as the musical sound, the subject matter of the songs is strikingly different. Many of the lyrics are rooted in the black consciousness movement and its Jamaican religious offshoot Rastafarianism. The lyrics are echoed by the singing voice of Perry and his artists, who feature strong Jamaican accents.

The Pistols' first single, 'Anarchy in the UK', sounds stripped-down even for the 1970s. Its basic instrumentation of guitars, bass and drums harks back to the basics of Memphis rock & roll, and the short guitar solo reproduces the condensed single-notes style used by Elvis' first guitarist. In 1976 the music was understood in the context of existing styles, and this single was everything mainstream rock was not. It was short, built on a frantic shifting beat, the vocal was shouted rather than sung (Laing 1985) and the production sounded like it was recorded in a practice room rather than a recording studio (which it was) (Savage 1991, 205). The lyric seems consciously created to shock. It almost rhymes 'I am an antichrist' with 'I am an anarchist'. The half-spoken half-sung delivery draws particular attention to the words and yet also rather artificially emphasises the final '-ist' of each line. This makes the rhyme more feasible, but possibly also reflects a playfulness with the spoken sounds themselves (Laing 1985, 54). The released recording was – unusually for the time – made without the assistance of a record company. The finished package of record and group image was then sold to EMI, then the leading British record company. The band's manager, Malcolm McLaren, arranged each step in the group's progress (Savage 1991).

These three artists are usually chosen for histories because at the time they represented dramatic shifts in popular music. To understand these differences from the dominant music of the time we need to understand the political-economic context. During the 1970s European and North American record markets were experiencing unprecedented expansion and concentration of control. In the USA receipts from record sales outstripped those from cinema seat sales for the first time, European and American record companies focused upon a small number of high-selling artists who received royalty payments that were 70 per cent up on those received just a few years before, and the six biggest labels, owned by massive entertainment corporations, controlled over 80 per cent of sales in the USA and 60 per cent in Britain (Laing 1985, 1–7; Sanjek and Sanjek 1996, 549). The bureaucracies of the majors were shadowed by a series of entrepreneurs who often moved from company to company, or allied their independent companies to a major through the release of a single record or a packaged distribution and promotion deal.

In America and Europe the record companies organised their promotional activities around the idea of two main markets: pop and rock. Pop was understood to be based mainly on the sales of 7-inch singles aimed at younger buyers, and centred on top 40 sales charts. Rock was perceived to be for an older, more male, group of consumers, and delivered through 12-inch LPs. These core markets were paralleled by a series of smaller markets for soul, reggae, country, jazz, classical and soundtrack records. With the exception of reggae, these markets were larger in the USA than Europe, but in both territories they provided valuable additional profit, though not on the scale of the pop and rock markets. Disco, reggae and punk all offered a significant challenge to the certainties of this rock and pop music culture, although throughout the 1970s there were many examples of dance, reggae and proto-punk rock records making the pop charts through what was called 'cross-over'. However, this was understood to be a process of individual records crossing from parallel markets into the pop mainstream, and hence adding to the profits of the specialist record company subdivision. These records were always seen as novelties, and so did not disrupt the certainties of record company knowledge which, mapped onto the pop/rock division, structured the record companies and their markets.

In their own ways the records of the Bee Gees, Lee Perry and the Sex Pistols disrupted these certainties. With different degrees of transparency, each of these artists owed a significant debt to the possibilities of the individual in the corporate world of the music industry. And each produced music that drew heavily on traditions of popular music that had been marginalised by the pop/rock binary, and was linked to significant senses of cultural identity.

Disco was built around the night culture of gays in North America's major cities. The music itself drew upon Philly (Philadelphia) soul, funk, and latin salsa and soul hybrids (Brewster and Broughton 1999, 182–220). In the disco this music was consumed as a celebration of 'eroticism, romanticism and materialism' (Dyer 1979/1990), and the music culture's combination of showbusiness glamour and the energy and sexual expressiveness of the dance floor could easily be turned into conspicuous consumption. This was the basis of disco's cross-over from black, Latino and gay clubs, through high-society clubs like New York's Studio 54, and the suburban clubs of Italian America and eventually into the mainstream pop charts (Brewster and Broughton 1999, 182–220). Stigwood understood that the music and dance of disco culture could easily be used to update the rock musical form that he had worked with in the decade before. A more contemporary feel was achieved in *Saturday Night Fever* by combining a Scorsese-derived directorial style with the ethnographic claims of the New York magazine article on which the storyline was based (Cohn 1989). In doing so he simultaneously articulated the ideas of disco culture to a wider audience, and promoted the artists he controlled as the defining sound of that culture (see Gilbert and Pearson 1999, 7–12).

Reggae in the late 1970s drew heavily on the repertoires of the African-American tradition. For Perry, like a large number of Jamaican musicians at this time, his music was both a very personal and a very cultural expression of black identity (Davis and Simon 1983, 59–71). Although he followed the Jamaican practice of producing covers of American soul and pop hits, he increasingly and self-consciously tried to produce music that would be perceived as more 'African'. To do so he utilised Burru drummers from the African-orientated religious cults of Jamaican marginalised society. The drums added to the deep, textured feel of his music, which was also emphasised by the prominent bass guitar typical of reggae. But like most reggae its roots are not monocultural and he also drew on the Jamaican obsession with the exploitation cinemas of the spaghetti western, the horror film and the kung fu movie (Katz 2000). These musical qualities also signalled his own Rastafarian beliefs, and his desire for creative freedom and business independence. His location in Jamaican popular music culture is paralleled by his popularity in Britain, and to a lesser extent at this time, in the USA. Although many of his records were played at the sound system dances for black Britons of West Indian origin, his records were also distributed by the British independent label Island. The label's owner, Chris Blackwell, an expatriate white Jamaican, had started his music business career selling imported reggae singles to newly migrated Jamaicans and members of the skinhead culture of the late 1960s. In the intervening years he had built up his record company into Britain's leading independent, first on a roster of key British art rock bands, and later and most significantly through the reggae star Bob Marley. Blackwell's innovative strategy was to sell reggae not as novelty pop but as rock music. He was successful too, but Marley's early death and the disruption of the rock aesthetic brought about by punk undermined this stratagem (see Bradley 2000, 103–7). The opportunity for reggae to have widespread mainstream success was lost, and in Jamaica the music mutated into ragga and dance hall. Even so the 1970s 'roots' sound seeped into all parts of the world, eventually becoming a key music in all continents. Perry's own influence was not to be felt fully until 15 years later when a new generation of musicians manipulating sound on computers used his 1970s records as a reference point for their own production experiments.

Punk, like most labels of popular music, referred to a range of styles of music and music practice. Laing has pointed to the diverse range of music and musicians who contributed to the formation of punk, including the London pub rock scene, 1960s US garage bands, and New York art rock groups (Laing 1985). While pub rock – a scene of small-scale music venues in British pubs – drew explicitly on the African-American tradition and especially the rhythm & blues music of the 1950s, which had been a cornerstone of rock & roll, the contributions of art-school culture were just as strong (Frith and Horne 1987). When first a number of fanzines, and then specialist music magazines, defined this diverse music as 'punk' they set the boundaries of its meanings, and placed the Sex Pistols at the centre. As punk, the music was just part of a wider homology of meanings in which dress (safety pins, bondage trousers and spiky hair) and behaviour (spitting and swearing) were just as important as musical style (Hebdige 1979, 23–9). An anti-establishment stance was so important to punk sensibility that insiders were declaring that punk was dead within a few months of its appearance in the mainstream media (see Burchill and Parsons 1978). Looking back, 25 years on, the DIY culture of forming a band, playing live, and recording and releasing records independently of the major music corporations was to be hugely influential over the next decade's indie rock scene (Hesmondhalgh 1999). Punk's legacy to late twentieth-century music is also to be found in the notions of spectacle and irony that were particularly apparent in the Sex Pistols. Their manager, McLaren, revelled in, and made explicit, the manipulation of the media he believed he was orchestrating. This is particularly apparent in his contributions to the film *The Great Rock 'n' Roll Swindle*. The film, directed by fellow art school graduate Julian Temple, constructs one version of the Pistol's myth. The preoccupation with the mediations of popular music, and the linkage of sound with cultural style, which was central to punk along with an ironic glorification of the Tin Pan Alley tradition, were to form what in the 1980s would be called postmodern pop (see Storey 2001, 161–4).

The Bee Gees, Lee Perry and the Sex Pistols, then, simultaneously represented new forms of excitingly different entertainment, new ways to manipulate the consumer through an understanding of the organisation of the music industry, and key indexes of the increased visibility of the marginalized identity of African-Americans, gays and an ironic youth in popular music culture.

Naming black music charts: 1942 to 2002

The way that we understand popular music is in large part organised by the sorts of language we use to talk about it and the way we categorise it. A revealing example of these categorising processes can be found in the naming of record sales charts for music of African-American origin. Taking as a primary source the titles of black music charts in *Billboard* magazine from their inception in 1942 through to 2002, it is possible to contextualise these changing terms by drawing on secondary sources in the historiographies of popular music culture.

Billboard is the American music industry's main trade publication, and its charts are the most widely cited national calculations of record sales in the USA. Starting with a pre-war 'Honor role of Hits' and later a 'Hot 100' list each week, *Billboard* has calculated and presented the best-selling records in descending order. As well as these national best-selling lists, it offers a series of other charts including, from 1942, a chart of music that sells to African-American audiences. The names of this list have changed over the past 60 years as shown in Table 4.1.

1942	Harlem Hit Parade	1963	[no separate chart]	1982	Black
1945	Race Records	1965	R&B	1990	R&B
1949	Rhythm and Blues	1969	Soul		

TABLE 4.1 *Billboard* charts for music of African-American origin, 1942 to 1990

The term 'hit parade' was already in use in the 1930s to describe the pop charts and the prefix 'Harlem' gave it a nice alliteration as well as connoting the African-American audience whose tastes this chart was designed to represent. Harlem, at the northern end of Manhattan Island in the city of New York, hosted the major black community in the city, and has a key place in the history of African-American music. By the 1920s the district had become the centre of a distinctive African-American intellectual and cultural movement termed the Harlem Renaissance (Floyd 1990, 1–28). It was here that band leaders Duke Ellington and Fletcher Henderson fused black blues forms and hot jazz styles with dance band music (Chilton 1979, 47–56).

On the edge of Harlem was the Cotton Club. It was here that Ellington made his name fulfilling the exotic notions the club's white middle-class clientele had of African-Americans with his 'jungle music'. The sophisticated, ambitious music was presented as primitive and sexual in the club's jungle setting and cabaret of dance and music (Haskins 1985). The noun Harlem, then, articulates the paradox of one part of African-American music in the first 40 years of the twentieth century: for the black musicians it represented an attempt to construct a culture the equal of that of white Americans, but for the latter group it was a symbol of the primitivism of sexualised escape.

The use of the term 'Harlem Hit Parade' represented an attempt to define the records bought by African-Americans from the perspective of the New York-based Tin Pan Alley traditions of the mainstream music industry. From their position just off Broadway, in Midtown Manhattan, the white industry executives felt the world of black music was as alien as the streets of Harlem just a short subway ride uptown. Although in the 1940s Manhattan was becoming an important place for the development of small-group bebop jazz, most African-American record buyers bought a very different type of music, made in other industrial cities of northern USA.

Billboard tried to signal this by changing the name of its chart to 'Race Records'. From the position of the twenty-first century, learning that the music of African-Americans was organised as 'race' music is quite a shock. This had been a widely used term in the music industry since the very early years of recorded music, although by the 1940s it was limited to the white industry establishment. The connotations of the term race are complex. Today it is associated with a now generally discredited approach to understanding the peoples of the world, which under the cover of a supposed scientific investigation sought to prove that white-skinned peoples were biologically superior to dark-skinned folk. In the early twentieth century, though, 'race' was widely used in the same way that the term ethnicity is used today. That is to say it represented a particular group of people with distinct cultural qualities. In the 1920s, African-Americans used the term positively as a collective noun defining their own cultural identity. In these terms, then, race music would articulate the distinctive culture of African-Americans (George 1988, 8–11).

The term 'race records' entered the vocabulary of the music industry in 1920 when white record producer Ralph Peer used the term to describe a new series of record releases of classic blues singers like Mamie Smith and Bessie Smith aimed at an African-American audience (Sanjek and Sanjek 1996, 31). Up until 1930 this was a major market for records, as there was little African-American music to be heard on the radio (Barlow 1995). African-American record buyers were sufficiently numerous to keep several independent companies, including black-owned ones, in business. However, the Great Depression and the resultant widespread unemployment led to the collapse of record sales and the companies that supplied them (Garofalo 1997, 46–50).

It was not until the industrial expansion created by wartime production in the 1940s, which led to rising prosperity among African-Americans, that the market for black music grew again. By then, though, the women singers of the classic blues and male singer/guitarists of the country blues were being eclipsed by the new urban music of the electric guitar-based bands of rhythm & blues. By the late 1940s the African-American communities in the northern industrial cities had grown dramatically as people migrated in search of jobs created by the post-war boom. These communities became a significant market for music, initially met by a new generation of independent record companies like Chess in Chicago, Atlantic in New York and King in Cincinnati (Gillett 1988; Garofalo 1997, 78–80; Cohodas 2000)

Sales of records to black consumers were, from 1949, tracked by a rhythm and blues chart. For over a decade, hundreds of rhythm & blues record companies were set up in cities and towns with black populations, producing the R&B and doo-wop music that was to contribute to the foundations of rock & roll (Gillett 1971, 23–37). The rising prosperity of the 1950s and the increasing prominence of African-American sporting and entertainment stars in wider US society suggested to young blacks that it was possible to integrate into mainstream American society. Brian Ward suggests that these integrationalists aspirations were reflected in a shift in popular music tastes, with an increase in sales for black pop, rather than R&B, along with white pop among black buyers (Ward 1998). *Billboard* obviously thought so as well, and in 1963 stopped publishing a chart listing sales among African-American buyers, presumably because the pattern of sales was so similar to that of the Hot 100. Detroit-based Motown was the defining record label of this period. Owned by black entrepreneurs and releasing music by black singers, it nevertheless declared itself 'the sound of young America' and modelled its releases far more on the white-produced girl group sounds of the early 1960s than the R&B of the decade before (Early 1995; Smith 1999).

However, the 1960s is also well known for another form of black music much more rooted in the changing views of the African-American communities. *Billboard* recognised these changes, but returned to an earlier terminology, reinstating its black music chart as R&B. Brian Ward and Nelson George both cite Ray Charles and Sam Cooke as key artists in this musical change in the way they brought together R&B and gospel music into what became known as soul music. But there was more at play here than a shift in musical form. Soul was an articulation of a distinctive, culture-affirming, black way of life: 'Soul style, as manifested in distinctively black ways of walking and talking, eating, dressing, joking, thinking, working, playing, dancing and making music, defied analysis or imitation by outsiders' (Ward 1998, 182). James Brown was emblematic, the self-styled 'Godfather of Soul', who proclaimed 'I'm Black and I'm Proud'. In 1969 this new music cultural form was recognised by *Billboard* and its chart was renamed 'Soul'.

It is no coincidence that soul remained the name for the black music chart for 13 years, on a par with the 'rhythm & blues' nomenclature. Although African-American music in the 1970s was diverse and fast changing, the term soul embraced it all. The idea of soul was self-consciously articulated through Africanised clothes and hair, southern styles of food, the search for 'black' musical forms, and support for the civil rights or black power movements (Ward 1998). While Memphis-based Stax records symbolised the early soul sound (Bowman 1997), the sounds of soul became increasingly varied. The increasing importance of the producer led to a studio soul championed by Isaac Hayes, developed by a raft of Motown producers and which achieved its most mature form in Philly soul (Cummings 1975). Experiments with earlier forms of jazz, R&B and rock produced funk – meaning dirty – from bands like Kool and the Gang, Ohio Players and Parliament (Vincent 1996).

Much of this music achieved wider popularity among white Americans and Europeans, and many of the artists were signed up to large music corporations. Such 'cross-over' from black buyers to white buyers had been a characteristic of the market for music since the mid-1950s but during the 1970s it became a highly politicised cultural phenomena (Perry 1988). George argues that it led to the 'Death of Rhythm and Blues' (1988), and the rise of a disco culture in the USA led to a dissemination of black musical forms into the mainstream of American pop music equal to that of rock & roll 20 years before.

In the face of the internationalisation of a strongly disco-influenced pop-soul sound, a new range of primarily African-American musical forms were developed in different cities of the USA. Hip-hop in New York, go-go in Washington, house in Chicago, techno in Detroit all reinterpreted the past of soul and funk forms into a new musical culture distinctive to the particular location, ethnicity and sexuality of its host culture (Rose 1994; Reynolds 1998; Sicko 1999). Together with the rising popularity of reggae and dance hall, the developments of studio soul into swing beat, and a continued interest in older forms of black music, the term soul could no longer cover them all. Reflecting the idea of black music produced for black consumers the chart changed its name first to 'Black' music, and then in 1990 returned to the term 'R&B.'

The reuse of the term R&B owes a significant debt to Nelson George and his concept of the 'R&B world', his role at *Billboard* magazine in the 1990s and his championing of a new generation of black entertainment industry entrepreneurs like Def Jam's Russell Simmons. For George the connections between hip-hop/R&B and post-soul black consciousness were this culture's most important characteristics (George 1998). R&B was taken up as a musical category for music firmly rooted in the tradition of studio soul/swing beat, but now infused with the vocal attack of hip-hop and production techniques derived from the break beat and house/techno manipulations. The political economy of contemporary R&B is indistinguishable from the Tin Pan Alley structures of mainstream pop, and the cultural articulations of soul have been replaced by a commitment to entertainment spectacle. Although it is possible to trace the musical sounds of R&B back to an earlier rhythm & blues, the sound and stance of contemporary R&B are as distinct from 1950s rhythm & blues as 1960s soul was from 1920s hot jazz.

It is hard to sustain the idea that the R&B chart still identifies what is selling to African-American consumers. The parallel economy of black music celebrated by

George – based on specialist record companies, regional distributors and small retailers, and promoted through local tours and black radio – and which sustained a musical culture, has gone. Black music entrepreneurs are most likely to work as independent producers for major record companies, and artists contracted to these companies and marketed internationally. While modern black music still sells significantly to a black audience it is far more widely popular, and the charts represent the sales of a type of music, rather than the purchases of a type of record buyer. For the record industry, R&B is now a marketing category and not a market, and for music fans R&B is just one sound among many.

SUMMARY

This chapter offers three case studies, each of which demonstrates an application of the model for studying the past of popular music culture outlined in Chapters 2 and 3. While many of the ingredients were drawn from existing secondary accounts of the time or recording artists, by combining them with primary materials and working through a structured analysis new insights are generated. This is not to claim that we have revealed the truth of the moment. Rather this is an attempt to open up the plurality of moments of popular music's past. We can then understand, for instance, that Presley and Davis, or the Bee Gees, Perry and the Sex Pistols, worked at more or less the same times, but operated with very different discourses of popular music, and drew on different repertoires to make very different responses to different social factors. We can also understand that our responses to them today are set within our own discursive practices.

In exploring the history of the music, we have also raised a series of questions about the institutions and industries that organise popular music, the meanings that it has, and how audiences consume it. These are examined in greater detail in the next three parts of the book.

Further reading

Bradley, Lloyd 2000: *Bass Culture.* **Viking.**

Carr, Ian 1999: *Miles Davis: The Definitive Biography.* **HarperCollins.**

Garofalo, Reebee 1997: *Rockin' Out: Popular Music in the USA.* **Allyn & Bacon.**

George, Nelson 1988: *The Death of Rhythm & Blues.* **Omnibus.**

Guralnick, Peter 1994: *Last Train to Memphis: The Rise of Elvis Presley.* **Little, Brown.**

Katz, David 2000: *People Funny Boy: The Genius of Lee 'Scratch' Perry.* **Payback Press.**

Laing, Dave 1985: *One Chord Wonders: Power and Meaning in Punk Rock.* **Open University Press.**

Savage, Jon 1991: *England's Dreaming: Sex Pistols and Punk Rock.* **Faber & Faber.**

Part TWO:
Industries and Institutions

Of all the aspects of popular music that we study, the industry producing the music is the least visible to us. There are clues to the organisation of this industry in the names of the record labels that we can find on the cover of any CD, cassette or 12-inch single, and in all the small-print detail of who recorded and distributed the record, who wrote the music, and who owns the copyright for the song and recordings. These clues are like the tip of an iceberg: a sign of the industry, but not one that prepares us for the massive hidden economic and cultural activity going on underneath. Central to this activity is the recording of music and its distribution in a form we can listen to. Although the term 'record' is now often used to mean vinyl discs, rather than CDs and MP3 files, it is a good term to use to cover all these formats of recorded music. Likewise, the organisations that produce and sell recorded music are still collectively called the record industry. Accordingly, these are the terms used throughout this book. To get a full understanding of the place of records in popular music culture we must study this industry in some detail to uncover who makes recorded music and what influence they may have in the wider culture.

There is a good library of books and published research on the music industry, so there is plenty of material for secondary study. In addition, in spite of the initial low profile of the industry, there are also many ways to access valuable primary material to test out the theories outlined in the published books and journals. Different writers, though, have emphasised different aspects of the popular music industries and so we need to draw on a range of studies and build up a rounded overall picture.

The analysis of the industries and institutions of popular music outlined in this part is divided into three main chapters. Chapter 5 is an overview of the production of popular music, identifying its dominant form of organisation and the main criticisms that are made of this dominant form. This chapter also includes a key analysis of the production processes and economic imperatives that drive institutional activities. Chapter 6 focuses on the record industry and looks in detail at the way that record companies operate, as well as examining the relationships between small record companies and the major global entertainment corporations. The final chapter in this part looks at the wider media and the relationships between record production and promotion, and the media forms that carry or comment upon popular music. This chapter includes a case study of popular music radio in the USA and Europe.

CHAPTER FIVE

An Overview of Popular Music Production

Before getting to grips with the detail of the music industry it is helpful to look at the bigger picture. This is best understood by working through the answers to some basic questions. What are the industry's main characteristics? What sorts of arguments are made about the industry? What factors led to this form of organisation?

The dominant organisation of music production, and its critics

Probably the most significant fact about the production of recorded music is that the vast majority of it is produced by a very small number of companies. By most estimates between 70 and 80 per cent of all the records sold in the world are produced by just five massive corporations. At the time of writing these corporations – collectively known as the 'big five' – are AOL Time Warner, Bertelsmann, EMI, Sony and Universal. Some of these names are recognisable from the record labels we regularly look at, and they appear in other media products like films, television programmes or the press. Others, though, may not be so well known. The reason for this is that all of these corporations are more than just producers of records; they are also involved in the whole range of media entertainment.

Each of the big five corporations has a division to deal with its music interests. The names of these major music divisions still reflect the corporate owners rather than the wider range of brands we are used to seeing on record sleeves and labels. They are Warner Music Group (WMG), Bertelsmann Music Group (BMG), EMI Music, Sony and Universal Music. In turn, these record divisions also release records using a range of label names, and so the identity of the major company is sometimes n in complex relationships of ownership. Record sleeves usually show something of these ownership relationships. For example, records released on the RCA label will say that 'RCA is a BMG company', or those on the Epic label that 'Epic is a division of Sony Records'.

I stress that this information about the dominant corporations was correct at the time of writing because the ownership and control of the production of music has been constantly changing, and the lists produced by writers in the 1990s are now out of date, so it is very likely that they will have changed again by the time you read this. However, even if the names of the corporations have changed somewhat, the patterns of ownership and control – characterised by their concentration, transnational organisation and multimedia activities – will not have changed. Control of recorded music is consolidated in the hands of a few corporations that operate in most countries of the world, and as well as records they produce products or services in other areas of the record industry, music business or wider world of media entertainment.

Using your own music collection as a sample, produce a breakdown of what proportion of your collection was produced by one of the five majors, and what proportion by smaller companies. In some cases this may take some detective work as the major record companies release records on a number of different labels. Does your collection mirror the 70 to 80 per cent control by the big five corporations?

The domination of the production and distribution of recorded music by a small number of corporations, and the way they devise their business strategies to coordinate their music and other media interests has understandably led to criticism. Such criticisms were being made well before 1950, even before the characteristics of concentration, globalisation and multimedia activities of music production had become so obvious. Two influential critics here were Theodor Adorno and Max Horkheimer, who were particularly concerned about the way that the commercialisation of music production would restrict the creativity of music-making, and that the very idea that music was an art would be lost. They saw the production of music as part of a wider 'culture industry' (Adorno and Horkheimer 1997; originally published in 1947). Today a variation on this term – now the cultural industr*ies* – is widely used in a descriptive or even positive way (Smith 1998). Adorno and Horkheimer, however, were making a critical point. They argued that if music was now an industry then it could not be art. Further, they felt that the ideology of commerce that dominated cultural production – and which is expressed in the very terms 'record industry' or 'music business' – had ensured that consumers would accept inferior forms of music. They proposed: 'The truth that they are just business is made into an ideology in order to justify the rubbish they deliberately produce' (Adorno and Horkheimer 1997, 31). Theirs, then, is a damning criticism of all popular music.

Since the 1970s popular music academics have highlighted the dominant form of production as a key characteristic of record production and, taking an anti-capitalist position, they have championed the independent record companies that existed after

1950 as a source of more interesting and socially relevant music (see for instance Gillett 1971). We can see this as a recasting of Adorno and Horkheimer's position. In this reformulation the attack is not on the whole of commercially produced music as the product of an undifferentiated culture industry, but instead only on the institutions of the dominant organisation of production in popular music culture. Marc Elliot's historical study of the US record business presents it as an industry that converts the oppositional meanings of popular music into profit under the ever-increasing control of the corporations (Elliot 1990). Elliot comes to the study from a very personal position, which he articulates at the beginning and end of his book. He contrasts the cultural meanings that music has for him with its use in advertising for major corporations as part of their branding processes. A similar position is taken by Dave Harker, who links his analysis of the music industry with a wider critique of capitalism. He argues that popular music is changed by the involvement of the music industry. In this context he claims that the potential for artists to express political positions are so compromised they merely become slogans that can not disturb the status quo: 'under capitalism, it will remain the case that most artists (if not most of the audience) will have to be content to succumb to the commercial sausage machine, and be compensated with cash' (Harker 1980, 111).

Often this later analysis has been combined with a belief that popular music could play an important cultural role in achieving a fairer and more democratic society if it could only be separated from the activities of major record companies. This is a particularly important position for a generation of academics who grew up listening to rock music in the 1960s and 1970s and who believed it had an important role in the counter-culture (see for instance Chapple and Garofalo 1977; Grossberg 1992a). In this position it is not just the creative possibilities of music that are seen as being constrained by the dominance of the corporations, but also its potential to be the 'voice of a generation'. A similar notion of the monolithic corporation and the creative possibilities of the independent record company was developed over the next 20 years: first, when punk rock became strongly aligned with independent record companies (Laing 1985), and then again in the mid-1980s when alternative rock even took its generic name, indie, as a sign of its non-corporate roots (Hesmondhalgh 1999).

However, not all popular music academics have accepted the binary opposition between major and independent companies. Writing with the anti-corporation, pro-independent approach in mind, Simon Frith has argued that they are based on two mistaken 'anti-corporate myths':

> Myth 1 pitched artists and their audiences against an industry that, supposedly, denied people access to their music with a series of greedy, profit obsessed gatekeepers. Myth 2 celebrated independent labels as rock's real creative entrepreneurs – the majors were accused of simply taking over and hemogenizing the original sounds and styles the indies developed. Neither of these myths made much sense about how the rock business actually worked – as a highly efficient organisation of market servicing.
>
> (Frith 1992, 66)

Frith makes an important point. It is easy when looking at the production of music to rely on very broad ideas and a generally negative disposition, rather than detailed analysis. Although Frith's point can come across as support for the major companies, that would be a very limited way of understanding it. Rather than taking a stand against the music business he invites us to critically understand how it works.

5.2 The dismissal of the music produced by major record companies and the celebration of the small independent record companies is not restricted to scholars of popular music, but is often found in the comments of music fans too. Read the extract from a letter to the music press reproduced below. What similarities to the positions of Adorno and Horkheimer, Elliot or Harker can you identify? How strong is the notion that music is something outside of record production?

I WANT IT MY WAY

I hate kids, they really annoy me. They should be banned from buying music until they're 16.

I remember the days when so-called 'indie' or 'alternative' music was left alone to people who appreciate it, but it's all now been colonized and popularised by loads of kids who haven't got a clue, and would buy anything if it was flavour of the month.

I recall the days, and great days they were too, when bands rarely charted and getting a single in the Top 40 was an achievement. Nowadays, all the bands that I once liked chart highly, thanks to the kids, and it therefore takes something out of the music I once loved.

I have anticipated the possible response to this, and I agree I am an elitist and I don't care. If I like a band and they become all commercial and popular they are then corporate sellouts and I don't like them any more. I'm with John Peel: I like my music to be uncommercial, unpopular and unappreciated by the masses – and I am proud to say that I am an elitist.

(Adapted from a letter in the *NME*)

Conceptualising the dominant form of organisation of music production

Popular music scholars have used a number of key concepts in order to critically understand the industry. The production and consumption of music is often presented as a 'global market', the ownership of production concentrated in the hands of a few corporations, and music production increasingly linked to entertainment and new technologies (see Burnett 1996). These academic approaches often share common ground with how the industry presents itself. Keith Negus has drawn attention to how the corporations characterise the organisation of music production within their annual reports to shareholders. He shows how these corporations actively link their future development with the idea of a global market and a growing demand for information and entertainment, of which music is seen as a key part (Negus 1992, 5–7). It is apparent that it is important to those who control the corporation to present their businesses as part of a multinational, multimedia future. It is certainly the case that these corporations operate in virtually every country in which records are sold, and they certainly have a dominant presence in every continent. Although the proportions vary, these major entertainment corporations control the majority of significant national markets. However, just because our initial observations, the arguments of critics and the rhetoric of the industry coincide, it does not mean that this is the full picture.

In the study of popular music culture we need to understand the complexity of this worldwide system of production. The public relations rhetoric of major organisations is aimed at keeping the support of their shareholders and the wider public by presenting the corporations as effectively responding to a new economic situation full of exploitable opportunities. In these simple terms, the ideas of 'the global market' and 'demand for media information and entertainment' are neither sophisticated descriptions of how the corporations operate, nor a sound enough basis for a critique.

As Negus stresses, behind the headline characteristics of music production as concentrated, global and multimedia there are a number of qualifications to be made. First, corporations are not monolithic structures, and they are constantly changing. We, therefore, need to understand how they operate as institutions, and how they work in relation to the various companies that they do not own or control. The corporations themselves are conglomerates, made up of tens of divisions, each organised for different markets and products, and for different national or continental operations. Second, the idea of the global market can be misleading. Sales of records and associated products are unevenly distributed across the world, and the majority of record sales are still concentrated in North America, Europe and Japan. This is reflected in the patterns of corporate ownership with all the conglomerates having their headquarters, and the end destination of their profits, in these centres of world industrialisation. It is also noticeable that within this uneven distribution of sales, Anglo-American music dominates. Such music constitutes the overwhelming majority of records sold in North America and Britain, and makes up at least a third of sales in Europe and Japan (Negus 1992). Finally, while other media – like radio, publications, film, television and video – have played an important, and some would argue dominant, role in the promotion of certain artists or musical forms, there are artists who never get a promotional video and genres that get little radio play or television coverage, yet they still produce large numbers of records and find willing customers.

When studying the industries and institutions of popular music culture, then, we have a dual task:

1. to explain the tendency towards concentration, globalisation and multimedia entertainment within popular music culture

2. to examine the complexities of corporate operations, the patterns of international music production and consumption, and the differences between the way different forms of popular music and artists are spread unevenly across different forms of media.

Simon Frith has pointed out that there are other problems with the way that the production of music has been conceptualised. He has argued that the sorts of criticism directed at the dominant form of music production we examined in the previous section are rooted in other assumptions about the processes of recording and distribution. He states:

> What such arguments assume ... is that there is some essential human activity, music making, which has been colonised by commerce. ... The flaw in this argument is the suggestion that music is the starting point of the industrial process ... when it is, in fact, the final product. The industrialisation of music can't be understood as something that happens to music but describes a process in which music itself is made.

(Frith 1992, 50)

His article, 'The Industrialisation of Popular Music', is required reading for anyone seriously studying popular music culture. The historical analysis he sketches out goes back well before the 1950s where most analyses of the industry usually start. In doing so he is able to show that the emphasis on independent record companies, while not unimportant, has been exaggerated beyond its usefulness. His is not an argument that popular music has no significant cultural role, but instead he believes that the music's cultural role is intimately connected to the way that it is produced within record production. Frith is not arguing that there are no important issues to be found in a study of the music industry, but that separating 'the industry' from 'music' or 'art' is not helpful in our attempt to understand popular music culture.

Overall, then, our study needs to avoid making independent and major record companies, or popular music and the record industry, into polar opposites. They are, rather, all part of the same popular music culture in which the record is central. As Frith has emphasised, popular music is 'the twentieth century popular record; not the record of something ... that exists independently of the music industry' (Frith 1992, 50). Records are not copies, they are popular music. Music does not just exist as sound; it is created as part of a process of production that is primarily orientated to the creation of records. Even genres of music that are not recorded and distributed on tape, CD or vinyl are overshadowed by the culture of recorded music. Just think about whether the covers bands who play at weddings or in pubs could exist without a relationship to records. We need to study not how music has been taken over by the industry, but how the industry orders popular music; not how music is copied onto record, but how record making, distributing and consuming creates popular music.

Our aim in doing this is to account for two counter-tendencies. On the one hand we need to explain why there has been a tendency towards concentration of ownership, transnational operation and diversity into multimedia entertainment within recorded

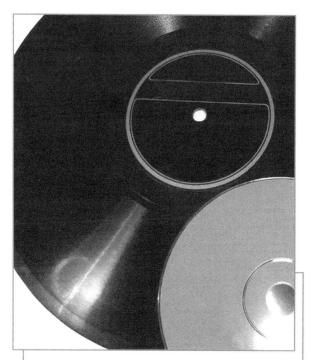

FIGURE 5.1 From the 10-inch shellac to the CD, the record has been central to popular music culture
Photo: Edward James Stokes

popular music production. On the other we need to explain the opposing trend towards the departmentalisation and devolution of corporate operations, a diversity in the patterns of international music production and consumption, and the differences between the way different forms of popular music and different artists appear across different forms of media.

Most accounts of the record industry deal with these issues through ideas of monopoly, globalisation and media integration. However, while these are important concepts they describe rather than explain the forces at work. A more productive analysis needs to identify the principles that underlie the industry. It is the economics of record production that benefits large, transnational, multimedia companies, and aspects of the culture of consumption that benefit the flexible, local and niche media companies. It is to these fundamentals of popular music production that we must now turn.

The fundamentals of popular music production

It is the distinctive economic and cultural characteristics of record production and consumption that account for the two counter-tendencies: towards concentration, globalisation and multimedia entertainment on the one hand; and towards corporate departmentalisation, a diversity of international music production and consumption, and differences in the way music appears across different media on the other. A clue to these economic and cultural characteristics can be found in the seemingly contradictory strategies of record companies. They simultaneously release large numbers of CDs, while at the same time they try to focus consumer buying on to a small number of releases. For instance, in Britain well over 100 singles can be released in a week, and there are thousands and thousands more artists who would like to release one. Yet only a very small number of these releases gain a high enough media profile to achieve sales success. However, this is not as contradictory as it seems. As we will see, the large number of releases is a response to the culture of consumption, while the focus of promotion on a few releases is a response to the economics of production.

An understanding of the fundamentals of popular music production allows us to see that firms have the best advantages if they are large, flexible and produce hits. Large firms can afford the high costs of both a high number of releases and heavy promotional budgets. However, monolithic organisations would not be flexible enough to know which music to record and which records to promote. Further, the economics of production reward the company that releases a top-selling record many times more than the company that produces the moderately selling record.

The next few pages, then, examine the fundamentals of the record production process, the way the economics of production operate in profit-maximising capitalism, and the way consumption and the cultural meanings of popular music act on production.

The stages of production: the record as product

A good place to start is to model the basic stages of production. In the simplest of terms we could represent this in a diagram like the one in Figure 5.2. Although there may be some variations in this basic linear process – composition and recording are often simultaneous processes in contemporary popular music, for instance – this diagram represents the consecutive stages involved in producing and selling recordings on CD, vinyl and MP3 formats.

Composition → Recording → Duplication → Distribution → Retailing → Consumption
→ Promotion:
        press
        radio
        television →   other forms
        concerts   of consumption
        clubs

FIGURE 5.2 The stages of record production

From here we can make some other basic analytical distinctions. First, it is valuable to distinguish between the record industry, the wider music industry and the still greater entertainment media. Because the major record companies cover all these activities this is more of an analytical distinction than a practical one, but it does represent a set of widely used concepts. By overlaying these concepts on the stages of production we can reveal some interesting characteristics of the popular music industries.

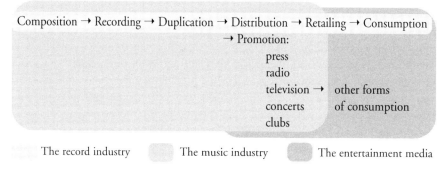

Composition → Recording → Duplication → Distribution → Retailing → Consumption
→ Promotion:
  press
  radio
  television → other forms
  concerts   of consumption
  clubs

  The record industry   The music industry   The entertainment media

FIGURE 5.3 The popular music system

It is possible to identify a wider network built around the production of records, which MacDougald (1941) termed 'the popular music system'. As well as recording, duplicating and retailing records, record companies also promote them, and in doing so they extend their activities into a wider music industry based upon live music or dance clubs, the music press and the elements of other media like radio and television. These other media are part of an even wider entertainment media that uses music as one of its raw materials. Likewise there is more than just an activity of physical production going on in the popular music system. Record companies do not just produce CDs, vinyl discs or MP3 files, they also produce economic and cultural value. In saying this we are making another set of distinctions. For analytical purposes recorded music can be understood as existing simultaneously in three ways.

1. As *artefacts*. This emphasises the physical properties of recorded music and the production processes used to create them. For instance, when we think of a CD or MP3 file as something containing a record of the sound that is produced in a recording studio, which is then copied, and finally listened to by us on a CD or MP3 player as sound, we are thinking about its artefactual form.

2. As *commodities*. This emphasises the value of recorded music within an economic system. Recorded music is commissioned, bought or sold between companies, and provided to consumers in return for payment. And of course it is used in other commodities like radio or television programmes.

3. As *texts*. This emphasises the status of media output within communication. Recorded music is a source of meanings, which we can examine to discover its structure. For instance, we may classify music into different genres – rock, hip-hop, soul, and so on – or we can examine the way they are meaningful to us as listeners.

We are talking about one piece of recorded music, but with three qualities: as artefact, commodity and text. The artefact of the record is a carrier for a textual form of music, and the combination of this artefact with the textual meanings produces a form that can be sold and so converted into a commodity with economic value. Each form is dependent on the other. The music cannot be distributed without its existence as an artefact (12-inch single, CD, MP3 file), but we would not buy the artefact without its textual content, and so the commodity value is only produced through the combination of artefact and text. Each stage of production outlined in Figure 5.2 is simultaneously a stage of physical, cultural and economic production, and the opportunities and constraints of each interact with the others through the practices of the industry. These practices themselves are codifications of the cultural values and common senses of the industries, as well as the legal frameworks, physical limitations and economic imperatives institutionalised in popular music culture. We can understand the relationship between music fans and the industry using the same distinctions. We are simultaneously listeners, consumers and sense-makers. We can likewise understand the production processes themselves. Record companies are simultaneously manufacturers, traders in commodities and manufacturers of meaning.

Studying the industries of popular music production, then, involves us analysing the physical, economic and meaning-making processes of the record as an artefact-commodity-text. We will need to understand how the music is commodified through the making of a record and how this commodification bears upon the textual form of the record. Central to this understanding is a grasp of the basic economic principles of record production.

Economic principles of music commodity production

The process of record production identified above is characterised by what economists call 'high fixed costs and low variable costs'. That is, even if only a few copies are produced, the costs of making a particular record are very high, while the costs of extra copies are relatively low.

If you think about each stage of production outlined above you can see why this is so. Before a record is sold the company must go through a number of very expensive stages: signing a band involves legal costs and company staff time; recording incurs costs of practice, studio time, production staff and additional musicians; artwork will have to be designed; a promotional schedule including press releases, promotional copies for radio, a video and displays for record shops will have to be produced. On top of this the general costs of staff and offices have to be covered in the costs of the records. Even if the release only sold ten copies the record company still has to face these costs. On the other hand the costs of producing single copies of the release are relatively cheaper. The blank CD, the costs of duplication and artwork printing, and royalty payments are all very small for each copy and are likely to go down the more copies are produced. The variable cost of duplicating MP3 files through the internet is negligible.

For this reason selling a million copies of a single release is massively more profitable than selling a thousand copies each of a thousand releases. In the first case there is only one set of fixed costs in the second a thousand, but both will have the same variable costs and the same revenue from sales. The differences can create dramatically different profits. In the hypothetical example detailed in Table 5.1, increasing levels of sales would return exponentially more profit.

Taking the hypothetical case of a small record company with fixed costs of, say, £10 000, variable costs £1 each and CDs priced at £15

Costs	Revenue	Profit
= fixed cost + (variable cost × production)	= £15 × production	= revenue − total cost
Selling 100 copies		
£10 000 + (£1 × 100)	£15 × 100	£1500 − £10 100
= £10 100	**= £1500**	**= £8600 loss**
Selling 1 000 copies		
£10 000 + (£1 × 1000)	£15 × 1000	£15 000 − £11 000
= £11 000	**= £15 000**	**= £4000**
Selling 1 000 000 copies		
£10 000 + (£1 × 1 000 000)	£15 × 1 000 000	£15 m − £1 010 000
= £1 010 000	**= £15 000 000**	**= £13 990 000**

So, selling 100 copies leads to a loss of £8600, selling 1000 copies gives a profit of £4000, but selling 1 million copies (a thousand times more) gives a profit of just under £14 million (three and half thousand times more). Selling 1 million records, but spread over 1000 releases, would give a profit of £4 million against the million-seller's £14 million. But if you were producing 1 million copies of a record you could probably gain economies on reproducing each copy and could get your costs down to, say, 50p a copy. This would cut costs to nearly half and so increase profit by £0·5 million more.

TABLE 5.1 Hypothetical example of record production costs, revenue and profit

---

Now, the economics of record production are far more complex than this. The costs of production are spread across the stages of production so that the artist bears some of them, the recording studio will bear others, the record company some others, the pressing plant, the distributor and the retail shop others. And, of course, the revenue from the sales of the records will be shared across these stages. In addition, different records will receive very different treatment: some may have major promotional support, with expensive videos and media publicity; others may sell over a very wide geographic area and have increased distribution costs.

Even so, these hypothetical and simplified figures show the primary economic imperative that operates in record production. It means that profit-maximising companies that understand the distinctive qualities of producing the record as commodity aim to get a small number of releases to sell a large number of copies by focusing record buyers on a small number of artists.

It is this basic principle of commodity production that explains the overall strategy of record companies. First, looking outwards to their record buyers, they need to distinguish their releases from those of other companies by building a distinctive brand. This is usually achieved by promoting the artist as a pop star and by using the cultural meanings that popular music has for the audience. The most profitable artists will be those whose image and music gain a strong response from as wide a range of consumers as possible because these are the artists that will sell a large number of copies. They then need to extend the image and the audience's awareness of it by promoting their records through a multitude of media forms. They finally need to extend the potential audience as far as they can by operating at an international level. Star-building, promoting across all media and operating internationally will increase costs of production, of course; but, returning to our example in Table 5.1, even if the cost is increased by ten times and sales increased by 100 times, the profit would be increased by over 96 times. The costs are getting so small a percentage of the revenue that the income is almost all pure profit.

Second, looking backwards to their production processes, record companies seek to order the production, reproduction and distribution processes so that they can be controlled and directed to ensure that profits are being maximised. They seek to manipulate the production process to reduce costs and capture as much of the profit as they can. These activities involve capital investment: buying new technologies of production, reproduction or distribution. By buying or establishing recording studios, pressing plants, distribution networks or other media companies, they can ensure that their desire to control production and capture profit at every stage is achieved.

So from the overall aim of maximising profits record companies are pushed in the direction of industrialising, professionalising and commercialising music production. It is these forces that create the corporations with their concentrated, global and multimedia dominance of record production. As these corporations grow they are able to use their size and scale of operation to increase their control over the music we hear, sell it to a larger number of people, and control as many of the aspects of the productive process as possible. They therefore simultaneously increase sales of their own music, and increase the profit from these sales by focusing on a narrower range of artists and recordings to ensure that they capture as much of the generated profits as possible. Profit creates scope for further investment that helps to increase control, concentration and further profit.

In the corporation's perfect world – and the music lover's nightmare – there would be a small number of artists who were heavily promoted through all the media to a global audience to generate massive profits for the corporation at every stage of production. But, again, the reality is more complex. The great paradox for the corporations is that the cultural meanings of music they try to utilise to attract consumers are in constant flux, and the economic principles of commodity production they seek to understand are matched by the economics and cultures of commodity consumption.

The economics and cultures of consumption

The economics of producing records as commodities explains why record companies focus their promotional efforts on a small number of releases, and why the greater the scale of the company the greater the quantity of profit will be realised. But production is not the only factor in determining the behaviour of record companies, and different aspects of consumption are also important. The distinctive nature of the economics of music consumption, and the culture of consumption, create different determinants of production.

The key economic principle of production is mirrored by a key economic principle of music consumption: music buyers are unlikely to buy the same record twice. Now, this may seem obvious, but it is the opposite of the consumption of other products outside the cultural field. If you like a particular brand of food you are likely to buy that same product again. If you like a piece of recorded music and buy it, you have no real reason for buying it again. There are perennial attempts to get record buyers to repeat-purchase a particular recording by offering it in a range of collectable special editions, or encouraging them to change the format from, say, vinyl to CD, but the principle still applies. The efforts made by the record companies to focus the purchases of consumers onto a small number of artists need to be constantly renewed. There is a finite limit to the number of copies of a release that can be sold, and once the profits from a new release have been realised, then the process must start again for another release to ensure that a stream of sales and profit continues.

The record companies therefore need forms of branding that go beyond individual records. This explains why record companies spend so much time and money investing in, developing and publicising a star image for an artist. If you bought a particular release by your favourite pop star, you may not buy the same release again but you are more likely to buy the next. It also explains why record companies are so interested in the idea of genre and, as we shall see, why they organise their record companies around both stars and genres. Again, liking a particular release will make you more likely to buy another release in a similar style. It also explains why the ideas associated with the Tin Pan Alley tradition (see Chapter 2) are beneficial to the aims of the record company. An emphasis on newness, star image, and success and celebrity continually renews consumption and encourages brand loyalty.

However, this culture of newness and celebrity also creates other cultural responses that are less beneficial to record company profits. Consumers often tire of a particular style, while each new generation of music buyers seeks new styles to differentiate themselves from their older siblings. Many music consumers seek out music specifically because it offers a set of different meanings from the mainstream. So, on one hand the record company needs to utilise the textual meanings of records among listeners as potential consumers in order to focus sales and so to realise large profits; on the other hand, these textual meanings are constantly changing. This is particularly true where the main market is young people. The record company needs to both control and direct the textual meanings of records into the most profitable forms of consumption, while at the same time understanding that this very control will undermine the long-term profits of the company, as increasing numbers of consumers shift their interests to new textual meanings of new types of music. The only way to respond to this is to seek out new artists and types of music that, in the future, may be popular.

In Paul Hirsch's (1972/1990) terms, record companies 'process fads and fashions'. He argues that record companies have to deal with an over-supply of creative artists compared with the restricted number of opportunities for promotion. To ensure that the artists most likely to be successful are selected, decision-making is delegated to staff closely involved in finding new artists or plugging records to the media. In addition, to ensure fixed costs are kept low, artists are paid on the basis of the number of copies of their records that are sold. Negus' (1999) analysis of corporate strategy suggests that 30 years later this is still the case. Interestingly, Hirsch contrasts the state of the record industry in the latter half of the twentieth century with its structure in the first half, where record companies had a greater involvement with films and radio, which could be used as marketing avenues. The earlier industry could be more bureaucratic, he argues, because its control of the media gave it more control over what would be heard, and so what would sell (Hirsch 1972/1990, 130–1).

For Hirsch, then, uncertainty about cultural choices has a number of organisational imperatives that we can see as running counter to the drives for concentration, globalisation and multimedia interests identified above. A larger number of records will be produced, organisations will become more devolved and departmental, and the opportunities for local success will be opened up. The implication of this is that in periods of uncertainty, when the meaning of a genre of music is less easy for corporate executives to understand, the smaller record companies will have an advantage as their staff have a better grasp of the cultural meanings of a new music. Support for this idea can be found in a series of empirical studies undertaken by Richard Peterson working with David Berger. They argue that as the concentration of record sales in the hands of a small number of companies increases, variety in music style declines, and when the sales of records are shared among a larger number of companies, variety in music increases (Peterson and Berger 1975/1990). This is not a cause-and-effect relationship but is linked to other social and institutional shifts.

It is possible to speculate from Peterson and Berger's analysis that when a small number of record companies dominate record sales they tend not to actively recruit new artists, but narrow their promotional strategies to support a small number of 'stars', and rely on the profits from their currently successful artists. However, this makes them complacent and they do not take sufficient account of the changing cultural meanings generated by consumers out of popular music. In these situations it is left to smaller companies to identify new artists with cultural resonance. Peterson and Berger identify the decline in control of the media of film and radio by record companies in the late 1940s and the rise of television and shift towards popular music as the basis for programming in radio in the early 1950s, as key changes that undermined the ability of companies to work on a bureaucratic management system, and they lost out to a set of more flexible, responsive small independent companies and new corporations. Peterson has offered an interesting case study of this idea in his analysis of the changes up until the birth of rock & roll in 1955 (Peterson 1990).

5.3 The internet provides access to detailed information about record companies and their record release strategies. Select a record company and find its internet site. How many records does it seem to be releasing in a particular week? Which records does it seem to be supporting with the most promotion? Why do you think it is promoting them? Are there any examples of strategies of star-building or genre in promotion? How strong are the ideas of 'newness' on the website? Is there any evidence that companies are releasing a larger number of records than they are promoting? Is there a link between the records they promote and an existing strong star image? Is there a link between the records they promote and the records in the charts? Finally, how does this survey research support or undermine the theory developed in this chapter?

SUMMARY ● ● ● ● ● ● ● ● ● ● ● ● ●

This chapter has outlined the dominant form of record production. Most records are produced by one of five large corporations. This concentration of market power has attracted considerable criticism, as it is felt to compromise the music that is released. This domination was explained by examining the economic and cultural principles of music production and consumption. These principles also explain the paradox that record companies face in their desire to control music sales on an international level, but also their need to be flexible, devolved and constantly produce new musical forms to respond to changes in consumption culture. From this basic paradox it is possible to explore the details of how the record industry is organised, what strategies corporations develop, and how small companies survive in such an environment. This is the subject of Chapter 6.

Further reading

Frith, Simon 1992: 'The Industrialization of Popular Music', in *Popular Music and Communication*, ed. James Lull. Sage.

Hirsch, Paul M. 1972/1990: 'Processing Fads and Fashions: An Organisation-Set Analysis of Cultural Industry Systems', in *On Record: Rock, Pop and the Written Word*, ed. by Simon Frith and Andrew Goodwin. Routledge.

Negus, Keith 1992: *Producing Pop: Culture and Conflict in the Popular Music Industry.* Arnold.

Peterson, Richard A. 1990: 'Why 1955? Explaining the Advent of Rock Music,' *Popular Music* 9(1), 97–116.

CHAPTER SIX

The Record Industry

While in reality the distinctions between the record industry, the music industry and the wider media-based entertainment industry are blurred, there is much to be gained by focusing in this chapter on the particular economic organisation of recorded music, before widening the study in the next chapter. That means looking simultaneously at the economic imperatives that drive corporate growth and control, and the cultural factors that constantly undermine and fracture this control. Initially we will examine how record industry corporations are organised, then how they operate (including how they grow in size and scope), and finally how small independent companies survive when all the economic imperitives seem to be against them.

The corporations in the record industry

When studying the record industry we need to carry forward the recognition of the corporation as the dominant way record production is organised. This involves examining the relationships between three levels of organisation in the record industry: labels, record companies and corporations. From these distinctions we look in some detail at the music divisions of the five major corporations. Finally, we trace how the corporations are involved in other stages of production and how they are organised in different countries.

Labels, Companies and Corporations

Rather self-evidently, the key institutions of the record industry are the record companies. We have to be cautious, though, as there is not one single form of organisation that we can understand as 'the record company'. The public face of the record company that we see on records themselves – the record label – often hides a much more complex set of relationships. Record labels are brands within the record industry. Some of these brands are so strong that we associate them with particular types of music. Labels like RCA, Blue Note, Motown, Electra, Island, Stiff, Def Jam, Food, Creation, Metalheadz or Moving Shadow identify distinct types of music and qualities to particular record buyers. So strong is this branding and association that some record buyers will even buy a release simply because of the label, and many record collectors attempt to own all the releases on a particular label.

Test out how strong label recognition is among a cross-section of record buyers. Start by asking a few people to name some record labels and produce a list for a questionnaire. Try to choose labels that have distinct identities. Ask your respondents if they recognise the label name, if they associate it with any particular type of music, or with a particular period of popular music history.

However, rather than the industry being organised around single companies that produce records under single labels, there are an assortment of 'label' brands, record companies and corporate divisions, linked together in a variety of ways. To understand the different ways that record companies and corporations are related it is important to differentiate between the following factors.

- The *record label*, which is the public face of a record company. The term obviously derives from the label at the centre of a vinyl record with its distinctive logo. The characteristic imagery is used by a record company to establish a brand identity, often based on a reputation for releasing certain forms of music. For example, the Epic label.

- The *record company*, or *record division*, which owns and organises the releases of a record label, or a series of record labels. For example, Sony Music.

- The *parent corporation*, which owns all or most of the shares in a record company and controls the major strategic direction of the record company, even if day-to-day decisions are in the hands of staff at the record company. The parent corporation may own a number of separate record companies that operate independently on a day-to-day basis. For example, Sony Corporation.

There is no one model of the relationship between the label, company and corporation, and the variation covers virtually every permutation possible. Sometimes a company only releases records on one label and has no direct ownership or control relationships with a corporation. The status of these companies is usually signalled by the term 'independent'. As we shall see, the concept of 'independence' is an increasingly unstable one for scholars of the record industry. It is more common for a company to produce music under a label identity, but to be owned by a corporation along with a number of other semi-autonomous companies, each with their own label. These companies could, alternatively, release records on a range of labels, each with its own distinct 'label identity' and style of music. Or, again, the company could be part of a larger division that coordinates the activities of a number of labels or companies. In other instances, ownership is shared between a corporation and the person who runs the company. Most often corporations have a range of relationships within their own organisation covering all the possibilities outlined above. Just to add a final richness to the analysis, these relationships change over time and the corporations constantly reorganise their own internal structures, and buy and sell labels and companies.

The Organisation of the Main Corporations

At the time of writing, the 'big five' corporations organise their record companies and labels in a number of distinct ways. It is useful to run through an overview of each.

AOL TIME WARNER

The music interests of the multimedia corporation are brought together under a music division, Warner Music Group (WMG). In turn the group is organised into a number of companies. This is a fairly standard practice as not only are the labels felt to have distinctive brand identities, but it also allows for the feel of a small record company – important for artists and label strategy – within a large corporation. The names of the corporation's main American record companies reflect the original distinctive independent companies taken over by Warner Brothers in the 1960s and 1970s. The key companies here are the Atlantic Group, Elektra Entertainment Group and the original Warner Bros Records, together with its later subsidiaries Rhino Entertainment and London-Sire Records. Each of these companies has a named record label. In addition, WMG operates in 68 countries of the world through its Warner Music International division, releasing records on local versions of its labels and through affiliate companies. On top of that it has part ownership of a range of key niche record companies that have distinctive brands of their own. These include RuffNation Records, Strictly Rhythm Records, Sub Pop Records and Tommy Boy Records.

BERTELSMANN

The Bertelsmann corporation has interests across a wide range of publishing and broadcast media, and its music interests are collected under the Bertelsmann Music Group (BMG) division. The two main record companies within the group are built on the biggest music interests taken over by Bertelsmann. The first, RCA Victor, is one of the oldest US record companies, and the other company, Arista, was one of the most successful of the 1970s independent labels. RCA Victor has a range of labels including Windham Hill, Private Music, Blue Bird and DHM. Arista also has substantial holdings in two more recent labels with 'independent' identities: Bad Boy Entertainments and LaFace Records. Both RCA and Arista also have divisions working in Nashville producing country music.

EMI

EMI Music is one half of EMI Corporation's activities. The division is made up of three main record companies: EMI, Capitol (EMI's US division since 1955) and Virgin (a major British independent until it was acquired in 1992). EMI and Virgin both operate through further subsidiaries in over ten countries. EMI records includes the Chrysalis label, which was also an important British independent until 1989 when it was sold to EMI. EMI and Virgin also run subsidiaries for classical, country, and easy listening. In addition, the music division owns a number of smaller subsidiaries or labels that deal with niche musics. Blue Note, Food, Hemisphere, Java, Matador, Parlophone and Real World are perhaps the best known.

SONY

Sony Music Entertainment was organised from 1994 into four companies: Epic Records Group; Columbia Records Group; Relativity Entertainment Group; and Sony Classical. Sony, a Japanese hardware corporation, took over Columbia records, one of the oldest and 'most American' record companies. Epic has been a subsidiary of Columbia since it was established in 1953. The takeover of the Columbia Company by the Sony Corporation followed 20 years of corporate collaboration in Asia.

UNIVERSAL

Universal is the newest of the big five. Its music is organised by Universal Music Group, which has the most complex history and current organisation. It was formed in the late 1990s when the Seagram distillery company took over first MCA (which had previously taken over Decca US records, Universal Pictures, ABC records, Chess records, Geffen records and GRP records) and then Polygram (formed out of Polydor and Philips records in 1972, and which had previously taken over independent record companies including Verve, Decca UK, Island, A&M, Motown, Def Jam, and Rodven). The music subsidiary currently organises its activities around 11 main companies that draw together its various label interests, which now also include Interscope, Celtic Heart, 10 records, Hip-O and Lost Highway.

These profiles were produced by looking at the companies' websites, and you can find out more information and up-to-date detail by visiting them yourself. These overviews reveal a number of very different ways the corporations organise their record companies, from the relative coherence and more monolithic structure of Sony, to the diversity and devolved system operated by Universal. Keith Negus (1999, 31–62) has related these corporate structures to distinctive corporate personalities and strategies. He suggests that in the late 1990s, both EMI and BMG tended to benefit most from their back catalogues and established artists, but did not seem to break many new acts. Although they are both constructed out of well-known European and American companies, they tended to be more successful in Europe, in contrast to WMG and

Sony, which dominate the US industry. Both the corporation and its strategy make Universal a difficult corporation to rate, but its constituent parts have had very mixed histories, and a failed strategy to tie music hardware and software on the Sony model had almost bankrupted MCA's previous owners. Increasingly the companies see their music division as just one part of a multimedia strategy in which music becomes content for a range of media including film, television and video, the press and radio, as well as the emerging interactive, online, medium of the internet.

Even within the record industry, though, the corporations are not just involved in this one level of record production, and their corporate status comes from their involvement in more than just the releasing of records.

Corporate Control of the Stages of Production

Looking across the big five corporations we can see that they not only own a range of record companies and labels, they also often own the companies that are involved in other stages of production: they often own publishing houses that hold the rights to record a song; it is common to own recording studios where the original recording is made and mixed; they frequently own pressing plants that produce multiple copies of a record; they almost always own distributors, which make sure that sufficient quantities of a release get to the record retailers in time; and it has been the case that they own retail shops themselves.

 CASE **STUDY**

C A S E S T U D Y **EMI Music**

EMI is now the corporation most focused on the music industry, and so it is not surprising that its interests are the most developed at each of the stages of production. In the last ten years EMI has changed significantly. After being part of a larger industrial conglomerate with Thorn Industries for 20 years from 1979, EMI separated off and concentrated on its music industry activities. This seemed to represent the very opposite strategy to the one followed by Sony when it took over Columbia. However, while Thorn did offer a hardware division to match EMI's music software, Thorn's music playback equipment just could not compete with Japanese companies and this contributed to continued losses in Thorn industries.

EMI's record industry activities can best be summarised by linking them to the stages of record production, as outlined below.

- Publishing: EMI Music Publishing
- Recording: Abbey Road Studios, London
- Record labels: EMI, Capitol, Virgin, Chrysalis, Blue Note, Food,

                      Hemisphere, Java, Parlophone, Real World
- Manufacturing: Major CD and vinyl plants in Britain and worldwide
- Distribution: Caroline Distribution; Chordan Distribution
- Retail: (until 1998) HMV record shops

It should be apparent from the sketches of the major corporate record divisions outlined earlier, and from the case study of EMI, that the major corporate record divisions have grown primarily through a process of taking over existing businesses involved in either signing artists and releasing records, or in other stages of record production. This is to make a distinction between two dimensions of corporate growth. Economists talk of the takeover of other smaller record companies by a larger record company as a process of 'horizontal integration'. That is to say it is the joining of two companies involved in the same level of production. Where a record company takes over a recording studio, record pressing plant or distributor it is termed 'vertical integration' because it is the joining of companies at different levels of the production process. One of the best ways to establish these dimensions is by visual representation (see Figure 6.1).

Production of records

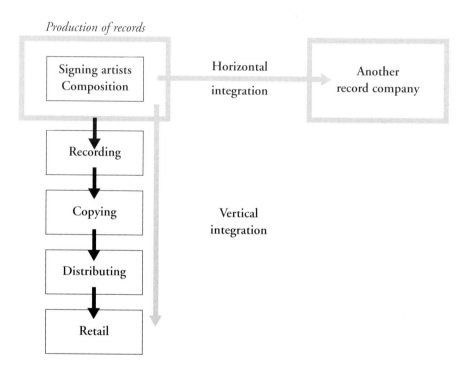

FIGURE 6.1 Vertical and horizontal integration in the formation of record industry corporations

The original reasons for these sorts of takeover were primarily to gain control in order to minimise risk and maximise profits produced at every stage of production. Record companies understood that if they controlled distribution, for instance, they could ensure that copies of one of their popular releases would get into the shops. It also meant that any profits made by distributing a successful release would come to the record company. As record companies grew they also realised that owning more companies would allow them to cut their costs of production. Size in itself has benefits.

As we have seen, increasing the scale of manufacture and distribution lowers the cost of each copy of the release, so producing a lot of copies will lower costs. So the more copies a company produces, the cheaper it is to manufacture, promote and distribute each one. This is what economists call 'falling marginal costs because of economies of scale'. These economic benefits are more likely to be realised by large companies that can afford the massive costs of promoting a single release, have the capacity to produce and distribute large numbers of copies, and have the scale to realise the cost savings.

We should add a further example of integration in the takeover of companies in what the industry tends to call 'other territories'. The term originates in the language of record companies in the USA, which used to organise their activities on a regional basis so that different clusters of geographically based record markets were called territories. It is now used to mean taking over companies in other countries (Negus 1999 152–72). Operating across the world exponentially increases the potential market.

X 6.2 It is quite possible that since writing this section, the details of the big five corporations' structure have changed. Fortunately, the internet gives us access to the most up-to-date information. As the corporations' websites themselves change on a regular basis, you will first have to locate the most recent information using an internet search engine. Each corporation may have a number of websites that you will have to visit in order to build up a comprehensive picture. Once you have found information on the corporations, their music divisions, record companies and labels, produce a diagram for each, showing the ownership and organisation of labels, companies and divisions.

The primary motivation of a record company is to maximise its profits. As we have seen the economics of record production and consumption reward companies that can sell large numbers of copies of a single release because the profits are disproportionate to similar sales over a larger number of releases. A greater scale of production also allows companies to reduce the costs of producing copies of each record release, and by diversifying its control into other spheres of production it can ensure that all stages operate for the benefit of the record company, and that all the profits from record production and distribution come to them. These are the central tenets of the second area of study in the record industry: corporate strategy.

Corporate strategy

The objectives of minimising costs, maximising income and taking over any other companies that contribute to primary costs or income, brings forth two other tensions. First, there are questions about how growth is to be achieved while still ensuring staff remain flexible enough to remain responsive to fickle audiences. Second, there is the challenge of maximising the benefits of a worldwide operation, while simultaneously taking local differences into account.

Building Corporations: Growth, Takeovers and Integration

Keith Negus has argued that record company strategies can be distilled into 'a desire to increase market share, either through so called gradual "organic growth" or through the purchase of labels, catalogues and companies' (Negus 1999, 45). Market share refers to the percentage of sales of a particular product made by a particular company or group of companies. In simple terms, to increase your share you can either increase the sales of your records relative to other companies, or buy up other companies and take over their sales as your own. It is generally easier to take over another firm than to generate extra sales within your existing company, but it takes considerable capital to do so. As most reasonably sized organisations operate as public limited companies anyone can buy shares in a record company. So when a record company wants to take over another existing company it merely has to buy a controlling share to dictate how it operates. As the profits of a company are distributed among shareholders in proportion to their stakeholding, the more shares you hold the larger proportion of the profits you get.

Corporations, then, are quite complex organisations. The holding company – so called because all it does is hold shares in other companies – will own and control a number of different companies to different degrees. The status of ownership and control will range from a wholly owned subsidiary (where the holding company owns all the shares and has full control), through a partnership holding (with one or more other shareholding companies), to a minority holding where the holding company cannot exercise substantial control (because there are companies with a greater stake involved in the business).

The brief overview of the big five corporations presented earlier in this chapter reveals something of the origins and process of corporate growth in the record industry. New companies have continued to enter the business of record production and as they have become successful they have been systematically taken over by the larger corporations, which have therefore increased in size. So while the international sales of records have increased over the last century and into this one, the number of firms that control most of those sales has hardly changed. As each newly acquired company joins the corporation it is integrated into the operation of that organisation. The possible ways that a corporation can control its subsidiaries vary considerably. The corporation may simply convert the acquired company into a label, and use its brand identity. Alternatively, it may, at the other limit, give the company complete autonomy to decide who to sign and which records to release, even though any profits the company makes will be passed on to the owning corporation.

Negus has suggested that we should understand corporate strategy as a way to control and order three categories of uncertainty about the output of the company, its reception by the audience, and the technologies used to distribute the music (Negus 1999, 32–5). The history of popular music shows, how swiftly the popularity of particular artists or styles of music can change, and how the 7-inch 45 and LP formats replaced the 10-inch 78, to be replaced in their turn by first the cassette, the CD and then MP3 files. On top of that there are uncertainties about how workers within such a large organisation will do their job, particularly if these workers have joined the corporation because the firm they work for has been taken over.

Uncertainties about what music will sell to whom are dealt with through the concept of genre. For Negus, 'genre provides a way of linking the question of music (what does it sound like?) to the question of its market (who will buy it?)' (Negus 1999, 47). On the other hand, uncertainties about the organisation and its workers are dealt with by a strategy of firm control of finances within the corporation, and delegation of power to divisions on a day-to-day basis (Negus 1999, 50–2). The management of the corporation seeks to build up a portfolio of artists, music types and label brand images in order to spread the risk that a successful artist/genre might decline, or that a new trend could take off. Organisationally this is achieved through the establishment of a number of business units, each of which is accountable for delivering profits but given different degrees of independence on a day-to-day basis.

Negus' contribution (1992; 1996; 1999) to the detailed analysis of corporations in the music industry is easily the most significant to date. He builds on Richard Peterson's (1976) contention that we should avoid the polar ideas of popular music as the creative work of the artists or the product of a mass production industry, and instead study the distinctive ways in which the 'production of culture' is organised. This emphasis looks to identify the distinctive organisational structures and imperatives within sectors like the record industry. Most significantly, Negus has added an interest in the 'culture of production' with its emphasis on understanding the ideas, motivations and working practices of personnel within these organisations. We can identify two key dimensions to his analysis, and a central tension he seeks to investigate. He focuses on the relative independence of the artists and repertoire (A&R) functions within the corporation, and then on the interdependence of the national and international operations of the corporation. In doing so he explores the tension between creativity and industrial control that has preoccupied popular music scholars and music fans for over a century. This approach is the basis of the next two sections and the case study that follows.

Creativity, Music Production and A&R

A&R stands for artists and repertoire, which of course means the singers and musicians, their songs and music. The term is a long-standing one within the music industry, indexing the old Tin Pan Alley practice of finding separate individuals to perform songs from those who wrote them. It refers to the department within a company that finds and signs artists to the company, or licenses recordings from independent producers, foreign divisions or other smaller companies, and then decides which records should be released on the label.

A&R staff tend to express their role in relation to the artists they work with, succinctly summed up by one A&R staffer's self-description as 'a groupie with a cheque book' (Frith 1983, 102). But they often also share the notion with popular music scholars that they are gatekeepers who decide who to sign, what to record or license and what to release, with a keen sense that only one in eight of the records they release will make a profit (Negus 1999, 32). Following the analogy of a gatekeeper, who decides who will go through, some theorists have examined the way that the discourse of A&R workers constructs their activities as a transformational process in which music is turned into other organisational products – 'property', 'demo', 'tape', 'cut', 'master', 'release', 'product' and, finally (they hope), 'hit' – through each stage of production (Ryan and Peterson 1982).

Negus argues that the analogy of the production line is too superficial, and instead casts A&R staff following Bourdieu (1984) as 'cultural intermediaries'. This emphasis shifts the attention from the function of A&R as part of a popular music system and to the relationships of A&R within a wider popular music culture. Negus suggests that

> the boundary between the recording industry and potential artists is not so much a gate where aspiring stars must wait to be selected and admitted, but a web of relationships stretched across a shifting soundtrack of musical, verbal and visual information.

(Negus 1992, 46)

This allows him to present such record company workers as far more creative and autonomous than in other analyses (Negus 1996, 36–65). He is particularly interested in the way that the roles of A&R staff, musicians, other intermediaries such as DJs, managers and journalists, and the roles of fans are blurred, often within the person of a single individual, and how networks of contacts, and knowledge about pop's past and potential future are utilised to exchange information (Negus 1992, 47).

Musicians themselves are often presented as working with an idea of creativity and commerce as polar opposites. In an interesting ethnographic study of bands playing in Liverpool in the 1980s, Sara Cohen observed that the musicians made strong distinctions between the creativity in music that they wanted to pursue and the commercial restrictions they felt limited them (Cohen 1991). Of course Cohen's study focused on local bands who did not necessarily have a record contract at all, and it may be one of the characteristics of commercially successful performers that they do not make such a distinction, or that they are far more concerned with the pursuit of celebrity and fame than they are with their own creativity. Jason Toynbee has attempted to rethink the idea of creativity through the notion of 'agency', and what he sees as 'institutional autonomy' (Toynbee 2000). In his analysis, agency is the possibility to 'select and combine' musical material, and to speak with a distinctive musical 'voice' within the restrictions set by the popular music system and popular music culture.

However we understand A&R staff – either as gatekeepers in a production process, or as parts of an autonomous and amorphous network of cultural intermediaries – an issue remains about the implications of their ideas and practices for the kind of music the corporation records and releases. Negus suggests that staff classify artists into one of two groups that more or less map on to the classic distinction between rock and pop music (Negus 1992, 54). The first category, which he defines as an 'organic' ideology of creativity, positions A&R as discovering and nurturing new talent, while in the second, A&R is seen as bringing together different talents (writing, choreography, image-making, singing, playing, producing) to synthesise a new star image. For Negus these two ideologies fit with a wider notion of the rock tradition that was still prominent in the 1980s when he conducted his research. Under these conditions even a mediocre rock band would find it easier to get a record contract than music-makers outside this polarity.

Of course Negus' analysis is now well over ten years old, and his work is based on interviews with staff who probably joined the industry in the late 1970s or early 1980s, bringing with them a rock-versus-pop binary that was dominant in their adolescence. The landscape of popular music culture has changed quite radically since then. Rock no longer has the same resonance for young audiences, and has been replaced by a postmodern sensibility in which the 'inauthenticity' of 'manufactured' pop groups is not perceived as a negative quality, and no-group, no-star, no-song dance music is the most common form of music-making. If anything, the notion of networks of information and the blurring of boundaries suggested by Negus are even more prominent than they were in the mid-1990s. Ideas about creativity have themselves been transformed. And yet the major corporations still seem much happier with the idea of a group with a lead singer, and which writes its own songs, than it is with the new sensibilities of dance music.

A&R departments rely far more on independent producers and small labels for dance tracks than they do for the mainstream popular music. This reflects another level of the major corporations' organisation. Working on an international level, contemporary record corporations organise their A&R activities by dividing up artists and music into global, territory and niche markets.

Global, territory and niche strategies

The third aspect of record company strategy is the way that recordings are made for different audiences on a geographical basis. Record companies have always operated through a combination of local and international strategies. In the USA, a country that crosses a continent, popular music was traditionally a regional activity. Each territory of musical activity represented a particular taste culture, with bands playing in geographically limited regions and records selling in very different ways in different territories. Radio (and then television) was similarly organised, even if some output was networked to larger broadcasters in the major cities (Hilliard 1985, 1–14). Likewise each region had its own clutch of small record companies, which were often successful locally although the economics of distribution prevented them from operating more widely (Gillett 1983). Music did cross over from territory to territory, and national pop hits were often built from accumulating regional successes or from the niche markets of country or African-American music. The major record companies therefore worked both at the national level and kept an interest in local territories. In Europe the language differences between nations exaggerated this territorialism, and national markets were the norm; crossover hits from other countries were mostly restricted to novelties. However, record companies started operating internationally almost at their inception by setting up overseas branches or affiliations with companies in other countries (Sanjek and Sanjek 1996, 117–46).

By the end of the twentieth century record companies were not simply part of transnational corporations, they had added a global dimension to their earlier territory and niche market strategies. For the corporation a multinational hit increases sales many-fold on a single release. For individual A&R departments, a release that is a hit in one territory suggests it could be a hit in another. For the national record company, an international hit has such low fixed costs that revenue from sales is almost all pure profit.

By the 1980s these economic advantages led to the idea of international repertoire: music that could sell in all the territories in which a record company operated. This was reflected in the establishment of international marketing departments, which converted the corporations' international administrative strategy into an international marketing strategy. Particular artists who were believed to have the potential for international sales were given massive investment in high media profiles and strong media promotion. By the 1990s such music made up 40 to 45 per cent of non-US record sales, with 75 per cent of those sales being US-originated repertoire (figures cited in Negus 1999, 157).

Given that almost all of this international repertoire will also have been produced by the big five corporations it will come as no surprise that the situation has been criticised. The most searing criticism is that international repertoire represents a process of cultural imperialism. The analogy here is that just as European states and the USA had historically built political and economic empires out of the domination of other peoples in the nineteenth and early twentieth centuries, the culture of the former imperial powers – and particularly the highly commercialised culture of the USA – is now, through the control of the modern media, dominating the cultures of the rest of the world (Schiller 1969). The analogy has been very useful in highlighting the political questions that are raised by the operation of music industry corporations. However, it does privilege the idea of economic domination apparent in the role of the major record companies, and simplifies the cultural meanings of popular music.

More recent writers have argued that, rather than an American hegemony, we now have a new global culture created by the activities of transnational corporations (Tomlinson 1991). This idea of globalisation seems to sit more comfortably with the idea of international repertoire, and the process through which record companies construct an idea of a global market and a global music capable of being consumed by this market (Negus 1999, 155–62). Negus emphasises how the global market is defined in terms of criteria of commodification – primarily strict copyright legislation and high-priced CD consumption – and as a set of textual qualities that it is believed would sell in these areas. This leads to a geographically very limited definition of the global market that includes affluent Asian countries, Europe, America and Oceania, but excludes the Indian subcontinent and North and Central Africa, and to a narrow range of textual qualities – primarily the ballad form and English lyrics with no discernable local accent – as the basis for selecting music and artists.

It is important to note that these ideas of cultural imperialism and globalisation are not just restricted to the pages of academic studies, but are also found in the rhetoric of music fans. The growth of interest in so-called 'world music' has been significantly connected to the idea that such music from localised music-makers from different countries of the world is more authentic than that of the international repertoire produced by the major corporations (Mitchell 1996; Taylor 1997).

Equally, discussions of global markets should not detract from our recognising that regional and national musics are also seen as important as sources of profit for major record companies. The corporations have been as adept as any record company in responding to musical developments, even if they are sometimes slower to recognise the change. All major record companies have divisions or departments for black music and country, now joined by others for salsa – reflecting the increasing importance of Latin Americans as a consumer group in the USA – and alternative rock aimed at college students (Negus 1999). In Britain the Dance music scene is perceived to have significant potential for record sales, and this is reflected in the specialist divisions in many companies (Hesmondhalgh 1998). While these divisions are organised around the idea that these distinctive musics represent a particular niche market with an associated structure of record retailers, radio stations and venues, the music is also seen as a potential source of music that may 'cross over' into the mainstream of big sales pop. They also represent popular music cultures in which record companies that operate independently of the major corporations have been successful. As such, these are popular musics in which debates about corporate domination and the potential for alternative music culture are rehearsed.

6.3 Using the internet, or a trade paper, find the record sales charts for a number of different countries. At the time of writing www.lanetlv/misc/charts/ allows you to do this for most major territories. For many countries you can examine charts going back at least a year and sometimes over longer periods. For each territory identify which is domestic and which is international repertoire and calculate the percentage of each category. Then calculate the percentage of international repertoire of American origin and finally the percentage owned by each of the big five corporations. How do your figures compare with the mid-1990s figures for releases across the world of 40 per cent international repertoire? How significant was the percentage of American-originated music within the international repertoire, and how did this compare with the 75 per cent of IR in the 1990s? How significant were the big five corporations? What explanations could you suggest for the differences in figures between territories and over time?

Small companies and the concept of independence

The corporations, and their strategies to grow and yet remain flexible, are not the only important organisations in the record industry. There are also thousands of small record companies that, between them, share the remaining 25 per cent of sales of records. In Britain alone it has been estimated that there were 600 small companies in the mid-1990s (MMC 1994) and, given the marginal nature of these companies, it is likely that this is a underestimation. These companies are widely termed independents to indicate their autonomy from the economic activities of the major corporations. Stephen Lee's proposition that 'independent record companies have long held a cultural status that far exceeds the actual economic impact they have in the market place' (Lee 1995, 14) is as true of the record industries across the world as it is of the American record industry he studied. The critics who attack major corporations for reducing music to a profitable commodity, usually also champion these smaller companies for their pursuit of creativity, artistic freedom and unusual music. In studying independent companies, then, we need to investigate the proposition that they are 'better' for music than the major corporations. As we will discover, more recent writers have raised questions about the very idea that small companies are independent of the major corporations in any meaningful way. A study of small companies therefore needs to examine the discourse of independence utilised by the companies and many music fans, as well as those who have challenged the usefulness of the concept. These debates are the basis of the next two sections. They are then applied in a case study of the independent dance music sector.

The discourse of independence

There is a rich range of studies of such small companies that in itself reveals how important they are to the writers of the histories of popular music culture, and to music fans and record collectors. All of these studies associate the independent record company with distinctive or innovative music. Good examples would include American jazz pioneers Gannett (Kennedy 1994) and Blue Note (Cook 2001), American R&B, rock & roll and soul labels of the 1950s, 1960s and 1970s like Chess (Cohadas 2000), Atlantic (Gillett 1988) Sun (Marcus 1975), Motown (George 1986; Early 1995; Smith 1999) and Stax (Guralnick 1991), British independents of the

FIGURE 6.2 Independent labels are particularly popular with collectors. Copyright © Glenn A. Baker/Redferns. Used with permission.

1970s and 1980s like Factory and Rough Trade (Hesmondhalgh 1997a), as well as more recent labels like US dance independent Wax Trax! (Lee 1995).

Behind all these studies is the notion that the economic independence of a record label allows its staff to produce music that provides an alternative to that produced by mainstream companies restricted to their formulae by their corporate owners. In his history of popular music since the 1950s Charlie Gillett (1988) apportions a central role to the independent record company in creating sites for innovation in popular music. Such celebrations of independent companies tend to be influenced by one of two positions. In the first – exemplified by Gillett – an interest in small labels is based upon a passion for record collecting. This often reflects an attempt to understand the roots of contemporary forms and a range of alternative forms of popular music, which are seen as being more 'authentic'. The second position is rooted in the generation of popular music scholars who grew up in 'the rock era' of the late 1960s to late 1970s. This position – exemplified by Chapple and Garofalo (1977) – also uses the idea of authenticity, but recast in cultural and political terms. Here small record companies are seen as part of the counter-culture of alternative lifestyles that flourished among some young North Americans and Europeans during the late 1960s and 1970s. Here the attack on the majors is part of a general anti-capitalist, and pro-counter-culture position.

The idea of the independent reached its zenith in the late 1970s, becoming the central idea of some strands of punk ideology – probably best represented by the independent company Rough Trade (Hesmondhalgh 1997a). By the 1980s the term for a company's economic independence was being applied to a musical form, and shortened to 'indie' (Hesmondhalgh 1999). More recently, contemporary dance music has been similarly concerned with the idea of independence as a virtue for record production (Lee 1995; Hesmondhalgh 1998). Other writers have also celebrated the role of the independent record companies, but from other perspectives. Nelson George, for instance, has argued that some companies represented a form of black capitalism that was based on a powerful sense of self-empowerment as part of what he terms the 'R&B world'. He proposes that this world could have been a continuing engine for African-American equality had its economic and cultural success not have been undermined by the intervention of major companies when African-American musical forms became established as the basis of the disco boom of the later 1970s (George 1988). He also sees more recent independent companies involved in hip-hop as the new hosts for African-American empowerment (George 1999).

The juxtaposition of major record companies with independents is probably the key way in which the music industry is discussed by academics and in the wider commentary of music journalism. This discourse constructs a binary opposition for the majors verses the independents and then develops it through by connecting each pole to a series of other oppositions. Diagrammatically it would look as outlined in Table 6.1.

You may well be able to add to the binary oppositions listed in Table 6.1 yourself. The polarity is based on the assumption that the list on the right carries more positive connotations than the one on the left, setting the majors up as the enemy of all the

Majors	Independents
Safe	New/risky
Distant	Intimate
Profit	Art
Fake	Real/genuine
Standardised	Innovative
Conventional	Radical
'Whited-out'	Ethnically assertive
Middle-aged	Youthful

TABLE 6.1 The binary oppositions in discourses on the popular music industry

qualities signified, and made possible, by the independents. This sense of polarisation has placed independent companies in a romantic position as champions and guarantors of authenticity in popular music.

Using the internet or some of the books cited in the text, research one or two of the classic independent companies involved in the development of popular music; the website www.history-of-rock.com/independent.htm is particularly useful. Identify the areas of popular music that they were involved in, and the musical changes introduced by their artists. How is the record company characterised in the history? Is the independence of the company seen as important? If so, in what way? Does the account use any of the binary oppositions identified above?

Questions about the relationship between independent and major companies often surface when music fans are discussing the changing career of an artist or the development of a music genre. The movement of an artist or genre from the underground of a small group of music fans to the mainstream is often accompanied by a move from small independents to major companies. The A&R departments of majors constantly look to independent companies to discover new artists and musical genres, often seeing them as a testing ground, with majors picking up a contract once an artist or a particular record has proved itself on a minor label. It is this sense of linkage of the alternative values of underground scenes with independent production that develops a general disposition against commercial activities within popular music culture into a developed critique.

However, as Simon Frith has argued, these positions were simplistic and lacked a sense that production of popular music is 'essentially contradictory' (Frith 1983, 91). Such a position is part of a rethink of the role of independent companies within the record industry.

Challenges to the notion of independence

Keith Negus has noted that independents are seen as 'closer to the street' than majors, challenging both their artistic practices and, on occasion, their market domination. And while he recognises that, historically at least, some independents have clearly been associated with the production of alternative forms of music, he argues that binary oppositions such as these are unhelpful in understanding the relationship between different forms of ownership and control (1996, 43). In an earlier analysis he presents the relationship of such companies as a 'web of major and minor companies' (Negus 1992, 18). In part, the argument is that you cannot use a model established to understand the 1950s, 1970s or 1980s to understand the production of recorded music today. But it also emphasises the point that 'independence' is far more an ideology than it is an analytical model. This position has some important virtues, especially as it emphasises that the different record companies do not exist in isolation from each other, but rather that their activities are intimately related.

Robert Burnett has developed this emphasis on the relationships between companies into a sophisticated model of analysis. He uses the ecological concept of symbiosis – defined as the way that organisms live together within an ecological system – as an analogy for understanding these music industry relationships (Burnett 1996, 77–80). Burnett draws on the work of scholars in organisational theory, who have themselves drawn on biological explanations of how organisms live together. The major–independent binary we have just discussed does, of course, often use an ecological metaphor of symbiosis when it suggests that the majors are parasitic on the independents, taking away new musical forms as soon as the independents show that they can be successful. In this context, the independents are often described as the 'A&R departments of the majors'.

Burnett contrasts this parasitic model with ones of mutualism or commensalism. That is to say, in the long run companies of different scales have a mutual benefit in co-existing, or one benefits from the existence of the other without harm. Ecological theory suggests that dominant organisms will take generalist strategies for survival that allow them to occupy most of the available living space. Other organisms can survive by becoming very specialised. Applied analogously to the record industry this suggests that a small company will specialise in supplying a segment of the market that is too small to be of interest to the dominant, generalist companies. If sales of a particular type of music rise to a certain level they will be perceived to be of more general status and become of interest to the major/generalist who will attempt to contract artists to make this music for its labels. If sales remain low, the independent benefits by the major's neglect of the specialist market niche. Independent companies share a discursive construction of a general mainstream against which their music is perceived to sound alternative. This mutualist theory is more dynamic than the parasitic model and it explains changes in the industry as well as the relationship between dominant major and marginalised minor companies.

Negus' notion of a web of relationships between companies is important in a further respect. It not only emphasises the interrelatedness of small and large companies, but also seeks to undermine the notion that majors are large, monolithic institutions. In this context the smaller divisions or semi-autonomous companies of the big corporations are not necessarily that much greater in scale than companies labelled as independent. This was certainly the case in the 1980s when a series of large independent companies – Island and Virgin in Britain, and A&M and Motown in the

USA – did exist. However, as we have seen, all these companies were taken over by one or other of the corporations by the end of the last century as the market share they controlled became large enough to be of interest to the majors (Lee 1995). Often, though, the previously independent company was established as a separate company within a larger corporation to maintain a strong brand identity or encourage flexible decision-making. Lee argues (1995) that after the takeover of the largest independent companies the remaining market share controlled by other small labels was just not large enough to be of interest to the majors. Instead, most of the contact between the majors and minor companies has been through one of a series of economic relationships outside total ownership.

These major–minor contacts result from the relatively small scale and under-capitalisation of the independent company. Traditionally small companies have not had the resources to sell a release in overseas territories and have relied on majors for international marketing. Likewise it has usually been beyond the financial and managerial ability of a minor company to produce and distribute enough copies of a release that is becoming a sales success outside its usual niche market. This has usually led the small company to license the release to a larger company for a royalty fee, or to conclude a production and distribution (P&D) deal, where the corporation pays for copying and distributing the record in exchange for a share of the profits. As a small company becomes increasingly successful it may be able to agree an even more financially favourable agreement with a corporation, but only by letting the corporation take a share in its company.

Some theorists have pointed to the similarities between these changing characteristics of the record industry economy and structural shifts in other industries. Most often these are expressed through ideas of post-Fordism: the idea that traditional production lines long associated with the car production techniques instigated by Ford, have been replaced by flexible firms, with multiskilled workers, network relationships between producers, and niche markets (see Bagguley 1991). Initially this idea seems to be productive in understanding the new way that the record industry is organised, and a new way of thinking about the commensal relationships between firms.

However, not everyone is convinced by these challenges to the notion of independence. David Hesmondhalgh, for instance, has taken issue with both the rejection of independence as an analytical concept, and the suggestions that flexibility, autonomy and post-Fordism are useful ways to think about the contemporary relationship between small and large record companies (Hesmondhalgh 1996). 'Independence' remains an important concept for Hesmondhalgh, as he links it to aspirations to offer alternative, more democratic, forms of economic and cultural organisation in industries like record production. It is a position shared by Stephen Lee in his study of the transformation of one particular Chicago-based small independent company into a semi-autonomous label in a corporation. Lee argues that the idea of 'independence' allows record company staff to take part in the construction of cultural communities in which the label will become a signifier for alternative values within a subculture of music fans (Lee 1995). Additionally Hesmondhalgh argues that ideas of post-Fordism, while indexing shifts in the organisation of the media industries, do not take sufficient account of the distribution of power or benefit within the relationship between major and minor companies. Centrally he wants to counter the implicit claim that the shifts described as post-Fordist offer opportunities for more democratic and participatory production. Hesmondhalgh argues instead for a careful analysis of the modes of independent production, and their relationship to distinct popular music cultures. He has convincingly applied these insights to a study of the dance music sector of the record industry, and his work provides an excellent platform to produce a case study of contemporary independent record companies.

CASE STUDY   C A S E   S T U D Y   **Dance music independents**

The sector of the record industry that deals with contemporary dance music is particularly worth studying because at first sight it seems to turn the economic imperatives of the mainstream industry on their head. There are a very large number of independent record companies producing dance music – one source claims that there were as many as 8500 dance labels in the 1990s (cited in Hesmondhalgh 1998, 249) – and they produce a very large number of record releases that sell very few copies. In the late 1990s, for instance, 61 per cent of British single releases were in the dance sector, but only 22.2 per cent of sales (cited in Toynbee 2000, 155). To understand how the dance music sector is able to sustain so many companies and produce so many low-selling releases, we must look at the way that the distinctive cultural characteristics of the various dance music scenes interact with the political economy of this record industry sector.

For many writers, including Hesmondhalgh, the activities of these small independent company labels are part of a wider economic and cultural transformation around post-1980s dance music. Jason Toynbee has suggested that these changes can be seen in the five interconnected areas summarised in the following list.

Changes in the economic and cultural forms of popular music:

1. the transformation of the music-maker from the auteur of rock music to the producer/DJ of dance styles

2. the postmodern qualities of the music, especially its characteristic pastiche and textual depthlessness

3. the transformed subject of dance music (by which Toynbee means a new way of understanding our self in relation to a new culture)

4. the new social formations of dance music, which reject hierarchy and are characterised by flat networks, connectivity and accessibility

5. the new economic relationships characterised by a high rate of innovation, relative lack of stars and the low costs of entry into production.

(Based on Toynbee 2000, 131–3)

This list emphasises the way in which the dance sector of the record industry, which developed after the mid-1980s, can be understood as relating to a distinctly different popular music culture than that found in the rock era. These differences are to be found in all aspects of the culture including the music-makers, texts and audiences, and the cultural and economic institutions.

In economic terms, dance music record labels are a classic case of the company that serves a niche market that is far too specialist for the labels of the major corporations. It is possible for the small companies to operate successfully in this niche because of a series of economic advantages: the 'bedroom studio' form of music-making using sampling and domestic computers creates a massive output of tracks; the cultural emphasis on 12-inch vinyl singles has allowed companies to take advantage of the massive capacity in vinyl production brought about by the shift to CD among major companies and mass audiences; a preference for new sounds encourages a high turnover of records; records are sold through specialist record shops, often supplied by companies from the boot of a car; and a pervasive anti-star disposition within the subculture means that traditional forms of corporate promotion are not possible. All these factors have massively lowered the fixed costs of production as well as the cost of entry into record production and distribution. Profits for most companies remain very low, and so the corporations are not attracted to the main field of underground dance music.

The cultural practices in the dance scenes themselves also make it difficult for major record companies to operate: there is a general disposition to be antagonistic to the mainstream media and the major record companies, and there is a strong emphasis on what Sarah Thornton has called the subcultural capital of the participants (Thornton 1995). By this she means the sorts of knowledge and awareness of practices produced within a particular dance subculture, genre of music or even particular club, which give the holder a cultural status. This idea is explored in greater depth in Chapter 13.

As we have seen the idea of symbiosis says that if numbers of sales for a particular release or series of releases remain small, *and* the staff continue to understand the cultural practices of the dance scene, *and* the label's practices are felt to have credibility within the subculture, *and* the company can balance the costs of production against the low revenue of low sales, *then* the independent company will prosper in its niche. The profitability of these companies is improved further, argues Hesmondhalgh, by the licensing of tracks for compilation CDs and soundtracks for adverts, films or television, as the company will be paid a royalty for sales or media use (Hesmondhalgh 1998, 240–3). Although he also notes that this economic practice is perceived to be problematic in the wider music culture, because of its associations with the mainstream, the media and the major record companies who release the compilations.

There are further problems for small record companies as popularity widens – indexed by the sales of compilations to a more mainstream audience – and sales increase. The major companies – with their generalist approach – become interested in the music, and will want to release records in that style, and promote their releases hard to increase the sales even more. The major company aims to make the once niche music a mainstream form. The challenge for the major is twofold. First, the independence of record companies is a key means of defining the musical culture. Second, the subcultural capital accumulated by those involved in the dance scene constitutes the essential knowledge required to make contacts with music-makers, and to select appropriate records for release.

A short-cut for the majors to access the specialist subcultural capital required can be found in either licensing records that have already proved themselves in the scene from small labels, employing staff from small independents, or in working even more closely with such labels. While licensing a popular underground record may increase the chances of gaining a crossover hit, it will not allow the major company access to the scene itself. Equally, while employing staff with subcultural capital would give this access, issuing a release on a major label would alienate buyers from the subcultural scene and a release would not get the initial impetus of club exposure to build a crossover hit. For this reason the major companies set up labels for the niche music (often called pseudo-independents) or make closer relationships with existing companies.

There are also benefits for a small independent record company in working with a major. As we have seen, the difficulties of pressing and distributing on a greater scale to meet increased demand, and of working outside the small network of dance record shops, increases costs dramatically, and involves different forms of expertise. Independents will quite often look to the major record companies for help at this point. Overall, then, an expansion of demand within the niche will push the interests of both the independent and the major record companies to work together, usually into a production and distribution (P&D) deal, possibly connected to a financing agreement enabling the smaller company to pay off debts or expand staff numbers (see Lee 1995). In return for this support, the major will often ask for a share of the record's profits or even the company's ownership. As Lee's study shows, though, such relationships do not need to go as far as a stake in ownership for the major company to exercise control over the smaller company. In the case of Wax Trax! the major merely held back financing if it disapproved of the smaller company's actions. Lee is also able to show how the ideas of company staff converged with the thinking of the major's mainstream marketing departments, and how they justified a sense that they are still independent by emphasising the A&R role that they had retained.

This detailed analysis suggests that, in the long run, small record companies will not be able to sustain rising success within a niche market, and that niche markets will themselves be seen by major record companies as raw material for the mainstream as they grow in popularity. While economically the major is now in control and diverts profits from the smaller company, the staff seek to sustain a continued belief in their own independence. This in itself allows the major to keep the necessary credibility with the underground scene that is required to build a crossover hit. Just as importantly, it also suggests that the ideas of post-Fordism do not adequately explain the sorts of relationships that have developed between small and large companies. What may seem initially to be a network of different forms of organisation – small record companies and small divisions, both linked to the primary record companies of the five major corporations, working with niche markets and looking for music with crossover potential – is in fact a set of power relationships that benefit the corporation. The variety of deals from licensing, through P&D to joint stake, or the establishment of a dance subsidiary, are not examples of flexibility or more equal relationships between small and large firms. They are, rather, ways in which the major has learnt to deal with the anti-corporate rhetoric of the dance music subculture. Such deals offer the audience the pretence that their records are on a label with credibility, and offer the staff the belief that they have managed to maintain autonomy and closeness to the scene while gaining improved financial rewards and access to corporate power. However, these gains are on the terms set by the major company, which hires and fires staff, continues or terminates the licensing or P&D deal, and increases or decreases the flow of finance (Hesmondhalgh 1998, 243–9).

Furthermore, the imperatives of major record production require that the abundance of independent record releases are cut down, and that a smaller number of releases are given increased promotion to maximise sales per release and increase the likelihood of the next release also being a hit. This requires the establishment and building of stars, one of the very qualities absent in underground dance scenes. Just such activities are apparent in the diverse practices of the star DJ personal appearance and CD collection, the DJ *auteurs* of drum & bass like Goldie and LTJ Bukem, the big beat pop stars like Fat Boy Slim, and the rock-band-as-dance-music-makers like the Prodigy. These activities may, initially at least, benefit individual small companies, but, argues Hesmondhalgh, they undermine the independent dance music sector as a whole (Hesmondhalgh 1998, 247).

**X
6.5**

Research the range of independent record companies, labels and major corporation divisions associated with a particular genre of popular music. The internet is a particularly useful tool for this sort of research. Websites like www.record-labels-companies-guide.com/links-indie-record-cos.html are very useful. Can you find out which companies are entirely free of the major corporations? How open about their links are those labels that are affiliated to major companies? Do the major labels that target niche markets present themselves in similar ways to independent companies? How do they do so?

SUMMARY

The record industry is in a paradoxical position. While the economics of record production give massive advantages to large-scale production, and provide corporations with substantial market power to control consumption, the culture of consumers is more dynamic and often purposely fickle. This is the main reason for the complex organisation of the record industry around labels, divisions and companies that is characteristic of the industry. The major corporations constantly aim to grow in size in order to control profit at every level of music production and promotion in every country. However, corporations are mainly generalists focused on mainstream popular music, leaving independent companies to operate in niche markets. As a genre of music increases in popularity, the connections between the independent and the major increase, often leading to complete takeover. Nevertheless, as we have seen, the idea of independence remains a vital concept within popular music culture, if only because it helps us understand the culture of production in small companies.

All record companies operate within the wider context of the entertainment media. These media are the main vehicles for the promotion of recorded music, and the music provides cheap, popular programming for the media. This mutual benefit is the key to understanding the operation of record and media companies as well as their corporate owners. This is the subject of the next chapter.

Further reading

Frith, Simon 1993: *Music and Copyright.* Edinburgh University Press.

Hesmondhalgh, David 1997: 'Post-Punk's Attempt to Democratise the Music Industry: The Success and Failure of Rough Trade', *Popular Music* 16(3), 255–74.

Hesmondhalgh, David 1998: 'The British Dance Music Industry: A Case Study in Independent Cultural Production', *British Journal of Sociology* 49(2), 234–51.

Lee, Stephen 1995: 'Re-Examining the Concept of the "Independent" Record Company: The Case of "Wax Trax!" Records', *Popular Music* 14(1), 13–31.

Negus, Keith 1999: *Music Genres and Corporate Cultures.* Routledge.

Sanjek, Russell and Sanjek, David 1991: *American Popular Music Business in the 20th Century.* Oxford University Press.

Toynbee, Jason 2000: *Making Popular Music: Musicians, Creativity and Institutions.* Arnold.

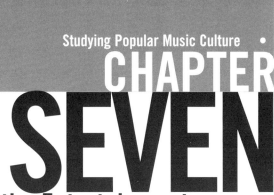

CHAPTER SEVEN

Popular Music and the Entertainment Media

Popular music can be found in all the mass media: it is the key element of most radio; it is the soundtrack to films, adverts and television programmes; it is the subject of newspaper and magazine articles and photographs; it is an element within websites and computer games; and frequently a common thread across all media as an artist appears in videos, on websites, in the press and on television. It is hard to think about popular music without the media, and hard to think about the media without popular music.

To understand the relationship between popular music and the entertainment media we need to focus on two aspects. First, we need to examine the way that the primary text of popular music – the record – is utilised within the entertainment media. Second, we need to explain how the relationship between the record industry and the media is organised for their mutual benefit. These are the topics of the initial two sections of this chapter. The ideas are then applied into a detailed examination of the main medium for popular music: radio.

The music industry and the entertainment media

There are a number of ways to understand the relationship between the music industry and the media-based entertainment industries. In the basic sequential model of production introduced in Chapter 5 the entertainment media are simultaneously an economic and cultural space for popular music culture. On one hand they are the promotional avenues available to record companies for increasing awareness of records in the hope of increasing sales and, on the other, they are the means through which popular music is consumed. Keith Negus constructs them as 'mediators' and their activities of broadcasting or publication as 'mediation' between production and consumption (Negus 1996, 66–71). By this Negus has in mind three interacting processes of meaning-making: as technologies of transmission like broadcasting or print publication, which allow popular music to be distributed over time or geography; as organisations whose staff operate as intermediaries, directing and ordering the way that these technologies operate as cultural institutions; and as part of the broader social relationships in which the role of popular music as entertainment is established.

The idea of 'mediating' popular music can be helpful, but it results in too strong a distinction between the record industry and the entertainment industry. From most consumers' points of view, they feel they are consuming the same popular music whether it comes from radio, television or a walkman. That is not to say they do not constitute distinct ways of experiencing music – they do – but they are collectively understood as being 'popular music'. Popular music is music produced for, and through, the modern mass media. Extrapolating Simon Frith's argument that records are popular music; not transcripts of a pre-existing music (Frith 1992), radio broadcasts of records are one of the ways the meanings of popular music is created, not how it is changed.

Following Timothy D. Taylor we can understand all the different ways we experience popular music as forming a metatext (Taylor 1997). That is to say, the meanings we apply to a piece of popular music are not produced simply by the primary text – the record – but by our engagement with all forms of consumption. The record is contextualised by which radio station we hear it on, how the press write about it, and how a video visually presents the record. The collective meanings of all these contexts and experiences are the broader, and often richer, metatext. This is a useful concept and we will return to it in Part 3 when we study forms and meaning.

In the same way that consumers experience popular music across the entertainment media, the industries think of music in this way as well. Although the record remains the primary commodity of the music industry – and the primary text for consumers – the industry increasingly treats the media as producing what we could call, developing Taylor's idea, metacommodities. Those staff who control the major corporations constantly point towards the need to see artists as operating across a range of media, and across the most developed nations of the world (see Burnett 1996, 8–28). To achieve this the corporations need to systematically direct the whole range of entertainment media that use popular music. Of course this is not a new phenomenon. Looking back historically we can see that music production has always been connected with the wider world of public entertainment. As music was first commodified systematically in the music halls of the nineteenth century, ownership and control of live music was quickly concentrated into a small number of hands. The companies that owned the theatres, managed and booked the artists, and published the songs they sang, then became integrated with the companies that produced and distributed films, which in turn acquired companies producing the hardware and software of radio, the record and then television (Sanjek 1988; Sanjek and Sanjek 1996). This drive to concentrate the ownership and control of public entertainment was based upon the same forces that drive modern corporations in the new media of DVD, the internet and video games.

The power of the corporations that dominate music production is not just over which records are recorded and released, but which ones are reviewed, heard on radio or television, featured in films and stocked in shops. These corporations usually have other subsidiary companies involved in other aspects of the entertainment industry, acquired through the lateral integration of music production with other mass media. Looking across the major corporations this includes companies that produce magazines, run radio and television stations, and make films or videos, as well as manufacture CD players, television or radio sets and video recorders. On top of this they control some of the formats that recordings are released on or promoted through. The Bertelsmann organisation, for instance, is also a major player in publishing and broadcasting, Sony and Universal own substantial film and broadcasting interests, and AOL Time Warner is a major publishing, film, broadcasting and internet conglomerate. Although for the music divisions of these corporations the record remains the primary commodity, the metacommodity is becoming increasingly important. In the 1990s half of the income generated for the music industry in Europe related to the sales of records, but nearly a quarter came from income that included royalty payments from radio and television, and concert ticket sales (Laing and Tyler 1998). If we add to that the boost in sales for other media created by the presence of popular music material, then the importance of the idea of the metacommodity becomes very clear. Just as, earlier, we looked for theories and models to explain why the record industry is organised as it is, and what the implications of this organisation are, we need to do the same for the corporations' role in the wider entertainment industry. The concept of synergy is most helpful here.

Undertake a survey of your media consumption for a few days to see how many of the media products you consume are made by one of these corporations. Start by listing the products and then use the internet to research the companies that produce them. What proportion of your consumption was produced by companies that are part of the big five music corporations?

Media synergy

Robert Burnett has drawn attention to how widespread the concept of synergy is within the music industry and the media itself to explain corporate strategy. He notes that, 'In the 1990s synergy has been the preferred topic of conversation amongst entertainment industry executives. Here we refer to the economic gain caused by the ownership or control of various media by one media company' (Burnett 1996, 22).

Burnett's own account of this idea of synergy draws upon organisational theory work on media corporations (Turow 1992; Sanchez-Tabernero and Denton 1993), and reflects the rather narrow sense that this concept is used within entertainment corporations. It is not unusual for corporate employees to use concepts from academia in a narrower sense to justify their own strategies. The difficulty for our study is that these restricted applications of the concepts often lose their descriptive and analytical richness as they are limited to the PR rhetoric of corporate headquarters. So, while there are significant gains to be had for corporations that can exploit synergies, there is more to synergy than simply the benefits of multimedia ownership or control.

Synergy is, like the concept of symbiosis introduced in Chapter 6, an ecological metaphor. Synergy refers to the way that a number of processes work together within a single ecological system in such a way that they create greater benefits for those involved in the synergy than would be achieved if they lived outside the ecological system. When applied to the music industry and entertainment media, this can explain how different companies working together can create greater benefits – in terms of larger listenership, readership or sales, and so profits – than working independently. Synergies can exist between record companies and radio stations, for instance. When a radio station plays a record because it is popular both the record company and the radio station share a synergy: playing records is a form of promotion that is likely to increase record sales; playing records people like attracts radio listeners. Likewise the press and record companies can have synergetic relationships. Writing features on popular artists sells copies of a magazine and promotes the artists, possibly increasing the artists' popularity, record sales and magazine sales. Synergies can extend to the film industry. Featuring a song on the soundtrack of a film promotes the song to all the cinema-goers and the song's place in the film will increase the public profile of the film. These synergies, then, simultaneously lie in the area of record or artist promotion for record companies, and audience building for other media companies. If the two activities can be brought together, then both types of company will benefit.

Sadly, Burnett's discussion of these relationships simultaneously narrows down the idea of synergy only to benefits achieved through ownership, and broadens it out to any benefit of greater scale achieved through takeovers. A statement from a senior corporate figure quoted by Turow shows this well:

> A media company that intended to compete successfully in the environment would have to be heard and big enough to hold consumer attention. It would have to propose products and synergies that only a large, versatile organisation could offer. It'd have to be able to move its products through the emerging global market place and amortize its costs over as many distribution networks as possible ... What we wanted was solid vertical integration so we could offer synergies that would bring together magazines, publishing ventures, studios, cable channels and other activities into a coherent operation.

(Quoted in Turow 1992, 688)

However, this statement reveals more about the processes of justification that go on in organisations than it does about the way the corporation works in this multimedia environment. Synergies are a different kind of benefit to the economies of scale examined earlier, in Chapter 5, and while both synergy and economies of scale can be produced through corporate growth and takeover they are distinct concepts. In fact as the examples of radio, press and film show, many synergies exist independently of consciously coordinated activity, let alone cross-media ownership. The problem here is that talk of synergy within the corporation has simply become a term to describe any sort of benefit, real or perceived, that comes from taking over another company.

For a greater insight we should understand synergy as the product of the way in which different companies involved in different sorts of media activity are related within popular music culture. The metaphor is a useful one in that it draws our attention to the media as a system in which all the parts are interrelated. As such it takes us beyond the simpler idea that records are produced and then marketed through the media. Synergy focuses our attention on the interrelationships: record companies want to produce records that will be taken up by the entertainment media, as they believe they will sell well; while the media wants to take up records that are going to be popular, and look to the record companies to indicate which ones they will be. The potential gains of synergetic relationships motivate corporations into certain types of action. First, they will want to involve themselves in practices that are synergetic. For instance they will want to encourage radio producers or magazine editors to feature their records. Second, they will want to try to control and direct the activities that produce and increase synergies. Finally, they will want to increase their share of the profit from all aspects of the synergy by owning both the rights to use the recordings and the other companies in other parts of the media that are involved in the synergy.

The concept of synergy, then, allows us to understand three areas of interest in the study of the industries and institutions of popular music culture: the promotion of records, the drive for control of copy and performance rights and, finally, the forces behind corporate lateral takeovers.

Promotion

Record companies see the other media as promotional avenues for their music. Most people buy records that they know about. If they have no knowledge that a recording exists, they will not buy it. Keith Negus has identified the marketing department of a record company, and its conscious activity of constructing an audience, as central to this process. For Negus this involves an attempt to ' "articulate" the relationship between the identity of the artist and the lived experience of consumers' (Negus 1992, 62). This is achieved through ideas of market segmentation. That is, audiences will be subdivided into groups that are associated with particular genre forms. Each audience/genre coupling will then be targeted through different media products seen as suitable to that audience/genre. Dance music is most likely to be promoted directly through club DJs, by giving them free promotional copies of a record before it has even been released, or even before the label artwork has been printed (which has given rise to the term white labels). In Britain a mainstream rock band will most likely be associated with an older male consumer, and promotion will be focused on record reviews and interviews in magazines like *Mojo* and *Q*. If the core audience is perceived to be younger university students the promotional focus will be on Radio 1's evening shows, and interviews and photographs in the *NME*. Record companies would link younger consumers with boy/girl pop bands and emphasise videos and personal appearances on Saturday-morning children's television.

One of the best examples of promotion in a synergetic relationship is the television show *Pop Idol*. It updated the talent competition, which has been a staple of popular music and light entertainment television, but it also tied directly into the record business with the show's winner gaining a record contract. The popular press covered the show extensively with several pages of tabloid papers given over to *Pop Idol* stories in the run-up to the final. The final three contestants all recorded the same tracks three weeks before the last show, and the winner's record was rushed out within days, making number-one sales the following week. This is an exemplary case of promotional synergy, with the television show, the record company, the tabloid press and the radio stations all gaining massive benefits from the carefully choreographed activity. (This example is used as one of the case studies in Part 5.)

Music Rights

Simon Frith has argued that 'for the music industry the age of manufacture is now over. Companies (and company profits) are no longer organised around making *things* but dependent on the creation of *rights*' (Frith 1987, 57). This is a premature description of the facts of economic activity because even 12 years later in Europe at least half of the income within the music industry came from the sales of records while 12 per cent was generated by ownership of the different rights associated with music production, distribution and sales (Laing 1998, 34). However, as a description of the primary strategy of the corporations it is insightful.

In law, individuals are awarded the right to perform, transcribe or reproduce a piece of music. These are known respectively as performance, publishing and mechanical rights. As Frith has shown, these rights are the product of a long history of ideological manoeuvring between the state and different commercial and cultural interest groups. In Britain and the USA rights were first assigned by the state to producers of cultural goods because it was recognised that if anyone could copy and distribute someone else's creation without rewarding the originator this would undermine general creative activity (Frith 1987). Writers and composers pass on their rights to performers in exchange for a payment made through the Performing Rights Society (PRS), and the right to record through the Mechanical Copyright Protection Society (MCPS). The record company extends the right to play the record outside of a domestic setting through Phonographic Performance Limited (PPL).

Frith perceptively notes that interests in different sorts of rights have changed as commercial circumstances and technological possibilities have altered (Frith 1987, 57–63). So as radio grew and record sales declined in the 1920s, record companies in Britain secured the ownership of performance rights for records. In America, though, record companies felt that, on balance, the promotional gain from broadcast record plays outweighed the likelihood that they undermined record sales. Instead, by the 1940s the struggle for ownership rights was between the music writers and composers and the radio stations, which led to radio stations setting up their own rights agency for music played on the radio (Ryan 1985).

Increasingly the corporations are recognising the economic value of the rights for existing and new texts. In the UK alone around £80 million a year is generated through the use of music in radio and television broadcasting (Laing 1998, 47). This is likely to increase massively in the next few decades. The potential for increased rights income is driven by three converging cultural and technological changes that are taking place in the media:

1. consumption of media products of all types is increasing as spending power and leisure time increase

2. traditional carriers of popular music – the record, the video and the radio play – are being replaced by new digital technologies distributed by networks

3. the products carried by these new technologies are not restricted by the old constraints of limited frequencies, real-time distribution or the calculatable costs of reproduction.

These new technologies allow an almost unlimited number of channels for audio-visual entertainment and so a massive increase in demand for content. To this end the corporations have been building up ownership of rights in new corporate divisions, and then promoting their use in the traditional and new media. In turn these imperatives are driving the acquisition of companies that own publishing rights, produce media products or distribute content.

Lateral Takeovers

When a company in one production sector takes over another company in another media sector this is termed a lateral takeover, to distinguish it from the vertical and horizontal takeovers that occur within a single sector. But by owning and controlling the agents involved in the synergetic relationships of musics, metatext/metacommodity corporations will be able to both direct and benefit from them. It is easier to create synergy if you control the record company that releases the record and the company that runs the radio station, the television station, the music magazines and the film company that will be used to promote the records. As we saw in Chapter 3, the origination of such multimedia cross-promotional activities is usually credited to the independent producer Robert Stigwood in the 1970s, and his control of the key products of the film, music and rights to *Saturday Night Fever*.

It is the change of scale and increased recognition of the importance of rights that distinguishes more recent economic synergetic relationships. When the Sony Corporation took over the film, publishing and music interests of CBS records and Columbia/Tristar Pictures in the late 1980s, it was recognising the potential for synergies between its music, television and video hardware and Columbia's past and future ownership of music and films. When Sony developed a new format for music or video playback, it would have a ready back catalogue of material to release on that format. The takeover of Time Warner by the internet provider America On Line (AOL) updates this same principle for the internet age. The management difficulties faced by Sony, and the failure of the similar merger between the Japanese Matsushita company and the American MCA (which controlled Universal pictures as well as MCA records), shows that such corporate strategies do not always succeed (Negus 1999, 40–5), but it remains a driving force in popular music and the record industry, and the entertainment media of which it is now an integral part.

X

7.2

Plan out a hypothetical promotions strategy for an entertainment conglomerate centred on the release of a piece of recorded music and using a range of media. Identify all the points at which profit could be made, and the points of synergy within and outside the corporation. Produce a diagram to show the flow of profits from sales and rights income.

CASE
STUDY

C A S E   S T U D Y   **Popular Music Radio**

Music radio is simultaneously the music industry's key channel for promotion and one of the main ways in which we experience popular music. Equally, music offers radio programmers a number of significant advantages: it is relatively cheap; it is well suited to the secondary and mobile listening made possible by radio technology; and the appeal of music gives stations readily identifiable audiences. These were the reasons why, when television took over from radio as the primary domestic medium in the USA of the 1950s – slashing radio's audiences and taking away the quiz shows, dramas and comedies that had been its staple programming – radio moved over to playing records. Radio executives sought out audiences that did not want, or could not afford, the domestic cosiness of TV: the young, less affluent rural whites and poor urban African-Americans. These were cultural groups that articulated their social position through the distinctive popular musics of rock & roll, country and rhythm & blues (Rothenbuhler and McCourt 2002).

In Britain the change was far less dramatic because radio was controlled by the monopoly of the BBC. The BBC's commitment to public service broadcasting was interpreted by its management to mean a middle-class, middle-aged version of radio's traditionally broad output, and a reluctance to play records of commercial popular music. It was not until 1967, with the establishment of BBC Radio 1, that a legal station concentrated on pop records. Even then it remained a centralised, national, universal provision, rather than the regional and diverse pop radio of the USA (Barnard 1989, 50–68). When advertising-funded radio was introduced in 1973 it was based on local urban communities, but initially at least there was only one station per area and the music played was, like that of Radio 1, heavily influenced by the idea that it was broadcasting to a wide listenership who wanted to hear familiar voices and music (Wall 2000).

Modern music radio is relatively cheap because the costs of producing the recorded music are carried by the record companies and not by the radio station. They do not even buy the records, but are sent promotional copies by the record companies. The notion that the costs of radio programming can be deferred by record company promotional budgets has not always been universal, though. For the first decade of Radio 1's existence the BBC agreed with musicians to play only eight hours of recorded music a day, and record companies, songwriters and musicians have tried to get radio stations to pay significant sums for the right to play their records. Radio stations have countered that they indirectly promote the records they play, and that this benefit to the record company more than compensates for the benefit to the radio stations of cheaper programming. There is some evidence to support this claim in the case of the Radio Luxemburg English-language service in the late 1950s, which was able to sell blocks of airtime to record companies in which they played their own records (Barnard 1989, 32–49). Today there is an acceptance of the mutual benefits of the synergetic relationship between the different vested interests. Although radio stations have to pay for the right to play records, these rights payments are significantly less than the true benefit of the music to the radio station.

This raises questions about the influence of this relationship between the record industry and music radio. Rothenbuhler and McCourt have gone as far as making the proposition that 'radio largely determines which records become popular and which remain obscure' (Rothenbuhler and McCourt 1992, 101). Their analysis is useful in the way that it demonstrates how radio is part of a popular music system that systematically filters hits from the over-production of records. Radio stations, they argue, want to find records that listeners will not object to (rather than ones they like), while record companies produce and target them at radio play. They conclude from this that 'contemporary commercial radio actively discourages significant stylistic innovation in popular music and the communicative potential that such creative endeavors would produce' (Rothenbuhler and McCourt 1992, 114). Their polemic is a useful counter to the claims from radio executives that stations just play what people want to hear, but it does not capture the complex and dynamic nature of the interaction of radio and popular music, nor the diverse ways in which different national radio systems or regulatory regimes impact on the popular music system.

In a more developed comparative analysis of North American and British music radio, Keith Negus has argued that American radio is characterised by the dominance of station formats that determine the type of music that any particular station plays (Negus 1992, 101–14). The largest format group – both in terms of the number of stations and number of listeners – is contemporary hits radio (CHR), which plays records from the top 40 sales charts. These stations are so numerous that they are further divided into three graded categories: parallel one (P1, with over a million listeners), two (P2, with fewer than a million listeners) and three (P3, with fewer than 200 000 listeners). Other formats include: adult contemporary (soft rock/middle-aged listeners); urban (black music and dance/young urban listeners); alternative (more diverse music/young, white, middle-class listeners); country (contemporary Nashville music) (see Barnes 1988 for more detail). Negus's analysis places an emphasis on the centralised, routine and information-led nature of music programming with these formats.

The records played by a station are chosen by a music programmer, who organises them in three playlists. Records on the A list get played as much as once a programme, or even once an hour, B list records get less play, and C list records may only get one play per day. Records are programmed so they will not jar with the listening audience, repeat style or tempo, or place unfamiliar records together. As there are well over 2000 record plays in a week, most stations use a computer program like Selector to allocate records to each time slot. The decision about which records to select from each list is usually based on information about record sales, plays on other stations and the views of actual or potential listeners. However, these music programming practices are undertaken within a paradoxical context. P1 CHR stations only play music that gets into the charts, while the charts themselves are constructed by surveying what records are being played by radio stations and which records are selling in large numbers, sales which are in themselves influenced by radio play.

Negus identifies two main strategies used by company staff to break a record. Most common is to try and get the record played on the smaller P2 or P3 CHR stations, and build a regional hit into a national hit. Music programmers in radio stations are constantly checking trade press charts compiled from the playlists of other stations, and so the momentum of a record being played by an increasing number of stations will in itself cause other stations to start playing it. Alternatively, a promoter can try and get heavy play for a record on one of the niche-format stations and then hope it 'crosses over' to CHR stations. Interestingly, Negus suggests that the very act of putting money into promoting a record can in itself attract a P1 station's music programmer. The logic of this is that if a record company is 'getting behind' a record – signalled by the employment of expensive independent record promoters – it must have the qualities of a potential hit, and so be worth playing. And, of course, through airplay, it does become a hit.

Negus contrasts the situation in the USA to that in Britain. He argues that the dominance of BBC Radio 1 among UK radio stations, and the freedom of individual programme producers to choose music for their own shows means that 'the idiosyncrasies and tastes of particular producers and disc jockeys can have far more influence on what is broadcast' (Negus 1992, 110). However, it is perhaps only in the contrast between the US and UK radio systems that the role of the individual becomes so significant. During the period of Negus' analysis the daytime output of Radio 1 was, like that of the US P1 CHR stations, overwhelmingly guided by the top 40 charts. The interest of individual radio presenters or producers in being part of the process that gets an artist into the charts should not detract from us understanding the 'overwhelming allegiance to the sales charts' as the criterion deciding which tracks are playable (Barnard 1989, 129–30). As Barnard has shown, evening and weekend programming on Radio 1 has always provided a significant space for specialist and alternative music. Station management used the idea of 'ratings by day and credibility by night' as a way of articulating a particular notion of public service (Barnard 1989, 51–62). It is this distinction between ratings and credibility that characterises the central role of Radio 1 in the British music industry.

There have, though, been significant changes in British radio since Negus' research was conducted in the late 1980s. First, the number of commercial radio stations – both as a national total and within each region – has increased dramatically. At the time of writing there are over 200 terrestrial commercial broadcasters in Britain (Radio Authority 2001) and all the indications suggest that we are about to experience an explosion in the numbers (Radio Authority report 2001). This expansion in commercial radio has been paralleled by an increase in listenership, and a commensurate decline in listenership to Radio 1. Second, Radio 1 has undergone a dramatic transformation since 1996, radically altering the station's programming and presentation practices, which were established at its inception in 1967 (Garfield 1998).

FIGURE 7.1 The tracks played by radio stations are one of the main ways we experience popular music
Photo: Stefan Klenke

David Hendy's analysis of the changes at Radio 1 also reveals a more complex relationship between record companies and the station, and between the 'popular music system' and popular music culture (Hendy 2000b). While his analysis still assumes that radio influences record consumption, by studying this relationship at a time of transition he picks up more of the contradictions and disjunctions. Hendy shows how changes in music programming (the idea of 'new music, first'), the style of presenters, and the role of staff with knowledge of music from outside the pop mainstream, changed the type of music that was played, and blurred the distinction between 'daytime pop' and 'evening serious' programming. It may even have altered the pop mainstream itself. Certainly his analysis suggests that during the mid- to late-1990s Radio 1 did increase the proportion of pre-release and pre-chart entry records it played, as well as significantly increasing the ratio of British-produced records to international repertoire. Hendy locates these changes in the context of the BBC's public service traditions, increasing competition from commercial stations, and a series of flourishing local music sounds – including Britpop, trip-hop, and British R&B and garage.

Hendy's analysis also shows a significantly different picture between Radio 1 and commercial stations, whose playlists seems far more strongly weighted to known bands and musicians, current success in the charts and international repertoire. Although these programming characteristics are an application of the key principle of commercial radio – that a playlist of well-known records is more likely to attract listeners – we should not forget that in Britain commercial stations have a legal obligation to follow similar principles of public service to those of the BBC. Although the regulation of commercial stations has become increasingly 'light touch' over 30 years, during the late 1990s stations still had to meet a legal 'promise of performance' that outlined which genres they could play and in what proportions (see Wall 2000). In fact, nearly all new commercial stations that were given a licence from the mid- to late-1990s were obligated to play musical forms from outside the national charts as part of a state attempt to broaden the variety of broadcasting within local areas (Radio Authority 1999).

However, there is evidence that some commercial companies applied for licences based on niche musical programming, but were not genuinely seeking to extend the variety of music radio listening available (Wall 1999). More recently the British radio regulator has replaced detailed promises of performance with general 'statements of format', giving stations even more latitude in the programming of records (Radio Authority 2001). For Stephen Barnard, commercial music programming is neither simply guided by record companies or regulation, but at heart is,

> a professional judgment of what the listener will prefer to hear at a particular time, informed by a variety of factors including a record's appropriateness for the station's target market, when either it matches the brand image of the station and its generic base, and perhaps only incidentally its sales performance as reflected in the charts.
>
> (Barnard 2000, 130)

Yet, while this emphasis takes us away from the crude idea that radio merely responds to record company promotion, or that record companies simply produce what they think radio stations will produce, Barnard's analysis makes such programming seem obvious and, however, as Jody Berland has argued:

> Format music programming styles ... appear to spring from and articulate a neutral marriage of musics and demographics, and to correspond opportunistically to already established tastes, whose profiles are discovered through the neutral science of market research.
>
> (Berland 1993a, 107)

Berland counters such an assumption by arguing that only certain types of music to certain types of audience are catered for by commercial radio. She sees the practice of radio broadcasting as an attempt to construct radio listeners and their musical tastes as communities tied to senses of space and time produced by the regular forms of music programming, time checks, travel news and other presenter talk.

Many commentators have suggested that it is in unlicensed broadcasting that we find a greater sense of adventure in music programming, and a stronger link between broadcaster and popular music culture. This is certainly the theme of most books and articles on what has come to be called 'pirate radio' (see Hind and Mosco 1985; Keith 1997). It is true that such stations do usually provide extensive airtime to music genres not heard on mainstream radio; they do not usually have the highly centralised music programming systems of licensed broadcasters, and their presenters are usually heavily involved in other aspects of the same music culture as club DJs, promoters or journalists. However, many stations are as commercially orientated as their licensed competitors, and they can often broadcast to smaller audiences because they do not pay for the right to broadcast recorded music, and do not usually pay their DJs.

The obvious tension between commercial interests – which seem to push music programmers towards the playlisting of well-known, currently charting, international repertoire – and the cultural considerations of musical innovation, diversity and local distinctiveness can be found in a further case study in European broadcasting. Geoffrey Hare's fascinating study of French radio draws on exactly the same ground as Hendy's British case study, but in a dramatically different regulatory context (Hare 1999). The Broadcasting Reform Act 1994 set a compulsory quota of 40 per cent of French-language songs at peak listening times, with half of these tracks to be by new artists. The motivation for these quotas was to promote the traditional French popular music form of *chanson* and support the French music industry. Hare argues that while French youth are fascinated with American culture, and so English-language music, the French elite see this music as a form of cultural imperialism. While this period of regulation created much tension between the state and commercial radio, there were some interesting by-products for French popular musical culture.

The youth-orientated stations did not believe they could attract their desired listenership with *chanson* and in looking for ways to circumvent the quotas some national stations sought out French-language music that they hoped would have the same appeal as the international repertoire they had previously played. They found distinctive forms of French rap, North African–African-American hybrids, and French-language reggae. All these musics could be counted in the French-language quotas, and as stations started to play them these records moved out of the underground of unlicensed broadcasters and small independent labels. At the same time, music from these genres took a more prominent place in the French charts, and major record companies signed up artists like MC Solar in these genres.

Case studies like Hendy's and Hare's on the relationship between popular music and music radio reveal that radio clearly is part of a wider popular music system, which does have major implications for popular music culture. Radio play does feature significantly in the processes through which music becomes more widely known, which records are purchased and, ultimately, which ones are made and released. However, this is not the overwhelming determinism that Rothenbuhler and McCourt suggest, rather it is part of a complex interaction of record and radio industry production processes, institutional practices and the regulatory context.

Produce a survey of music played on radio stations you can hear in your locality. Most stations now have a website that lists the programmes and the music genres they play, and sometimes even the playlists. Identify which genres are played most often and which are neglected. Is it possible to say why certain types of music are being played often and others less so? How far do the tracks played by the radio stations reflect those currently in the sales charts? How far do the tracks played by a specific station seem to fit with the brand image of the station?

SUMMARY

Records are not the only way that we consume music. The wider entertainment media are important channels of promotion for the record industry, and sources of cheap programming or content for other media. This relationship produces a synergy of greater benefit when the media and the record companies work together, and is one explanation of why record companies are increasingly part of vast entertainment media corporations. Music-making and music culture are intimately connected to these industrial processes and forms of organisation, and the way they operate fundamentally influences all other aspects of popular music. The broader contexts of consumption, and the cultural activities of listening, looking, dancing and buying, are the subject of Part 3.

Further reading

Burnett, Robert 1996: *The Global Jukebox: The International Music Industry.* **Routledge.**

Frith, Simon 1993: *Music and Copyright.* **Edinburgh University Press.**

Negus, Keith 1999: *Music Genres and Corporate Cultures.* **Routledge.**

Rothenbuhler, Eric W. and McCourt, Tom 1992: **'Commercial Radio and Popular Music: Processes of Selection and Factors of Influence', in** *Popular Music and Communication,* **ed. James Lull. Sage.**

Part THREE:
Form, Meaning and Representation

Everyday conversations about music very often concentrate on the styles of different musicians or singers, the characteristics of particular types of music, the way we respond to individual records or whole categories of music. We choose to listen to certain types of music, and these choices are often linked to how we think of ourselves as individuals. These activities relate to the meanings that particular music has for us. Of course, we also hold views on the value and meaning of music we do not like. This part takes these processes of description and sense-making and turns them into systematic processes of analysis.

Chapter 8 concentrates on the forms that popular music takes. Focusing on the song as the most common form, the chapter introduces ways to understand this form, its development and its alternatives. There is also an exploration of the (mostly negative) judgements that have been made about the song form. Chapter 9 moves from questions of form to questions of meaning. After a discussion of how meaning is generated in popular music, the chapter explores some ways in which the performance of music, its place in the wider meanings of our society and the role of genre contribute to meaning. The final chapter in Part 3 aims to introduce some straightforward approaches to the way star images are represented, and how a particular music represents an identity for the people who make and consume it.

EIGHT

Form

One way to start our analysis is to identify some of the main characteristics of popular music, to produce some general observations about the music and attempt to draw some conclusions. This chapter looks at the dominant form of popular music: the song. It introduces some straightforward ways to understand the structure of songs, and examines the implications of the dominance of songs within popular music.

The dominance of the song form

While there are many examples of other musical forms and interesting variations, the song is the most common basis for composing and performing popular music. Charles Hamm has argued that the song was established as the dominant compositional structure as early as the late nineteenth century (Hamm 1983, 256). Most major styles of twentieth-century popular music – including ballads, ragtime, jazz, big band, rock & roll, rock, soul, reggae, punk, metal, indie – have either reproduced this structure or been based upon some modification of it.

The song form is so widespread that we often take it for granted, and use the term as a synonym for popular music as a whole. But the song form is distinctively structured around a number of components, most notably the verse/chorus structure, patterns of melodic repetition and change and, finally, lyrics. Describing these elements as dominant does not mean that they are universal. There are millions of variations or exceptions, but the idea of a dominant form is very useful for analysis because it allows us to identify both the common features and the cases where something different has been produced. The next three sections examine these characteristics in some detail.

Verse and Chorus

Songs are structured around a sequence of verses and choruses. The verses tell an unfolding story, while the chorus is a repeated refrain. The repeated verse, chorus, verse, chorus pattern is also usually interrupted by an instrumental section before a final series of choruses are repeated to the end. There have been some significant historical shifts in the way songs are written and performed (Hamm 1983). For instance, the chorus, as the name suggests, was originally always sung by a group of singers. Increasingly, in the early twentieth century, it became a role of the solo voice, which also sang the verse. The chorus also became longer and now usually contains the stronger melodic element, usually called 'the hook' (the melodic and linguistic part we sing along to) (see Burn 1987). As the chorus became the main musical focus, the verse took on a secondary role, and the story-telling function of popular songs was commonly reduced. Often songwriters made no attempt to construct narratives, but instead utilised other poetic devices that emphasised imagery or whimsy.

These formal characteristics of songs are strongly linked to differences in techniques of composition, the commodity form the song takes and the way it was intended to be consumed. Historically, the song form became standardised as songwriting itself became professionalised and industrialised around writing 'hit' songs where the melodic hook in the chorus was used to lodge the song in the listener's mind. Communal singing, and the rise of the star in the music hall of the early twentieth century also motivated this change in musical form (Bratton 1986). These, of course, are the formal structures and cultural practices we associate with mainstream pop songs, and they remain as strong in today's manufactured bands as they were in the music halls.

The variations and exceptions to this standard verse/chorus form are also rooted in different conditions of song production and consumption. Generally the less professionalised the songwriting the less strong the hook tends to be, and the greater the importance of the verse. This is particularly the case when composers think of themselves as artists rather than craft workers, as is the case with singer-songwriters, or songwriters within self-contained bands. Music aimed less at the one-off hit and more at becoming a long-term seller, will also place less emphasis on the hook. African-American forms have tended to keep more elements of the group chorus, influenced by the particular forms of religious communal singing prominent in black American culture, and the solo voice is often shared within a group of singers. This is prominent in soul and contemporary R&B. A similar characteristic is also noticeable when the industry is trying to promote a group of singers as equal star members, and particularly when the musical resources are derived from African-American repertoires. Think about the structure of the songs of contemporary boy or girl bands. The songs usually feature both shared solo singing of the verse and communal chorus singing, added to a strong hook in the chorus.

FIGURE 8.1 Dance music and the performances of DJs have changed the very form of popular music
Photo: Stefan Klenke

Musical forms that are consumed through dancing rather than listening place less importance on the verse, and often downgrade the importance of the song, or even singing, as a primary musical characteristic. However, most dance music of the twentieth century has still been based on the musical structure of the song, and, particularly before 1950, dance music was based on rearrangements of well-known songs. The obvious exception here is to be found in contemporary dance music. Here the dominant form is usually some distance removed from traditional song structure, or rejects it completely. The main reason for this significant shift away from the song form can be found in the way dance music in the late twentieth and early twenty-first century is produced and consumed. Contemporary dance records are usually made by producers with backgrounds as club DJs rather than being trained musically, and the formal structure of the music is built around computer programs, and synthesised or sampled sounds rather than older traditions of composition. These important shifts in production are mirrored by new social practices in dancing, where the whole physical experience is valued more than the individual piece of music, and the music is remade at the mixing desk of the club. These new conditions have lead to some completely new formal structures for music.

The best way to develop analytical skills is to practise them. Select six or so different styles of recorded songs and analyse their basic song forms. A short-cut to this is often to look at the lyrics printed on the CD insert. Identify how the verse and the chorus alternate. Identify who sings which parts, if any other voices are involved and how they relate to the lead voice. Is there a musical bridge? How does it fit into the structure of the song? Try listening to the song to see where the dominant melodic line is. Does it take the form of a hook? How important is the structure to your enjoyment of the song? Finally, try comparing the songs you've analysed. How much commonality is there? How much divergence? Can any of these features be explained by the suggestions given above?

Patterns of Melodic Repetition and Change

Both the formal and melodic structure of songs are standardised ways of securing certain sorts of response in the audience. They are based upon repeating patterns, then changing the pattern, then returning to the original pattern. So, a standard song would go through an initial pattern of verse, chorus, verse, chorus, verse, chorus. After this repetition we are aware of the pattern, so the songwriter shifts into a different melodic structure and the backing instruments play an instrumental section. After this variety we return to the repetition of the most important melodic element, the chorus, which is repeated at least twice to the end of the song.

Repetition and variation are also produced in the song's tune through what is called the AABA structure. The melodic line (the tune) is based upon the repetition of a single melodic (A) phrase, which is then repeated; variety is injected by a new melodic (B) phrase, before finally returning to the initial phrase. In Tin Pan Alley songwriting each melodic phrase is a stanza of the chorus or verse lasting eight measures, with each measure being four beats of the music. This is usually called the classic 32-bar structure (four × eight bars). These sections often use clever harmonic relationships to increase both the sense of repetition and variation that are part of the central pleasures of the popular song form. As Hamm has again shown, these formal properties became dominant within popular music, but in this case in the 1920s and 1930s, the heyday of Tin Pan Alley songwriting professionalism (Hamm 1983, 359–75) (see Chapter 2).

Again, though this describes the dominant form there are many exceptions – the most notable and influential is found in African-American music. Here the melodic line is often based upon a much reduced number of 12 measures, most characteristically in the so called '12-bar blues'. Like the Tin Pan Alley form there are many variations, but the basic 12 measures are usually spread across three stanzas with four measures to each stanza, the first two lines sharing the same melodic line and the third a different one: AAB (Southern 1983, 330–6). For simplicity, then, we could represent two songs, one in each form for comparison – both use four-beat measures, represented in Figure 8.2 by the vertical strokes separating the sets of four dots.

```
Tin Pan Alley song                      Blues song
I....I...I...I...I....I...I...I...I (A)   I....I...I...I....I...I....I....I (A)
I....I...I...I...I....I...I...I...I (A)   I....I...I...I....I...I....I....I (A)
I...I....I...I...I...I....I...I...I (B)   I....I...I....I....I...I....I (B)
I....I....I...I...I....I...I...I....I (A)
```

FIGURE 8.2 Structures of repetition and variation

Overall, then, the standard Tin Pan Alley form will have longer-length stanzas and four of them, while the blues has three stanzas of shorter length. Both, though, feature a form of repetition and variation, although the blues form will feel punchier and more repetitious. With a bit of practice you should be able to spot this basic form in pieces of music, and then use it as a basis to identify conforming songs, and the variations and exceptions.

Even music that emphasises improvisation has been based upon the song structure. Robert Townsend has shown how jazz improvisation developed among musicians in the big dance bands of the 1930s in their after-hours jam sessions. Here the shared repertoire of popular songs would be used as a basis for competitive 'cutting contests' where each musician would try to outdo the other in musical virtuosity or emotional expression. However, the shared understanding of the melodic lines of 'standard' popular songs or blues provided the structure for their playing, and the chorus length delimited their solo improvisations (Townsend 2000, 46–61).

There are thousands of variations on the very fundamental pattern introduced here. It is important, though, to understand how these variations fit with the dominant form. Just as the AABA and the verse, chorus, verse, chorus, bridge, chorus, chorus structure gives us pleasures of repetition and change, a song of slight variation on this basic form marks itself out and gives us another level of repetition–change pleasure, now at a level beyond the single song. At this general level, though, the dominant form needs to survive, because just as the B bit of a tune relates to the repetition of the A lines, or the instrumental section is the release from the repetition of verses and choruses, the non-standard song relates to the thousands of standard songs we have responded to in the past. We can understand other exceptions to the standard form as the result of very different conditions of production and consumption. White European and American musicians adopted the blues form in the 1960s as a self-conscious attempt to produce music that would be understood as more 'authentic' than the widely known forms of Tin Pan Alley professional music-writing (Hatch and Millward 1987). Others within rock music drew on European forms to develop what was called progressive rock using structures derived from symphonic or modernist art music composition (Middleton 1990, 27–32; Whiteley 1992, 103–18; Moore 1993, 56–103). Free jazz sought to reject these structural forms completely as a political and aesthetic statement (Litweiler 1990; Kofsky 1998). Finally, much contemporary dance music has departed from the 32- or 12-bar structure, but interestingly these styles are probably among the best examples of structures of repetition and change in the history of popular music.

Identifying patterns of melodic repetition and change is key way to understand how popular music forms are structured, and to spot both the dominant forms and their variations and exceptions. It is useful to start with pieces that others have identified as having these structures. Most public libraries now contain record libraries with knowledgeable staff who can suggest particular records with which to practise your analysis. Take a standard Tin Pan Alley song and a classic blues number and try to identify the structure as you listen. This is sometimes much easier when you are listening to records you are not familiar with. Once you have got the idea, repeat the process with songs you are more familiar with. Finally, it is worth seeing if you can recognise the structures in mainstream jazz and their complete absence in avant-garde jazz or pop.

Lyrics

The most common approach to examining the form of popular music has been focused on the words of songs. Early studies by John Peatman (1944) and by H. Mooney (1954; 1968) assume that the lyrics are the most significant part of a song, and that the psychological states of listeners, or even whole societies, can be divined by categorising the lyrics of the songs they listened to. Peatman's content analysis of songs broadcast on the radio in the early 1940s proposed that the vast majority of songs were simply variations on the topics of love and sex (1944, 370–7). Mooney's post-war analysis proposed that the themes in lyrics reflect the psychological state of the American people as they respond to changing economic and social conditions. This sort of analysis has been criticised by Simon Frith (1988). He argues that such analyses reduce the cultural significance of songs to the content of their words. This is fair criticism, but even these classic studies attempted to explore other aspects of the significance of songs. Later in his article Peatman interprets the choices of wartime soldiers as escapism among individuals who had a 'grim determination to see a nasty business through' (1944, 388), and argues that US popular song and jazz would signify 'Americanness' to opposing forces in Nazi-occupied Europe (1944, 389).

Other analysts have developed approaches similar to Mooney's, but for songs found in more specific periods of time, or forms of music less prominent in the mass media. Such work would include the significance of lyrics in the following musical forms: blues (Oliver 1963; Keil 1970; Haralambos 1974), doo-wop and black pop (Ward 1998; Gribin and Schiff 2000), girl groups (Bradby 1992), soul (Haralambos 1974; Hoare 1975; Larkin 1998; Ward 1998; Werner 1999), country music (Di Maggio *et al.* 1972), progressive rock (Whiteley 1992), punk (Laing 1985), reggae (Bradley 2000). The vast majority of these studies seek to assert the importance of the type of popular music being studied to a particular cultural group. For these studies, meaning is the collective creation of a cultural group of black Americans or Jamaicans, young women, southern white Americans or unemployed British youth, articulated in song by musicians who are also members of that cultural community. This celebration of music and identity for groups marginalised by society, as indexed by the lyrics of songs, is set in implicit contrast to the songs of Tin Pan Alley. Such analyses make an implicit distinction between a dominant form of song lyrics – produced by professional songwriters and conforming to Peatman's categories of love and sex – and alternative songs – produced in specific subcultures by members of those cultures. In this they share an antipathy to mainstream pop lyricism with other writers who have explicitly attacked them as banal for a variety of reasons (see for instance Hoggart 1958; Harker 1980).

There is obviously something significant at play when scholars can produce a quantitative analysis of lyrics and identify distinct patterns that relate to different time periods or different cultures. For this reason analysis of lyrics can be a productive way of comparing one widespread aspect of the form of songs.

Peatman suggested that the topics of the lyrics he analysed fitted into three main categories: happy in love, frustrated in love and novelty songs based around the theme of sexual romance. Reproduce Peatman's study from the 1940s by producing a content analysis of the songs played on a contemporary radio top 40 countdown show. You will find useful advice on doing content analysis in most guides to media research (like Deacon 1999, 114–31). You could then compare your categories and distribution with Peatman's late 1940s' findings. Many of the writers summarised in this section have proposed or implied that songs that are produced outside the pop mainstream will focus on other lyrical topics. Test out this idea by repeating the content analysis with songs played on an alternative music radio programme. Again compare your categories and distribution with your top 40 study and Peatman's.

It is another thing entirely, though, to move from identifying common patterns in lyrics to the proposition that they indicate a specific collective psychological response. This is to confuse the description of certain properties of the form with meaning. It is entirely proper to suggest that the lyrics of songs have some bearing on meaning, but as we will see in the next chapter we need a theory of how lyrics relate to meaning in popular music. Peatman's assumption that because songs sustain their popularity across a range of versions it must be the lyrics that are important, gets things the wrong way round. The existence of a multitude of ways to perform a song suggests that it is performance, and not lyrics, that is central to meaning in records.

Simon Frith has argued that 'Songs are more like plays than poems; songs work as speech and speech acts, bearing meaning not just semantically, but also as structure of sound that are direct signs of emotion and markers of character' (Frith 1988c, 120).

From this proposal he suggests three ways in which we should study songs that will take us beyond the existing work summarised here. First, he recommends investigating the way that different performing conventions used on a recording of a song construct a sense of the artist, and a sense of ourselves as the listener and part of a wider audience. Second, he argues for the development of a systematic genre analysis that would allow us to locate how different types of song construct different sorts of popular music community and what he calls their 'narratives of desire' (1988, 121). Finally he offers the suggestion that songs work on ordinary language, and even cliché, constructing a cultural form through which people can articulate their feelings. Here Frith is stressing that analyses of forms of composition are not sufficient in understanding popular music. He argues that performance, collective responses and aspirations, and everyday language and communication are all significant. Disappointingly, Frith never developed these suggestions, but they do provide us with a very useful set of approaches that are picked up in the next chapter.

Evaluation of the dominant form

The fact that popular music has developed a dominant or standard form over the twentieth century has been the basis for one of the most searing critiques of the whole popular music culture. Theodor Adorno's article 'On Popular Music' (1941/1990) uses a similar formal analysis to the one outlined above to make the claim that the standardised form of popular music is politically and culturally dangerous. He sees popular music as the product of a social system that aims to encourage conformity in people's thinking so that they will continue to accept the inequalities of society. His basic argument is that the whole of popular music culture is standardised. From this perspective all levels of music culture – production, music and consumption – are organised to produce predetermined forms.

This is a fundamental, and sometimes misunderstood, part of his critique. He is not simply arguing that all popular music is of the dominant form we have analysed, but that even the exceptions are part of the standardised musical culture. Part of the way that music-making operates, he proposes, is to produce music that hides its dominant form by highlighting other qualities. For this reason he calls these differences pseudo-individual qualities: they pretend to offer individuality, but this is illusory. Moreover, he argues, even when a piece of music actually is different, this difference is mentally substituted in the process of listening with the dominant form. He is therefore not simply saying that the music is standardised because it is produced by a production-line system of songwriting – he notes that songwriting is in fact a professionalised craft, rather than a unskilled production-line process – rather, he sees music composition as just part of a wider music culture that seeks to ensure conformity. He argues that 'The whole structure of popular music is standardised, even where the attempt is made to circumvent standardisation. Standardisation extends from the most general features to the most specific ones' (Adorno 1941, 302).

For Adorno, any song is written within this standardised culture where looking for novel ways to write the song are also standardised and even the most complex of musical elements is translated mentally into the standardised form. The way of understanding the form of the song is predetermined as a conformist response, either of obedience or romantic dreaming that ignores reality. He counter-poses this musical culture with the culture of 'serious' music in which production, the form and consumption all require demanding intellectual processes that encourage independent thought rather than conformity.

Adorno is obviously writing from outside popular music culture and is antagonistic to all aspects of the culture. It is easy, then, for those of us who participate within the culture to reject what he has to say as simply the ideas of someone who is expressing his own approval of classical ('serious') music forms and his hostility to other forms of music. Nevertheless, it is noticeable how many people reject Adorno's analysis of music they like, but use a very similar argument about music they do not like. It is common to hear people say that other forms of music are unimaginative, that they are simply the formulaic products of a manipulative media and music industry, and that those who listen to them are dupes or naïve. It is very hard for us to accept that Adorno might be correct and that the same criticisms could be applied to all popular music, even that we like. But that would be to accept that the music we invest with significance in our lives could simply be a standardised form full of elements to make us think it is different, and that the artists we favour are just part of a music culture that seeks to exploit us and make us conformist consumers and workers. It also suggests that our pleasures in listening, dancing and collecting are just hedonistic and predetermined reactions to stop us facing up to the realities of the world we live in. As Gordon Gendron (1986, 19) has pointed out, if this sort of analysis succeeds when applied to some popular music, it actually succeeds when applied to all popular music.

It is more fruitful to try and understand the usefulness of this critique, and its limitations, rather than simply reject or accept Adorno's position. In part, his approach is a product of his purposely extreme, contradictory and negative way of thinking and arguing (see Paddison 1996). It is rooted in a sophisticated understanding of the musical practices of European art music, which are then inappropriately applied to popular music. The best approach with Adorno's writing is not to see it as a description of a social phenomenon, but as an attempt to challenge us to think in new ways about that phenomenon. In this light, Adorno's emphasis on tackling production, forms and consumption in our study is central. He points us to examine cultural processes that operate through all these aspects of popular music culture, to analyse beyond the level of individual pieces of music, and to try and grasp the social significance of popular music culture. His was, then, one of the first attempts to understand meaning in popular music.

One of the greatest challenges is to try and apply Adorno's critique to your own favourite music. Try and construct the best argument you can that the production, form and consumption of this music is, as Adorno argues, standardised. Some of the things you know about a particular artist or group will no doubt support his claims, even if you are constantly tempted to see other aspects that prove him wrong. You might also discover, however, that there are whole areas about the making of the music you do not know about. It is worth asking yourself what is emphasised in your fan knowledge, and what neglected. What would be the implication of that other knowledge? In doing this analysis you will see the strengths of his case more clearly, and be able to see its limitations more clearly too.

SUMMARY

In this chapter we have seen how the dominant form of popular music – the song with verses and choruses, patterns of melodic repetition and change, and lyrics with themes of love – can be understood, analysed and critiqued. There was also a discussion of why and when alternatives to the dominant form have developed. Even though studying the form that popular music takes can be instructive, it is also restrictive. It is easy in describing form to feel that we have analysed meaning, but this is not the case. The next chapter explores questions of meaning and suggests ways that they could be incorporated into analysis.

Further reading

Adorno, Theodor W. 1941/1990: 'On Popular Music', in S. Frith and A. Goodwin, *On Record: Rock, Pop and the Written Word.* Routledge.

Frith, Simon 1988: 'Why Do Songs Have Words', in S. Frith, *Music for Pleasure: Essays in the Sociology of Pop.* Polity Press.

Gendron, Bernard 1986: 'Theordor Adorno Meets the Cadillacs', in T. Modleski, *Studies in Entertainment.* Indiana University Press.

Middleton, Richard 1990: *Studying Popular Music.* Open University Press.

Moore, Allan F. 1993: *Rock: The Primary Text: Developing a Musicology of Rock.* Open University Press.

CHAPTER NINE

Meaning

Richard Middleton has noted that examples of textual analysis of popular music are far less common than studies of other aspects of music culture (like its history or its fans) and are characterised by 'methodological hesitations which suggest deep-lying doubts about the viability of the enterprise itself' (Middleton 2000, 1). In approaching the study of music as a text – as a carrier of meaning – we are most likely to find a range of interesting and suggestive approaches, rather than a fully formed single method we can apply with certainty. This chapter aims to move from questions about form to questions about the social significance of music in popular music culture. After some discussion about what we actually mean by meaning, the chapter explores three areas that are significant to the generation of meaning. Performance, the idea of the metatext, and genre are each investigated, developed into analytical techniques and then applied in a case study. The final section draws these ideas together into an analysis of contemporary dance music genres.

What do we mean by meaning?

The idea of meaning seems less obvious when we are talking about popular music than when examining other media cultures. It seems a little artificial to look to popular music for 'messages', though it is clear that some popular music artists believe they have something to say about the world, and certainly music listeners and academics have expended a lot of time trying to isolate what a particular song is saying. Meaning in music culture, though, is a bigger issue than this. When we talk about musical meanings our discussions encompass how the music makes us feel, how we categorise it, how we associate places or moments with particular songs or styles, how we value it, how we relate collections of tracks to an artist or a group of musicians, and how we understand certain music as being significant in our lives and our relationships with other people.

This list of aspects of popular music's meaning is of course primarily rooted in our activities of consumption, and that is perhaps why so much of the literature on popular music culture has placed the emphasis on the way music fits into our lifestyle. Part 4 examines these approaches in greater detail, and we will return to the question of meaning there. These 'culturalist' approaches have, though, been criticised when they suggest that the meaning of popular music is produced solely by the cultural activities of the listeners. It is argued that such approaches do not pay sufficient regard to the 'sound of the music' (see Moore 1993). Intuitively it does not seem correct that the meaning of the music does not have anything to do with its 'materiality': with its rhythm, its melody, its harmonic structure, and with the way it is played, sung and recorded.

These musicological approaches, with their focus on the 'sound' of music, have not been without their own limitations. There are two connected issues here. First, musicologists have tended to isolate the musical text from its cultural context and, second, because of their technical training they hear and understand the music in very specific ways. These are criticisms shared by scholars who have had musicological training themselves, but even an attempt to develop suitable analytical tools for studying popular music, and to take greater care to include the cultural context in the analysis, has not led to fully successful approaches. This can be demonstrated by examining one of the most interesting attempts to theorise musical meaning and produce a systematic set of analytical tools. Philip Tagg has developed a rigorous and detailed semiology of music across a series of articles. Although I would want to recognise how careful Tagg's analysis is, and how he qualifies each of his culminative analytical stages, his analysis still produces results that seem to be a product of the analysis, not an explanation of meaning. For instance, in one part of his analysis he suggests that, for a particular song,

> whereas the words say 'if I had to go back and fight for freedom in Latin
> America, I would', the music expresses the affective attitude 'I may be longing
> for something here at home but I'm really quite content with things as they are'.
>
> (Tagg 1991, 96)

The song under analysis is Abba's 1970s hit 'Fernando'; and while I am entirely convinced by the analysis, and can see that these are prominent potential meanings in the materiality of the text, they are not the meanings in my mind when I hear the song, nor, I would surmise, are they the meanings made by most listeners to Abba. Like all forms of analysis in media and cultural studies we do not need the analytical tools to tell us what the text means – we already know that from our own interpretations – but we do need them to tell us how it means what it means.

Furthermore, we should not confuse the description of form with the analysis of meaning. In Chapter 8 we were able to identify the dominant form of popular music and then show how this was used by Adorno to make claims about the meaning of popular music. Identifying the standardisation of the music may have served Adorno's argument well because he was able to link it to other aspects of standardisation he identified or theorised, but that does not mean he fully understood the music's significance in the wider culture. A number of authors have suggested that this eliding of form with meaning derives from using tools established to reinforce the cultural assumption that art music is better than popular music. Such tools focus on music as sound represented through the notated musical score (Shepherd 1980; McClary and Walser 1990; Middleton 1990, 101–26; Moore 1993).

To demonstrate the fundamental differences between the form of art music and popular music, Andrew Chester has argued that while the former customarily works 'outwards from basic musical atoms', in a manner he calls extensional development, the latter primarily works intentionally through the 'modulation of the basic notes and by inflection of the basic beat'. He further argues that the language of popular music is derived from spoken language and gesture (1990, 315). Here he is emphasising that popular music, as a form, is more about the sophistication of performance than it is about the complexity of musical construction. Interestingly, these qualities of intentional performance are the same ones Adorno saw as the basis of popular music's pseudo-individualisation. Because of his musicological training Adorno seems to have recognised these devices, but misunderstood their role. If we followed Adorno we would be forced to conclude that the differences in performance of 'My Way' by Frank Sinatra, the Sex Pistols or a karaoke singer, or the differences between Oasis' rendition of 'Wonderwall' and the Mike Flower's Pops version, were unimportant surface details.

Chester has suggested that popular music has, at different times, drawn in different degrees on the repertoires of art music's extensional techniques and popular music's intentional ones (1990, 316). This suggests that a rounded analytical approach would identify the formal structure of a piece of music, but also attend to the performance, and evaluate the relative importance of the extensional formal processes produced in composition, as well as the intentional processes produced in performance. This approach moves us away from the form of popular music and towards an examination of how the music fits into the wider culture, particularly in terms of its associated production and consumption practices.

Drawing on all that has been said so far, we can conclude that to investigate meaning in popular music we have to:

- start with interpretations (and so avoid confusing form with meaning)

- recognise that different readings will be made

- work with an awareness of the context in which the music was produced and consumed

- recognise that the text is wider than simply sounds

- grapple with this wider sense of text using analytical tools suitable for the type of music being studied, and especially attend to performance.

The next section of this chapter is based on a set of analytical techniques that are aimed at doing just this. We will look at the idea of performance in popular music, at the idea of the larger text of popular music – what has been termed the metatext – and finally at those systems of coding usually understood to be genres of music.

Analysing popular musical meanings

Performance

A prominent part of our textual analysis, then, will be to examine how a particular piece of music is performed – particularly the performance created for, and captured on, records. We need to identify the distinctive sound and style of one recording against another. There is a wide range of elements we could study here, but three are particularly useful: the instrumentation, the vocals and the recording.

INSTRUMENTATION

This consists of the way the group of musicians is organised, the instruments they play and the roles they take. This can be achieved by examining four levels of musical

FIGURE 9.1 Levels of instrumentation and vocals are important in understanding the sound of particular forms of performance
Photo: Stefan Klenke

organisation (Moore 1993, 31–55):

1. rhythmic – the drum kit and percussion

2. low-register melody – usually the bass guitar

3. higher frequencies – a variety of instruments, forming 'the tune'

4. harmonic filler – instruments adopting sonic places between levels 2 and 3.

The descriptions of form produced through the analysis must then be related to the interpretations made by listeners.

VOCAL STYLE

Moore offers four qualities to be analysed:

1. register and range – the height and spread of the voice's pitch

2. resonance – the thin voice resonating in the nose against the full resonance in the chest

3. deviations from tempered pitches – including slides and slurs of notes

4. attitude to rhythm – including anticipation and delay, stress and accenting within beats.

Using these defining qualities allows us to express quite valuable distinctions between different styles of singing (and therefore singers), but these descriptions need to be connected to what Roland Barthes has called 'the grain of the voice' (Barthes and Heath 1977, 179–90). He develops this idea in a short but challenging article that has produced many interpretations. However, its usefulness probably lies in the simple point that we need to recognise that musical meanings are not just acts of producer-to-consumer communication, but are about an enveloping pleasure in the richness or 'grain' of the sound itself. It is a concept obviously applicable to the human voice, but in popular music with its emphasis on the subtle and individual qualities of performance, it can also be applied to the distinctive styles of instrumental players. In addition, the accent the singer adopts when singing is important (see Trudgill 1983). The accents of most British singers, for instance, are broadly North American, and Trudgill identifies a similar process of accent adoption in the USA, where northern- and eastern-born singers adopt some stylistic qualities of southern, and particularly black, Americans when they sing. The meanings of these singing accents need to be a prominent part of the analysis of audience interpretations of performance.

RECORDING TECHNIQUES

These are the qualities of recording that give particular records their distinctive style. Even though most of the analysis of popular music is based on listening to records, there has been almost no analysis of the processes used to produce the musical recording. A basic analysis of this area would involve examining four main factors:

1. mic'ing/sampling – the way that voices and instruments are converted into an electrical signal; includes the acoustics of the recording space, the distance of the voice/instrument from the microphone, and the source of the sound

2. recording – the way that the electrical signals are stored; originally done directly to disc, but after 1950 on tape; tape expanded the number of tracks that could be recorded, increasing from one to two to four, and eventually to 64, while digital recording in the last 20 years has allowed unlimited ways to layer sound

3. mixing – the relative volume of different sound signals in the recording; first achieved by the relative distance of the singer and instrumentalists from one microphone and later through a mixer; multitrack and digital recording allowed the sound signals to be manipulated after the moment of recording, and for additional recording

4. degree of overt production – the degree to which techniques and quality of mic'ing, multitracking and mixing dominate the textual qualities; highly stylised or controlled recording is sometimes interpreted as being 'over-produced'; on the other hand, late 1960s and 1970s rock, studio soul and Jamaican dub reggae, and 1990s computer-produced dance music forms are often celebrated as distinctive sounds.

These analytical techniques can be applied to single recording, or more generally to the work of an artist or even a genre of music. The James Brown record examined in the accompanying case study has been the subject of a number of analyses before (Wilson 1974; Brackett 1991; Slutsky and Silverman 1997; Brackett 2000). These analyses are incorporated into the case study, but they are combined with the conclusions drawn from the discussion about meaning outlined above. In particular, three of the principles outlined earlier are applied:

1. start with interpretations

2. recognise different readings will be made

3. recognise the production and consumption context.

In addition Simon Frith's three recommendations, introduced in Chapter 8, are followed:

1. investigate the conventions that construct a sense of the artist, and the listener

2. locate how different types of song construct different sorts of popular music community

3. examine the way songs work on ordinary language.

  C A S E   S T U D Y James Brown's 'Super Bad' (1971)

For most listeners, even though James Brown records are now widely heard in adverts and samples, 'Super Bad' is strikingly distinctive. It is also music obviously made for dancing (a point missing from most analyses of his records). In this context the music is packed with a fervent energy, coiled like a spring, building but never quite releasing a dense musical tension. The sound is strongly rhythmic, driving forward supporting the punctuation of vocals, guitars and horns, which stab, plead, cry and eventually reach moments of ecstatic delight. Brown is the dominant personality, sole vocalist and the dominant sound. His words encourage and direct us, and the musicians in the band. This record is part of a world of communal dance, creating a party atmosphere with an undertow of sex and sweat.

In the right cultural context these associations are triggered by specific formal elements of the music. The conventional verses/chorus structure has been collapsed into one dense musical theme, which is repeated three times with some minor variation, then interrupted by a bridge section, repeated, interrupted again, and finally repeated several times with variation until the fade-out. There is no strong melody, and the words are a series of hooks sung and played over a strong, driving rhythmic pattern. In European terms, the record is musically unstable: it follows a conventional blues form, but the emphasis is on the driving rhythm section and subtle emphases in the beat; the music builds harmonically over relatively long stretches of time, and the releases of tension are limited to short punctuations at the end of the bridge (Brackett 2000a, 134–6).

Brown's voice has a wide range and a full resonance, and he sings in his southern African-American speaking accent, with strong rhythmic effect. The band plays in a key that pushes Brown to sing at the very top of his register. Combined with the inflections drawn from blues and gospel styles, this creates a sense of yearning and emotion, which is often associated with his style. The words are delivered as exhortations, driving on in successive waves, punctuated by pitched grunts and groans (Brackett 2000a). He sometimes reinforces, sometimes anticipates, and sometimes responds to the propulsive drive of the band. All the instruments, including the voice, are mic'ed close, giving them a full resonance and highlighting Brown's diction. His voice is mixed to a volume that makes it prominent against the other instruments, but instead of being back in the distance, they are independently discernible and forceful. The communal, party atmosphere is reinforced by the crowd noises, which were overdubbed for the single release.

The drums are central to the rhythmic drive, with the kick drum hitting the first beat of the bar, and the other drums dancing around the beat to produce the jerky punctuations. The bass, guitar and horns constantly alter their role. In the verse/chorus sections the horns punctuate and the guitar moves between rhythm and the kind of fill role usually taken by the horns, while the bass emphasises the drum beats. In the bridges the singing continues and the horns return to a more traditional role of lead and harmonic filler, the guitar follows the drums in quadruple time, while the bass changes the feel of the section completely by punching into the spaces between the drum beats. All the instruments end the bridge section with a double-time staccato riff, which momentarily releases the harmonic tension, but simultaneously drives the bridge into a new verse. This verse leads off with a sax solo, which catches the emotional style of Brown's singing: full, forceful, and with untempered pitches and a slurring of notes. It is hard not to respond to the driving beat and the exuberance of the sound, and the musical tension creates a sense of expectation that is never fulfilled, never quite released.

But there is another, more culturally specific, level to the record's meaning that may only be available to some listeners. Brackett argues that what is important about these qualities of musical form is how they fit into African-American culture. He suggests that this record represents a 1970s revitalisation of black American forms after the assimilations of earlier R&B into the pop mainstream. The lyrics draw upon characteristic African-American expressions, where sound and performance are more important than the meanings of the individual words, removing the distinction between audience and performer (Abrahams 1976; Gates 1988). It is the intertextuality of the words and musical phrases – 'right on', 'brothers and sisters', 'I got soul', 'soul power' – to other James Brown songs, to African-American vernacular speech, and the rise of black power politics in America at that time, that is important (Brackett 2000, 128–34).

FIGURE 9.2 James Brown in the early 1970s when 'Super Bad' was recorded. Copyright © Gai Terrell/Redferns. Used with permmission

The instrumentation and lack of harmonic development also echo these concerns with a strongly affirmative black culture. The emphasis on rhythm and the relative demoting of harmonic development within the performance can be understood as an example of the 'double voice' of the African-American (Gates 1988). That is, using the 'language' of European society, but expressing it in an African-American way. The style of the sax solo draws heavily on the way of playing established by black power jazz avant-garde players like John Coltrane (see Litweiler 1990; Kofsky 1998). The recording style and overdubbed crowd sounds are most likely an attempt to present or suggest a live recording, perhaps to recreate the commercial success of LPs of Brown's live shows, but they also signal the importance of performance over composition. Most of Brown's recordings in this period were improvised in the studio, and the 'lyrics' consist of instructions to the band. This adds to the sense of communality reinforced by the use of African-American street talk.

This record will mean different things to listeners in different cultural contexts. I know there is a group of listeners that feel it is nothing more than an overly repetitious, musically impoverished cliché. They will probably say it is boring. To dancers it is a physically charged dance classic. To African-Americans (of a certain age) it is an articulation of an empowering cultural movement. Each of these meanings is culturally specific, but each relates to qualities within the materiality of the recorded sound.

Using the James Brown case study as a guide, undertake an analysis of a record of your choice. Remember to start with the meanings of the record as you perceive them, then try to identify the formal qualities of the record which are significant in that meaning. Keep Frith's proposals, outlined above, in mind. It is then very productive to share your analysis with others. Did they share your responses? Attempt to integrate these different readings into your analysis.

Metatext

The case study of performance in James Brown's record indicates the importance of factors outside the record itself. There has always been more to popular music than records. As we have seen, they did not become the primary text of popular music until the 1950s, and popular music has always been a prominent part of other media as well. Today the textual meanings of popular music are likely to be spread more widely across these media, and so across a wider range of forms of consumption. A full analysis, therefore, requires a wider sense of text. Timothy D. Taylor has coined the term metatext to refer to these wider senses of text (Taylor 1997). His emphasis here is on wider discourses that order our understanding of particular types of music. The music industry produces popular music across a set of commodities – radio airplay, promotional videos and DVDs, live shows, television and radio appearances, magazine interviews and photographs, advertisements and point-of-sale campaigns, and websites – which in turn become the texts consumed by the music's audience.

The relationship between these promotional media forms and popular music is well represented in academic literature. In particular, the role of the music press and pop videos has been well documented.

THE MUSIC PRESS

There are some good, succinct, historical surveys of the role of the media in popular music. Simon Frith's outline of the specialist music press up until the turn of the 1980s (Frith 1983, 165–77) is complemented by Roy Shuker's broader account, which updates Frith's history through the following decade (Shuker 1994, 72–98). It is fairly straightforward to produce an update based upon their analyses of the current state of the music press, and the music journalism websites that have been established since. Frith sees music journalists as performing the role of 'professional fans', and sees their readers as opinion leaders for the wider popular music culture. He argues that the music press constructs the nature of the relationship between its readership and specific popular music cultures. In particular he examines the role of the underground music press in the USA, and the slightly later split in the UK between the rock press like the *NME* and *Melody Maker* and the pop magazines led by *Smash Hits*. What he neglects are the specialist fanzines and small-circulation papers of specialist music journalism. These are Shuker's starting point. He is particularly interested in the way that music journalism is linked to more systematic academic analyses, and the way that reviews of records are constructed within existing knowledge of music culture.

X 9.2 Produce a survey of current music journalism available today. There are now so many specialist publications in print and online that it is easiest to select one type of music and to look at the range of smaller-circulation publications and websites. This can be contrasted with the field of higher-circulation, mainstream publications. An analysis of the basic editorial positions, and some judgement on their influence among music fans, will prove a very useful mapping exercise.

POP VIDEOS

The academic study of pop videos has faced the same sorts of problems that we found in the study of the sound of the primary record text. As videos became a more prominent part of promotional culture in the 1980s the academic interest in studying them increased, leading one commentator to argue that 'pop video is now more heavily theorised than pop music, and has generated more scholarly nonsense than anything since punk' (Frith 1988a, 205). Certainly, it is important to be selective when reading in this area. Many accounts rely too much on assumptions from film studies, and like a mirror of the musicologists who hear musical qualities that they are trained to analyse, scholars with film backgrounds see only visual metaphor and narrative structure, usually ignoring the music.

Even so, E. Ann Kaplan's film studies-based analysis of videos on MTV (1987) raises some interesting issues. While Kaplan felt that some videos reproduced the classic narrative forms of films and television, with beginning–middle–end stories, others emphasised performance or a montage of imagery. She argues that the traditional narratives used in pop videos portray love and loss, and mostly involve the objectification of women, while those that mix narrative with non-narrative forms produce a critique of society associated with the USA's 1960s counter-culture. Non-narrative videos cover a range of meanings, from straightforward group performance through a nihilism that Kaplan associates with metal groups, to videos she terms 'postmodern' for the self-aware way they seem to play with the traditional images and styles of film and television. These categories of 'classic narrative', 'performance' and 'montage' remain quite useful, and it is still possible to use them with videos produced today for TV, DVD enhanced CDs and websites.

However, the obvious criticism of Kaplan's study, that videos have a relationship to the music, became the basis for further studies. This is most developed in Andrew Goodwin's work (1992). His analysis focuses on the way that the visuals interact with the music, providing illustration (showing the topic of the lyrics, or mood or structure of the music), amplification (developing visuals from, but beyond, the song) or disjuncture (where song and visuals offer different meanings). He argues that we understand both the musical and lyrical meanings together in a process of synaesthesia (literally: 'experience at the same time'). Keith Negus has again adapted ideas from film theory to discuss the way in which what we could call 'the imaginary world of the song and its performance' relates to 'the imaginary world of the video' (1996, 90–3). He uses two sets of contrasts: diegetic and non-diegetic sound/visuals relationships (in the former, sound and visuals share the same world, perhaps by showing the singer or the instruments performing the music; in the latter, the two worlds are separate, usually where the song functions as a film soundtrack); and parallelism and counterpoint (in the former, the images follow the music; in the latter, the images offer a range of comments or alternative meanings to those expected).

Apply Kaplan, Goodwin and Negus' concepts to the analysis of a pop video of your choice. It is straightforward to develop such an analysis further by reading each of these authors in greater depth, and seeing the worked examples they produced. Once the analysis has been completed it is useful to ask some critical questions about the analysis. Do these approaches help you to understand any of the formal elements of the video? Do they assist in understanding what the video means? Are these approaches likely to help us understand how the video would be interpreted?

While these accounts of the role of the press and pop videos provide some very useful information about popular music in these media, there is a frustrating lack of analysis of how these texts generate meaning for popular music consumers. There are two main questions about meaning that are missing from these accounts, and that should be at the centre of such an analysis. First, how do all these texts work together with the primary record-based text as a holistic metatext to build an identity for a record or artist across media? Second, how do metatexts construct a general sense of what popular music is, and how it should be valued?

In attempting to answer these questions it should be remembered that the meanings of the metatext are not innocent. The record industry puts considerable resources into attempting to use these media forms as vehicles for the promotion of the artists and records they have under contract. However, the meanings cannot just be reduced to promotion. In addition, other media workers may have other aims that range from an attempt to produce a critical commentary on contemporary popular music and its culture, through the desire to create a polished piece of entertainment, to an attempt to attract a fickle audience with the lowest cost production they can.

The limitations of the approaches to metatext outlined so far repeat the problems of musicological analyses of the primary text. That is, they tend to privilege the analytical tools, and produce distinctive formal descriptions or categorisations, rather than attempt to locate the text in its wider popular music culture context. A good way to illustrate how the text and context of popular music operate is in a case study based on an analysis of mainstream terrestrial television pop programmes. Popular music has always been a staple of popular television, drawing on the light entertainment function of radio (see Frith 1988e) or back even further to the variety format of music hall. As the number of channels has increased so has the number of pop shows, but a selection of three will illustrate the approach I am arguing for here.

CASE STUDY *Top of the Pops*, *Night Fever* and *Later with Jools Holland*

These are three very different programmes, made to attract very different audiences, and they draw on very different ways of understanding popular music. *Top of the Pops* is most strongly connected with the practices of mainstream pop established in the age of Tin Pan Alley and updated by the post-rock & roll teen pop. *Night Fever* shares many of the same showbusiness values, but connects them with the more democratic arena of karaoke, recast as a television game show. *Later ...* takes music seriously, stripping out the glamour of showbusiness to offer itself as presenting unadorned musicianship captured as authentic performance.

These positions are apparent in the programme titles. While the phrase 'top of the pops' with its stripped-down rhyme could easily be connected back to the terminology of the 1960s, it seems more to articulate the programme itself, a clear sign of its institutionalisation. With its screening on Saturday obviously completing the title of a well-known film, *Night Fever* offers the excitement and glamour of the disco or karaoke club, but tinged with a little postmodern irony. *Later ...* not only points to its television scheduling, but also signals its analogy to the after-hours club where musicians meet to play the music they want to, freed of the demands of commercial culture. It is hosted by the king of television musos, pianist Jools Holland. The contrast of presenters is central to the way that popular music is given meaning in these metatexts. *Night Fever* has Suggs, once leader of the ska-meets-music-hall 1980s band Madness, with his pivotal place as ironic judge negotiating between the hyped glamour of singing C-list celebrities, faded pop star guests, and game-show tinsel, and the claims of democratic participation and musical nostalgia that karaoke offers. *Top of the Pops* showcases a rotation of television presenters who cross the line between children's programmes and youthful light entertainment. While *Top of the Pops* presenters seem to fight against the overpowering background studio sounds when standing and facing us to introduce the next act, Suggs orders the potential chaos of the *Night Fever* studio from his adjudicator's table-cum-scoreboard, and Holland is listened to in respectful silence as he paces round the studio-as-club.

While excitement and energy are articulated by the flashing lights, fast tracking/cutting cameras, and the visible, but anonymous, audience that *Pops* and *Fever* both use, *Later ...* is more sparse, white and basic, with the audience – a mixture of the anonymous and the well known, but music fans all – grouped between sets for the different performers, declaring its diversity and authenticity. Most *Pops* performers mime on a stage with pretend backing musicians or dancers, as most of the tracks are heavily produced and almost impossible to reproduce in the TV studio. They present themselves to the studio audience and through the camera to us at home, mostly as entertainers, occasionally with irony. *Later ...* artists always play live, usually with acoustic or rearranged versions of their compositions, frequently with Holland on piano, and often in combination with other guests from the show. While there are some pop performers on *Fever*, they – like the two panels of contestants – sing to pre-recorded backing tracks, while we see the song words (perhaps encouraging us to sing along like the studio audience). The gender separation of the contestants and studio audience is in marked contrast to the heterogeneity of the songs that can come from any time in the last 50 years and from any genre of popular music, as long as each one is widely known and has good sing-along choruses. *Later ...* has even greater heterogeneity as the programme purposely juxtaposes musicians usually segregated, arguing that there is only good music (which you'll see here) and bad music (which you won't). *Top of the Pops*, of course, only plays records rising in the sales charts, or predicted to do so. Newness is everything: 'new in at number 32', 'a new single', 'a new band', 'a brand new chart', and 'a new number one'.

The metatext of these programmes is so much stronger than the meaning of individual records or styles of music. This is not to say that the music is not important, but within the metatext it is inflected, rebuilt and recontextualised into a larger set of meanings that reach back into discourses of popular music culture. These shows do not play the same music – indicating that the selection of artists and music is as important to the construction of the metatext as any other element – but it is possible to imagine that a single piece of music would have been played on all three shows, but in each case its meaning would be very different.

X .4 Select an artist who might appear in an edition of *Top of the Pops*, *Night Fever* and *Later ... .* Thinking through the way artists are presented in each programme, identify the differences of meaning that would be constructed for your selected artists in each programme. For instance, Coldplay and their music could be presented as a hit-making band with a new single on *Top of the Pops*, a serious band of authentic musicians on *Later ...*, and as a great song to sing to on *Night Fever*.

Genre

This brings us to the third important factor for understanding meaning. The idea of genre is widely used within popular music culture, in discussions of music fans, and in the strategy debates of the record industry and the media, but it is also used within academic media and cultural studies and other associated disciplines. In basic terms, genre refers to the types of popular music, so that a categorisation of music into distinct categories like soul, rock, house, rap, ragga, trance, nu metal, or whatever, is a process of genre identification. In the context of this chapter we need to explore ways in which the concept could be used to understand meaning in popular music. To do this we again need to discuss some of the issues of the theory of genre before going on to apply it as an analytical technique.

At a fundamental level we can understand genre as a code. This gives two senses to the cultural role of genre. First, it is a means by which music is categorised – or codified – and, second, this process of categorisation sets the rules by which popular music is produced, distributed and consumed. Although the idea that genres are categories of popular music suggests that they therefore describe something about the form or style of that music, some of the non-academic uses of the idea have been countered by Alan Moore, who has tried to be precise about the concept from the perspective of the musicologist. Genre, argues Moore, relates to the musical form – he cites 'the up-tempo dance number' or the 'ballad' as examples – and he distinguishes this from the style that these forms are performed in. From this position Moore argues that rock is therefore a style, not a genre (Moore 1993, 2–3). His position, shared with many other writers, is an attempt to clarify in academic terms how we can categorise popular music. Although this achieves far greater precision for musicologists, the sense of genre that is widely used outside the academy is then lost. Rock, after all, is widely understood as a genre, with several subgenres: progressive rock, heavy metal, indie, grunge, and so on. It does not really take us much further in our analysis by saying 'Well you might think it is a genre, but in strict musicological terms it is a style.' We need a theory of genre that helps us understand how the categorisation of genres is meaningful in the whole of popular music culture. Simon Frith has put this succinctly: 'popular music genres are constructed – and must be understood – within a commercial/cultural process; they are not the result of detached academic analyses or formal musicological histories' (Frith 1996b, 88).

As Robert Walser has pointed out, genres are ideas that are 'constantly debated and contested' (Walser 1993, 4). They are not clear-cut; it is not a technical process to allocate music to one category rather than another, and considerable effort is expended by music fans to define and police the lines between genres. Conversations about music are often built around arguments about whether a certain record or artist is house, or techno, or break beat, or some new, interesting hybrid.

This line of thinking has led Jason Toynbee to conclude that genre (is) 'neither a textual essence nor a comprehensive code' (Toynbee 2000, 103). Instead he draws on similar arguments from film studies to highlight Steve Neale's definition of genre as 'not as forms of textual configuration, but as systems of orientations, expectations and conventions that circulate between industry, text and subject' (Neale 1980, 19). This is a valuable definition because it emphasises genre as not reducible to textual qualities, but as the product of specific (in our case, popular music) cultures that he terms 'genre cultures' (Neale 1980). These cultures are formed around the activities of the media industry, the text itself, and the individuals who produce and those who consume the texts. For Toynbee these activities are cultural processes, and ones that are the basis for the struggles over definition that are at the centre of concepts of 'creativity' within popular music (Toynbee 2000, 103). Two other writers pick up this emphasis on creativity. Keith Negus has sought to examine in some detail how music industry corporations have shaped the conditions under which musicians produce music, and within which the artists seek to realise a certain notion of creative production (Negus 1999). Simon Frith has looked at the different ways that genre definitions change according to who is using them. He argues that, for musicians, they constitute an effective shorthand for discussing music, while, for listeners, they organise the listening process; and for the different parts of the music industry the different genres integrate questions about what the music sounds like with questions about who will buy the music (Frith 1996, 75–95). The strength of Frith's approach is that he draws upon a wide range of cultural factors to understand genre as a process. It effectively combines the approaches we have studied so far in this chapter – form, performance, the ordering processes of the media in the metatext, and the role of the listener – into one analysis focused on the establishment and development of what he calls 'genre worlds'. In studying this he has argued that,

A new 'genre world' is first constructed and then articulated through a complex interplay of musicians, listeners and mediating ideologies, and this process is much more confused than the marketing process that follows, as the wider industry begins to make sense of the new sounds and markets and to exploit both genre worlds and genre discourses in the orderly routines of mass marketing. The issue then becomes how to draw genre boundaries. Genres initially flourish on a sense of exclusivity; they [are] as much (if not more) concerned to keep people out as in. The industry aim is to retain the promise of exclusivity, the hint of generic secrets, while making them available to everybody. It sometimes seems, indeed, as if genre is only clearly defined (its secret revealed) at the moment when it ceases to exist.

(Frith 1996, 88)

This may be a little overstated for all popular music cultures, as mainstream popular music cultures are by definition less concerned with notions of exclusivity. However, it is an excellent guide for thinking about the formation of more 'alternative' genre-based music cultures, and provides a good model through which to interpret the documentation of such cultures in other studies.

Most of these authors' discussions of genre highlight the work of Franco Fabbri (1982). He has produced a systematic approach to studying these cultural processes of definition in the wider context of the genre culture, which include, but are not restricted to, the narrower ideas of musical forms or styles. He suggests genre is a set of music cultural practices that are ordered by five broad categories of rules, as follows:

1. formal and technical rules direct the *performance* (playing and recording) conventions

2. semiotic rules order the way that the music (as a set of formal and technical rules) should be *interpreted*

3. behavioural rules guide the performance *rituals* of the audience, mediators and performers in a range of settings

4. social and ideological rules govern what the music *stands for*

5. commercial and juridical rules sanction the *rewards and critical valuations* made in the genre culture.

Fabbri's approach allows us to move analytically from the form of a particular type of music, through the way it is interpreted, performed, represents and is valued. In this formulation, genres are far more than types of music, but ways of understanding what music is. If we combine Frith's and Fabbri's approaches we can understand a genre analysis as looking for the ordering processes that govern a particular popular music culture. This involves identifying the rules that are established in a new genre culture, and then the subsequent record company and media practices that streamline and order the music and its culture for their own gain. These rather abstract ideas can easily be applied in more concrete terms in a case study.

C A S E   S T U D Y   Contemporary Dance Music Genres

There could be no area of popular music more suited to a case study of genre than dance music. The music's mutation into different genre and subgenre forms has been a pronounced characteristic, marking it out from previous music cultures. In a short survey of club culture, Ben Osborne lists over 40 genres, and suggests tens more subgenres, commenting that,

> genres have spread through and divided the dance scene like a plague. No sooner has a new form ... emerged, been tagged and appeared in the music press than a new sub-version branches off, gets a new name and spawns its own sub-genre which begets another, and so it goes on.

(Osborne 1999, 110)

No doubt by the time you read this there will be many others to add.

Genre names are in themselves revealing. Some name a music after a scene. 'House' and 'garage' derive from the clubs – Chicago's Warehouse and New York's Paradise Garage – where the music was first popularised (Osborne 1999), while gabber – Dutch for mate – takes this one step further by naming a music for a small group of friends (Sicko 1999, 177). Other terms have been produced by more obvious record industry intervention. Techno was coined for the title of a compilation album, reflecting the music-makers' preoccupation with futurology (Osborne 1999, 290; Sicko 1999, 97–104). As these terms became more widely known, new terms came in to usage among club-goers to differentiate a new music and its distance from the mainstream. Adjectives like 'hard', 'speed', 'dark' and then 'intelligent' were deployed as prefixes to denote the qualities of a subgenre from its parent genre (James 1997; Sicko 1999, 181). Other terms, like drum & bass or break beat, signalled the formal qualities of the music – low frequencies with percussion, and looped samples respectively – and the origin of their production techniques: dub and hip-hop (James 1997). Other terms, notably nu med, were ironic responses to the proliferation of genre names in the press (Osborne 1999, 208).

The musical changes that accompany genre shifts, suggests Fabbri, are created through the transgression of predictable rules of existing codes (1982, 60–3). Toynbee identifies the even beat of most house-derived music as a transgression of the syncopation rules of African-American music (2000, 135–6). However, this non-accented rhythm was derived from 1970s disco, which had already been incorporated into the African-American tradition. More productively, he suggests dance music is distinctive in the way it has changed through intensification of formal rules, where pleasure in certain formal properties led to their increasing emphasis (2000, 136–9). His comparison of hardcore and jungle is exemplary in this respect. The idea that house has changed through intensification rather than transgression allows us, in part at least, to understand both how quickly dance genres are replaced and why the differences have been so difficult to distinguish for those without the requisite cultural competence, leading to the claim that 'It all sounds the same!'

However, genre changes are more than mutations of form. They are processes through which cultural differences in practices of interpretation, performance, representation and evaluation are manufactured. The proliferation of genres since the mid-1980s suggests that a hyper-categorisation has a central role in music culture. The process of intensification can be seen in the paradoxical way in which dance culture works with the paradoxical pulls of 'democratisation' and 'elitism'. While the notion that dance culture offers some sort of proto-democratic space away from the domination of the mainstream and corporate industry has been rehearsed in many places (see Hesmondhalgh 1997b), the way that particular dance genre cultures build elite cultural spaces has been somewhat neglected. So while the access to music-making, and particularly the role of DJ music-makers has been discussed (Langlois 1992), the way clubs and genres exclude others is neglected. Dance genre mutations are a classic case of Frith's (1996) idea that distinctions establish exclusivity where new 'genre worlds' are generated to define a more exclusive music-cultural space away from the 'commercialised' predecessors now populated by 'weekend clubbers'. This aspiration to 'in-crowd' exclusivity has been the preoccupation of a subgroup of revellers since the nightclub was established in the 1920s. Contemporary club culture, though, is not without its ironies. Handbag house, a term coined to deride mainstream club music, became a genre that celebrated its disco roots and completed the circle when clubbers then danced round their handbags (Osborne 1999, 126).

The behavioural rules of clubbing are tied into the rules of dance music-making in distinctive ways as well. The continued demand in clubs for sounds that intensify certain formal qualities, and keep ahead of mainstream consumption, is met by a massive productivity. Here music production is again recast, with the production of records only part of the music-making process, which also requires the manipulation of records within a DJ set to create a dance music text (Langlois 1992; Haslam 1998). The productivity was made possible by an orientation towards the track rather than the song, electronic, sampled and computer-generated sounds rather than traditional instruments, and DJ-based manipulations and computer-based composition techniques rather than band-based music-making (Reynolds 1998). These production practices are rooted in 1970s disco and funk, and European art electronic music, the latter filtered through Kraftwerk, the Euro-disco producers, and early 1980s British electro-pop. Different genres have remade these influences in distinct ways. House and techno tended towards the use of basic electronic instruments like the Roland 808 drum machine, and the 303 bass machine for its solid 4/4 dance beats, together with an incestuous sampling process for its 'colour'. This is developed to its ultimate end in hardcore, created through the distortion of multiple resampling and a basic rhythm track to become little more than 'bass and bleep' (Reynolds 1998). Jungle draws more heavily on hip-hop, where tracks are built out of sampled percussive breaks taken from 1970s dance records like 'Apache', 'Amen' and 'Think' (James 1997; Reynolds 1998). They are then processed through manipulation techniques like looping, time-stretching/compressing, pitch-shifting and reversing (Reynolds 1998).

The ideological function of dance genres has changed significantly over 20 years. It is no coincidence that these new dance musics of the 1980s were first formed in the imaginations of people who inhabited new and often seemingly unstable social positions, produced in forms that broke with the dominant ways of structuring music, and celebrated in places that were experiencing the disintegration of a modern industrial society. Techno pioneers were part of a new upwardly mobile, sub-urban group of Detroit African-Americans (Sicko 1999), while original Chicago house DJs-cum-producers were members of a gay subculture who continued the tradition of disco into a new decade (Reynolds 1998). Neither of these subcultures took its identity from the ghetto-assertive blackness of the hip-hop genre, but mixed European art electronic music with disco's drive, and a fascination with cyber-culture (Sicko 1999). It is significant that the new music genres were first played in British clubs, just as they had been in the Chicago, Detroit or New York clubs, as part of an eclectic mixture of music that purposely broke the rules of genre that had governed the dancefloor. Significantly, though, this musical miscegenation came not from the industrial cities of North America, but via the open-air clubs of Ibiza, and was imported into Britain along with the practice of taking the drug MDMA/Ecstasy (Reynolds 1998, 34–68).

In Britain, house was taken up by a different audience, and while most of the formal, semiotic and behavioural rules were derived from previous dance cultures, the genre worlds were experienced as strikingly different. Perhaps the paradigm shift here was in the ideological and juridical rules that governed the way that dancing and dance music are valued. As Sarah Thornton has shown, these genres represent a reversal of the dominant notion in popular music culture that preceded it. They all share a newly dominant idea that dancing, recorded music and the DJ were authentic cultural experiences and not simply commercial or artificial exploitations of the real music of listening, live performance and the musician (Thornton 1995, 26–86). The multiple mutations of genres seem to be both the product of the hyper-productive world in which the music was made and consumed, and the need to make differentials *within* dance music, now that it is no longer necessary to defend it from the accusation from 'real' music that it is inauthentic.

Dance music genres exist in a cultural tension between the ideologies and practices of the dominant music industry and the utopian (and sometimes dystopian) dreams of their genre cultures. In these genre worlds texts are created, promoted and consumed outside of the processes that the record industry has understood for nearly 90 years. There is no original performance, no group, no star, the music-maker assumes an alias (sometimes a different one for each record), and makes the record on a computer, generating/sampling sounds and manipulating them in layers. The creators are most likely to be DJs with a record collection and knowledge of what makes dancers respond. If they release a record at all it will be on an independent label that is likely to survive no more that 12 to 18 months, but more likely to distribute DATs or vinyl white labels, consumed on non-licensed radio or as shop-bought DJ mix tapes. Finally, they are experienced on the dancefloor as part of a continuous physical experience.

Carry out an analysis of an established and an emerging popular music genre. When producing a generic analysis it is best to draw upon a range of primary and secondary material. The former can come from your own involvement in a genre culture, or from observations produced by original research, while the latter can be met by reading one of the many analyses of genres now published. Using these sorts of sources select a genre and apply Frith's approach and Fabbri's five rules. The analysis could be, for example, a historical examination of the rise of beat in Britain (Bradley 1992); the establishment of reggae in Jamaica or Britain (Hebdige 1987 or Bradley 2000); country (Malone 1985); or punk (Laing 1985); or more contemporary analyses of the genres of heavy metal (Walser 1993); house (Thornton 1995; Rietveld 1998); or rap (Toop 2000).

SUMMARY

A case study of a genre of music reveals how complex the elements that contribute to the meaning of popular music are. This chapter has outlined the debates about meaning that have been widespread within the academic literature on the subject, and the limitations of applying concepts from musicology or sociology. By emphasising issues of performance, the wider metatext of popular music, and the way that the production and consumption of music in ordered by genres it is possible to produce developed analysis of the meanings of a particular piece of music. How these meanings 'stand for' or represent aspects of popular music culture and of our wider society is the subject of the next chapter.

Further reading

Brackett, David 2000: 'James Brown's "Superbad" and the Double-Voiced Utterance', in R. Middleton, *Reading Pop.* Oxford.

Frith, Simon 1983: *Sound Effects: Youth, Leisure and the Politics of Rock.* Constable.

Goodwin, Andrew 1992: *Dancing in the Distraction Factory: Music Television and Popular Culture.* University of Minnesota Press.

Kaplan, E. Ann 1987: *Rocking around the Clock: Music Television, Postmodernism, and Consumer Culture.* Methuen.

Middleton, Richard 1990: *Studying Popular Music.* Open University Press.

Negus, Keith 1996: *Popular Music in Theory: An Introduction.* Polity.

Reynolds, Simon 1998: *Energy Flash: A Journey through Rave Music and Dance Culture.* Picador.

Tagg, Philip 1991: *Fernando the Flute: Analysis of Musical Meaning in an Abba Mega-Hit.* Institute of Popular Music, University of Liverpool.

Toynbee, Jason 2000: *Making Popular Music: Musicians, Creativity and Institutions.* Arnold.

CHAPTER TEN

Representations

In this chapter we move from questions of form and meaning to issues of representation. Representation is a standard concept in media and communication studies. It is often explained through the idea that the media represent the real world, and this usually leads to debates about how true to real life the media representations are, or what sorts of ideological position about the world these representations articulate. The question of how popular music represents the world is a challenging one. As we have seen, popular music cultures operate across different media and draw on a range of channels of communication, which include musical sounds, lyrics, performance styles, and media images and related transformations. Any discussion of how popular music's meanings represent the world has to take account of all these aspects.

Part of the challenge in discussing representations in popular music is that we most often understand music as either about the individuality of performers and artists or the abstraction of musical sound. Music therefore either seems to be about real people who produce music, or not to represent at all. However, we are also aware of the fact that the media and the music business produce images for artists, and that those artists not only perform music, but also perform a particular star persona. Furthermore, popular music is meaningful to different groups of people in different ways. Getting to grips with how popular music constructs the individual images of pop performers and relates to wider cultural groups will lead us to an understanding of how music – both as sound and image – represents in a wider sense.

How music performers become pop stars and how they represent

Given how important pop stars are within the music industry, and how important they are to our everyday discussions about pop music, it is surprising how little has been produced by academics on the subject. The very term 'star' is part of the hyperbole of media-based culture. It suggests a distant, but bright, shining presence, which we gaze longingly at, as it arches high above the mundane lives we live. But it also taps into a longer history of the 'marked' or 'chosen individual', someone whose talent makes them shine out from the crowd. Like many ideas that are widely used it lacks the precision that academics favour, and so it has been a difficult concept to use in systematic analysis. We need to understand how stars are signalled as special individuals, and how star personae are constructed.

Stars as individuals

Stars are famous individuals, widely known, and often admired and desired. These attributes are usually seen as the product of talent or personal magnetism; of charisma. We feel we know stars as individuals, but our experience of them is always mediated through the interviews, records, photographs and video appearances we consume. Our awareness of these individuals, and our knowledge of their fame and talent, is the product of carefully executed publicity campaigns. In turn our knowledge of the star is used to encourage us to purchase records and an array of secondary merchandise through which we are invited to express our commitment. The study of stars, then, has to encompass the way that our sense of an individual performer is being constructed by the media and for what purposes. But it also needs to explain why we are drawn to certain individuals, and the particular version of individualism they express.

The study of stars has tended to draw on work in film studies. One of the key analyses of stars has been produced by Richard Dyer (1997). He combines an economic analysis of the star in terms of the industry, with a cultural analysis of the meaning of the star for fans. In economic terms, argues Dyer, stars are forms of capital in which a record company invests significant sums to gain publicity and reinforce an image they believe will, in turn, ensure greater sales of that star's records. In cultural terms Dyer sees the star image not as a real person, but a representation of both wider social values and a constructed sense of 'individualness'. We feel we really know the performer's personality, but the star image is a media text, a constructed persona. In some cases this star image/persona may be built upon some facets of the individual's personality, but then again it may not. In approaches such as this, questions about how the representation of the star persona relates to the individual's personality are far less important than questions about the economic and ideological function the image performs. In other words, it is less important to be asking if the star is really like that, and far more important to ask 'What sorts of meanings does that star persona articulate?', 'Why should that star appeal to his or her fans?' and 'Where are these meanings of the star's persona taken from?' A concrete example can demonstrate these points well and one of the best star analyses – and therefore a model for analysing other stars – is to be found in a short article by Simon Frith.

CASE STUDY Bruce Springsteen

In the late 1980s Bruce Springsteen was one of the half-dozen most successful artists in the music business but, claims Frith, his star image related to that success in a paradoxical fashion. It is the ubiquity of Springsteen's records in the 1980s that, for Frith,

> enables an aging, affluent rock generation to feel in touch with its 'roots'. And what matters in this post-modern era is not whether he is the real thing, but how he sustains the belief that there are somehow, somewhere, real things to be.
>
> (Frith 1988b, 95)

Through a series of oppositions Frith explores the paradoxical nature of Springsteen's image. He is 'a millionaire who dresses as a worker', 'an employer-as-employee', 'a 37-year-old teenager', 'a shy exhibitionist', 'a superstar-as-friend', and a performer whose 'most successful "record" is "live"' (Frith 1988b, 95–7). Frith suggests that Springsteen is consumed as 'truth', indexed by his 'authenticity', and set against the 'falseness' of other rock music. But, argues Frith, 'to be authentic and to sound authentic is in the rock context the same thing. Music can not *be* true or false, it can only refer to conventions of truth and falsity' (Frith 1988b, 100).

Therefore the Springsteen persona is a representation, a set of meanings constructed through a contrast of his persona with the idea of a corporate-dominated mainstream, told through a narrative of songs and performance, in which the star speaks for 'the people' through everyday words about real emotions and situations. Springsteen's persona stands as a champion of those people excluded by American capitalism but, argues Frith, it provides only individualised solutions. The desire that is directed at him by fans is a response to his 'ordinariness' or 'naturalness'. These qualities work through basic signs in the star's image. So, for instance, Springsteen's sweating in performance is an index of his energy, but also a symbol of his naturalness.

Frith roots Sringsteen's star image of rugged, real, individualism in a particular American populist anti-capitalist tradition that has a long history in popular music. This is a repertoire of ideas and associated signs that articulates a particular sense of equality – 'us, the people' – against judgements based on economic success or aesthetic significance – fame signalled by wealth, or high art value. Ultimately, though, his own success is based on the economic success achieved by his multinational record company, and his image has, at best, a paradoxical relationship to that success.

Generally, what this sort of analysis suggests is that the meanings of star images are never innocent. Frith seeks to show how the star persona, articulated through image and sound, attempts to resolve an ideological problem for a certain group of music fans at a particular time. That is to say Springsteen offered a sign of 'the real thing' at a time when rock had become part of the entertainment mainstream, but it did so without any of the trappings of the wider social conscience of the counter-culture that had dominated alternative rock in the early 1970s. This general point strongly echoes Dyer's analysis of film stars of previous decades. In choosing a star like Springsteen, Frith is also able to investigate the way that some star images are constructed as 'not constructed'. Manufactured pop groups are more obviously star images – their music is written and produced by others, and their performances obviously choreographed – and this, to some at least, can make their persona seem false. Other artists are presented as being well known for being authors of their own music, rather than products of the media's hype machine. However, following Dyer's approach, 'authorship' is just as much a textual meaning as the glitter and froth of pop performers. As analysts we would be confusing our own tastes and desires with an objective truth if we set out to prove that our favoured artists were *auteurs* while bemoaning the lack of talent of other stars. In this case we should be asking 'Why is the role of song authorship so important in this particular star persona, for their particular audience?'

Recognition of the different relationships of different audiences to stardom does start to open up the question of stardom itself. There is clearly something to be analysed beyond the persona of individual performers and into the whole idea of celebrity and the processes of making stars.

Star-making

While there is a clear division between that category of stars like Springsteen, who have had long careers and whose personae are widely known, and those 'behind the scenes' music industry workers whose existence is not widely apparent, there is also a whole swathe of performers whose period in the spotlight is shorter-lived, or who seem to avoid the publicity machine completely. Stars are not a consistent, easily delineated group, and the epithets 'superstar' or the less fashionable 'starlet', while they may suggest a hierarchy of stars, are more a product of the industry's hyperbole than any attempt at greater clarity. These observations do raise two points that require emphasis.

First, the publicity machines of the music industry are linked to a range of economic strategies. At one pole the publicity is aimed at giving a personality to an artist who, it is believed, will have a limited period as a star. This is the classic pop strategy, often aimed at young mainstream fans. At the other pole are artists who sell consistently over several years and whose records are seen as catalogue material. Here the artists and audience are constructed as serious music lovers who have stayed with an artist over many years. Many artists, from Elvis Presley through the Beatles to Madonna, have started as the new 'seven-day wonder' later to emerge as kings and queens of catalogue. Up to the 1960s the route from the one to the other was seen to be through establishing the artist as a mainstream entertainer, while from the late 1960s onwards the strategy emphasised the artistic achievements of the performer and their qualities as a long-term *auteur*.

Second, there seems to be another category of fame that functions differently to that of stardom. We usually use the term celebrity, here. Celebrities are known for being known. It is because their image is circulated in the media that we know of them, and these media appearances associate them with glamour and wealth. The economic and cultural success of magazines like *Hello!* and *OK!* is self-evidently built upon these ideas. In their pages the 'lives' of the rich and famous are portrayed: a group that includes people from areas other than pop music, and only some of those in pop music. I am not aware, for instance, that Springsteen has appeared in either of these magazines.

These two points suggest that, although there is some value in trying to investigate certain performers who have some long-term success in the music industry, and particularly those who gain substantial fan reaction, we need a more general sense of performer image. Such a sense would allow us to deal with the very different meanings that different artists have, the different relationships that are created between fans and performers, and yet still treat artist personae as texts. It is in this wider sense that John Ellis has defined a star as 'a performer in a particular medium whose figure enters into subsidiary forms of circulation and then feeds back into future performance' (Ellis 1982, 1).

While Ellis had film in mind, the approach also works very well for pop stars. In his formulation stars are part of a process in which popular music cultures make music and its performers meaningful. It directs our analysis to two aspects of this process. First, to the 'subsidiary forms of circulation', where star images exist beyond the primary text of the record or stage performance in the metatext of media appearances. Second, to the way that these media representations of the star 'feed back' into the primary text, both in terms of its textual materiality, but also in the way that we decode its meanings. This is to emphasise star constructions as dynamic processes, in which the musical forms of the recorded performances, and our interpretation of artists, is altered by the developing star personae. In this approach the media, and their attempts to attract fan attention, have a far greater role in defining the star persona than the recording artist themselves.

At the time of writing, the first series of the television series *Pop Idol* was revealing itself as a classic case of this idea. While the story that the programme constantly repeated was that this was a process in which they were *looking for* a pop idol, in fact it laid out for us the process by which a pop idol *was made*. While essentially an updating of the talent show, the programme ties together a record company, a management and promotions company, and peak-time television into a synergy of star-making. The knock-out rounds of each edition not only whittled down the contestants, but built up an image for each of them. Viewers participated as they discussed the contestants, voted for their favourites, read the stories placed in the popular press, watched interviews or debated online. The star images formed week by week, eventually leading to the selection of songs that were considered to suit each contestant. Interestingly, the first single released by the winner was not selected with him specifically in mind, and there was considerable discussion about whether it was appropriate. As the process of building the winner's persona continued after the series had finished, the record company and management attempted to alter his records to reflect the persona. There is a more developed study of manufactured pop stars in Part 5.

The star is so central to popular music that we sometimes take their role for granted. However, there are moments when stars are downplayed, or even actively eliminated. The best example would be the post-1980s British dance culture. Partly because this was a subculture that self-consciously set itself outside of traditional media-saturated pop, partly because its theatre of performance was the record-based dancefloor, and partly because the music-makers were DJs and producers rather than musicians, stars (and star building) never played a major role in the music's development. It became a prominent practice for DJs to use aliases, and for music-makers to release records under a series of noms de plume, which acted to depersonalise the individual at work. As examples of the new dance music crossed over into the pop mainstream the need for artists to promote their records through the traditional means of the personal appearance, the interview and the video caused difficulties for mainstream record companies. They resorted to hiring actors to perform on *Top of the Pops* appearances, and found new sorts of imagery for videos. At the same time, individual DJs became a key reason to attend a club night and CD collections were branded in their names. By the mid-1990s some individual producers – Goldie, Roni Size and LTJ Bukem in drum & bass, for instance – were being seen as music *auteurs*. Meanwhile, in some dance subgenres, artists – like the big-beat pop star Fat Boy Slim and rock-band-as-dance-music-makers like the Prodigy – took the trappings of stardom. The star had returned to its place at the centre of pop music.

Using some of the suggestions from the writers outlined above, produce an analysis of a particular star or performer image. First, examine how they are constructed as an individual. Ask yourself what sorts of values do they seem to articulate? Think about their image, their performance and the characteristics of their music. Second, examine how they are constructed in the subsidiary parts of the metatext (i.e. media representations) and how these qualities feed back into the primary text of their records. You could do this by looking at the development of an artist across their career. Selecting artists whose persona has changed dramatically, or who have come out of contemporary dance music may be particularly interesting.

Star images, then, continue to point backwards into the individual performances and are part of the template we use to make them meaningful, but they also point forwards to general representations of cultural ideas that are part of the way in which the music takes its place in a popular music culture. It is to this general propensity of popular music cultures to represent values, identities and ideas that we now turn. As an example of how music can represent on a wider scale, the next section looks at how music culture has been involved in representing individual senses of identity.

Representing identity

The discussion of stars keeps returning to the question of image as a means of exploring ideas of identity for music fans. Popular music is linked to significant senses of ourselves, which we can call our cultural identity. This can be defined as the way we understand ourselves in relation to others with whom we come into contact. Such identities contain within them a sense of self we have as a member of a wider social group, and of ourselves as unique individuals. It is common in media and cultural studies to investigate these issues in relation to a series of dimensions of identity derived from nationhood, ethnicity, class, gender and sexuality. These are seen as fundamentals of identity and they are also issues that have been the centre of significant debate and political conflict. Some of these senses of identity are clearly articulated in the consumption of music with culture, and we will return to these in the next chapter, but identity is also represented in popular music texts.

For many readers of this book, identity will be a taken-for-granted idea. You may feel that you are just you, and discussions of identity will seem unimportant and possibly unnecessary. For others, though, identity will be something to assert. You may feel that who you are is marginalised within the wider culture and you wish to show that you, and others you identify with, are of equal importance. For others, identity maybe something confused or even fluid. Sometimes you will feel nearly one thing, other times possibly another. Whichever description seems to fit you best, it is important in our role as scholars that we recognise that identity feels different for different people, and identity functions differently for different cultural groups.

One of the key questions here, then, is how the texts of popular music represent the cultural groups who produce them. When we talk about American music, or the new Welsh pop, or Euro-house, or Britpop we are tying music in to certain expressions of national identity and their associated notions of ethnicity. Within the broad notion of American or European music there are a variety of ways that music is linked to identity. Sometimes these are overt expressions like the Afro-centricism of much black British music (see Marks 1990; Gilroy 1991), or the Latin Americanness of salsa (see Negus 1996, 115–23); others are naturalised as the taken-for-granted Englishness of British pop or the Americanness of country (Malone 1985, 369–416). Other texts present a musical synthesis linked to a synthesis of identity – for instance, the way that Indian folk forms and European pop are combined in bhangra to represent a British Asian identity (Bannerji and Baurman 1990). It is interesting to pose a similar question for identities that relate to gender and sexuality. For instance, is it possible to understand music produced by men as representing a sense of maleness, and that of women artists a sense of femaleness? Likewise will music produced by gay men or women represent distinct identities again? Whatever, it is apparent that what it is to be a man or a woman is a prominent theme within the texts of popular music in lyrics, musical form and performance, and it is hard to even imagine popular music without its preoccupation with the themes of love and sex.

These sorts of issues have direct links to political campaigns for greater equality. Feminism, black power and gay rights movements have all challenged dominant views about our social relationships, and debated the role that the media has in representing our world. Feminists in particular have examined popular music to see what roles it represents for men and for women. In the mid-1970s Sue Sharpe argued that,

> Almost all the significant and successful stars, individuals and groups are male, as are their managers, promoters, publicity agents and critics. Girls are cast as the inevitable followers, the fans and the groupies, who demonstrate acts of adulation for their idols.

(Sharpe 1976, 112)

Building on similar arguments, Simon Frith and Angela McRobbie produced an analysis of the way gender was represented in mid-1970s popular music. They argued that while, lyrically, most popular music dealt with romance, two distinct forms of music – 'cock rock' and 'teenybop' – represented masculinity and femininity in distinctive and unequal ways. They characterised the former as a particularly male form of popular music, which gives a prominent role to live performances in which bands are seen/heard as 'aggressive, dominating and boastful ... mikes and guitars are phallic symbols; the music is loud, rhythmically insistent, built around techniques of arousal and climax' (Frith and McRobbie 1978, 374) and presents men as active, in control, confident. By contrast, teenybop is seen/heard as 'the young boy next door: sad thoughtful, pretty, and puppylike ... male sexuality is transformed into a spiritual yearning carrying only hints of sexual interaction' (Frith and McRobbie 1978, 375) and presents women as passive, objectified, individualised.

Frith and McRobbie's article was written at the very time that these representations of fixed identities for men and woman were being undermined. The authors recognise this themselves and look at the way women may consume rock, the way that teenybop music texts can be used by women fans for an assertive identity, and the way that women performers have tried to make a positive music using musical form that negates the meanings of 'cock rock'. Equally they point to the way that the first glam rock artists like David Bowie used popular music as a way to explore sexual ambiguity, and then punk bands often gave prominence to assertive representations of women and their sexuality. There is also an interesting discussion about the way that lyrics and performance can project very different, and sometimes contradictory, meanings. Although Frith later expressed embarrassment with the article and offered a series of correctives and complications to what he felt were under-theorised positions (see Frith 1990), the original article remains an important starting point.

For instance, Mavis Bayton, in research into the attitudes of women musicians has posed the question 'Where are all the great female electric guitarists?' (Bayton 1997, 37). She answers by arguing that role models, the culture through which guitar techniques are shared, the musical forms in which the guitar is heavily featured and even the instrument's shape and mode of playing, are all dominated by a particular 'masculine' set of meanings and practices. Other writers have attempted to retrieve the role of women in the history of popular music from the usual *his*(s)tories (Stewart and Garratt 1984; O'Brien 1995). Amy Raphael has attempted to explore the attitudes and careers of a number of post-punk women musicians, all of whom have been eager to address the way that women are represented within performance (Raphael 1995). Studies by Marion Leonard (1997) and Mary Kearney (1997) have developed a detailed analysis of the riot grrrl movement, which challenged the notion that rock represented 'masculinity'. Riot grrrl bands appropriated the musical materiality of punk and recast it in a new way that highlighted issues of gender in popular music from a feminist perspective. Riot grrrl constituted a complete reappraisal of gender in popular music: women musicians played in traditionally male roles, men had to stand at the back at concerts, the 'feminine' and 'masculine' meanings of music, forms of dress and staging were all debated and reconstructed in performances, magazines and meetings. Kearney has also shown how the mainstream media coverage of the riot grrrl bands represented them as an exotic aberration or simply women taking up punk. She argues that aspects of feminism, lesbianism and the 'womyn's music' movement have been downplayed in accounts of riot grrrl. Ten years further on, it is also interesting to note how the radical intentions of this movement have been incorporated within mainstream pop. The assertive reappraisal of representations of women in pop signalled by the grrrl epithet, the playful exploration of 'femininity' in clothing and appearance, and the debates about the relationship between power, sexuality and image have all been recast in a band like the Spice Girls and their slogan of 'girl power'.

In another direction, Sheila Whiteley has developed an analysis of Mick Jagger as a 'cock rock' performer (Whiteley 1997a) and Robert Walser has explored the way that rock, and particularly heavy metal, has been constructed as 'masculine'. Here he shares the riot grrrls' contention that there is nothing essentially male about rock, but that it is made so through the cultural practices of excription, misogyny, romance and androgyny (Walser 1993). His first point reflects that of Sara Cohen (1991) who explored the way men exclude women from participation in music-making. His second and third show how the fantasy of rock music represents women as a threat to male control, and sees metal as an escape from the problems of the everyday. His final point is perhaps the most interesting, because it signals the contradictory way that metal constructs male identity out of many of the signifiers of 'femininity': make-up, display of legs, lace and other sheer fabrics. Walser points to the work that metal musicians put into countering suggestions that they are gay. The androgyny of some metal bands is not in the end a staged exploration of 'femininity' or alternative forms of 'sexuality', but instead the exercise of a male, heterosexual power over all imagery. It is possible to read this as the victory of patriarchy, rather than an exploration of other possibilities.

Musics outside of the 1970s and 1980s rock mainstream have increasingly been investigated in terms of their possibilities to offer alternative representations of gender and sexual identity. Richard Dyer has argued that 1970s disco, both as culture and music, offered an alternative form of sexuality to mainstream rock, and so appealed to gay men (Dyer 1990). The role of disco within the gay communities of North America and Europe since the 1970s has been an important part of the development of contemporary dance music (Reynolds 1998). However, this should not lead us to think that disco or more recent forms of dance music are in essence an expression of gay identity. Developing ideas from John Gill, Keith Negus has ironically asked: 'is disco more gay than Jazz?' (Negus 1996, 128). Negus' discussion of the singer KD Lang is also instructive here, as it allows him to discuss ideas of conservatism within country music, and the way that stars present their sexuality, and how it is interpreted by their fans (Negus 1996, 130–3). Assertions of alternative identities are particularly evident in the music of African-Americans; 1950s R&B, 1960s soul and free jazz, 1970s funk and reggae and 1990s hip-hop have all been built significantly on a strong sense of black, Afro-centric, identity (George 1988; 1994; 1999; Jones 1988; Rose 1994; Kofsky 1998). However, many theorists of black identity push us to rethink the way these musics represent forceful, empowering racial identity. Paul Gilroy argues that we need to understand black music not as an essence of an intrinsic black culture, but instead to view 'black culture' and its music as a means through which some people make sense of their world (Gilroy 1991; 1993). He suggests that there is a common culture of diaspora: the 'black Atlantic' that links Africa to America and the Caribbean to northern Europe. Black culture, and therefore music, is created through identities that seek to find a place within racist societies. Brian Ward has further suggested that the different dreams of 'integration' and 'separatism' can be linked to the changing popularity of black music over the latter part of the twentieth century (Ward 1998).

These very basic summaries reveal that popular music texts have a multidimensional relationship to identity. Identity itself is experienced differently for different individuals and cultural groups. For some it seems to be obvious and unchanging, for others it is a means to assert a sense of self that demands to be treated on equal terms with the cultural identities of others. Music is not a separate phenomenon of identity, but an integral part of the process of identity-making, part of the way we begin to understand and articulate who we are. Although it may be a useful argument for some to present a certain music as essentially belonging to, or articulating, an identity, the very politics of popular music has shown that the materiality of the music can be appropriated, its meanings interrogated or even altered. Popular music, in one of its many paradoxes, seems to commonly represent a rather conservative set of senses of cultural groups, but it is also a creative arena in which identities are hyphenated (black-gay-middle-class-Briton or white-straight-working-class-American), or even blurred (to identify with black gay Detroit men from the position of a white straight Essex woman). Such fluid identities are seen to be part of postmodern culture in which texts do not any longer relate to something outside themselves – in our case that a piece of music just refers to another piece of music through pastiche – and so we have lost our sense of ourselves (Baudrillard 1983; Jameson 1990). Sampling, covers of old songs, the spectacle of manufactured pop and the stripped-down nature of dance music, the ethnic-hybridity of contemporary music, are all given as examples of this phenomenon. In this context Stuart Hall has addressed the notion of 'the real me', arguing that we no longer have an essential sense of self (Hall 1992). Taking his own biographical journey as a metaphor, he has argued that while our identity has become fragmented, meanings are less certain, and we may feel geographically and culturally displaced, we still relate ourselves to important senses of individual and collective history. So, for Hall, identity has not been lost, it is just not to be found in some essential quality of ethnicity, race, sense of nation, gender or sexuality, but it will relate in important ways to these ideas.

Arguing from the other end of the identity–music question, Simon Frith has challenged the propositions of postmodernists – with their emphasis on sight and space, rather than music's reliance on sound and time – and proposed that we should not understand music as a way of expressing ideas, but as a way of living them. So he suggests that to read contemporary popular music solely in terms of pastiche is mistaken. Sampling, for instance, is not (to use Jameson's terms) 'blank parody'. He argues that we should understand contemporary musical texts not as new (meaningless) texts but, far more importantly, as new ways of performing texts. As such he suggests we may have new forms of musical activity producing new sorts of identity, but the way music produces identity remains unchanged.

Think about the musical forms you consume. Does there seem to be a connection between the music and performances that connect with your own self-identity? Do you understand yourself to come from the same cultural group that produces the music, or do you have a sense of identity that goes beyond your immediate cultural group? Do the texts you consume seem to produce a clear or fluid identity? Is the certainty or uncertainty of these representations an important part of why you like them?

SUMMARY

We have moved from the idea of form to that of meaning, and examined the way that performance, metatext and genre contribute to meaning. The activities in this chapter have encouraged you to approach the analysis of meaning by recognising that a piece of popular music is wider than just sound. It is possible to make a range of interpretations that will depend upon the way in which the music was produced and consumed. We examined the way that music represents those who produce it and those who consume it. The star image is at the centre of how popular music culture represents music-makers, although examples like underground dance music show how music can be produced without personifying the people who produced it. Consumers of popular music make it a significant part of their identity, and this probably explains why it is so important to us. It is to these issues of consumption that we must now turn in more detail in Part 4.

Further reading

Banerji, Sabita and Baurman, Gerd 1990: 'Bhangra 1984–8: Fusion and Professionalisation in a Genre of South Asian Dance Music', in P. Oliver, *Black Music in Britain: Essays on the Afro-Asian Contribution to Popular Music.* **Open University Press.**

Dyer, Richard 1990: *Stars.* **BFI Publishing.**

Frith, Simon 1988: 'The Real Thing: Bruce Springsteen', in S. Frith, *Music for Pleasure: Essays in the Sociology of Pop.* **Polity Press.**

Frith, Simon and McRobbie, Angela 1978: 'Rock and Sexuality', in *Screen Education* 29.

Gilroy, Paul 1991: *'There Ain't No Black in the Union Jack': The Cultural Politics of Race and Nation.* **University of Chicago Press.**

Negus, Keith 1996: *Popular Music in Theory: An Introduction.* **Polity Press.**

Raphael, Amy 1995: *Never Mind the Bollocks: Women Rewrite Rock.* **Virago.**

Walser, Robert 1993: *Running with the Devil: Power, Gender and Madness in Heavy Metal Music.* **Wesleyan University Press.**

Ward, Brian 1998: *Just My Soul Responding: Rhythm and Blues, Black Consciousness and Race Relations.* **UCL Press.**

Whiteley, Sheila 1997: *Sexing the Groove: Popular Music and Gender.* **Routledge.**

Part FOUR:

Audiences and Consumption

As consumers of popular music ourselves, the study of the different ways we can consume music is the aspect of popular music culture we are most familiar with. So commonplace are these experiences that we often take them for granted. Our study, though, demands that we go into these activities in greater detail to understand how they fit into the complex popular music culture we have started to map out in the earlier chapters. Paradoxically, while most of the popular music scholarship has centred on cultures of music consumers, there are only basic studies of the detail of how people actually consume music (Hesmondhalgh 2002). The interest of cultural studies academics in the consumption of popular music was the result of an attempt to understand how music was meaningful in relation to all the other aspects of the daily lives of different cultural groups, at different times and in different contexts.

In this part of the book, Chapter 11 examines some of this founding work on the relationship of popular music to culture, as well as discussing the numerous debates promoted by these first studies. Chapters 12, 13 and 14 look in more detail at how we could study the main activities of consumption: listening and looking, dancing and record buying.

CHAPTER ELEVEN

The Sociology of the Music Consumer

We can identify a number of general approaches to the consumption of popular music. In the first, which dominated the first 60 years of the twentieth century, cultural scholarship, there is a focus on popular music consumption as forms of socially maladjusted behaviour characterised by fanaticism. These scholars stand outside popular music culture, looking down at popular music consumption as part of a deviant social ritual, or an unhealthy psychological state, both symptomatic of new forms of society. The second strand, which became prominent after 1970, shared some of the assumptions of the study of fanaticism, but transformed these into an analysis of how certain subcultures within society use aspects of their lives to resist the norms of society. Finally, more recent approaches have attempted to understand a wider range of consumption activities and to grasp the meanings of music from within popular culture. Examining each of these in turn gives a good sense of how thinking about popular music has changed, and sets a good context for the more focused discussions of studying consumption that follow.

Fanaticism and mass culture

From the 1930s the audiences for new cultural forms like the movies and popular music were widely termed 'fans'. Although the term has since lost the strongest of its original connotations, the derivation of the word in the noun 'fanatic' reveals the way that audiences for popular culture were perceived at that time. Such thinking was related to a wider set of concerns among early twentieth-century intellectuals about what they perceived to be the development of a 'mass culture'. John Storey has characterised what 'mass culture' meant for these theorists as 'hopelessly commercial culture. It is mass produced for mass consumption. Its audience is a mass of non-discriminating consumers. The culture itself is formulaic, manipulative … and is consumed with brain-numbed and brain numbing passivity' (Storey 2001, 8).

These theorists analysed cultures that they did not participate in themselves, and the activities of popular music audiences were analysed largely to show the existence, and deleterious state, of mass culture. As such, this sense of a mass culture was a construction of the discourse of intellectuals as diverse as F. R. Leavis in Britain, Theodor Adorno and other Frankfurt School theorists in exile in the USA, and American intellectuals like Dwight Macdonald (see Storey 2001, 17–36, 85–93). All such theorists valued the production and consumption of what they saw as high art or folk forms, but attacked those forms they saw as commercialised, arguing that mass production created mass consumption and a mass society. While Leavis feared that such a mass society endangered the culture of intellectuals, and increasingly took an elitist line on the way to ensure it survived, Adorno felt that popular culture reinforced the 'social cement' that maintained the inequalities between rich and poor, powerful and subordinate. Macdonald's concerns were more with the way pluralism of American thought was threatened by the authoritarian societies of Germany and Russia in the 1930s and 1940s. These mass-cultural positions all took the idea of mass culture/production/consumption as a given but, as Raymond Williams has pointed out, 'there are … no masses; there are only ways of seeing people as masses' (Williams 1963, 289).

Joli Jensen has argued that such notions of 'the fanatic' and 'mass society' were still very influential in the study of fans well into the late 1980s. She asserts that, 'The literature on fandom is haunted by images of deviance. The fan is consistently characterized (referencing the term's origins) as a potential fanatic. This means that fandom is seen as excessive, bordering on deranged behaviour' (Jensen 1992, 9).

Jensen identifies two characteristic fan types that appear in such accounts of fan behaviour: the hysterical crowd and the obsessed loner. Fans and fan activities are constructed as being outside normal behaviour, and so beyond social control, prey to the siren voices of the media (and particularly popular music and its star performers). She suggests that fan activities are seen as a psychological compensation for the perceived inadequacies of modern culture, and characterises these approaches as constructing 'fandom as pathology' (Jensen 1992). The main characteristics of such approaches to popular music fans are outlined in the following list, which describes mass society characteristics of fandom.

Fans of popular music are seen as:

- emotional and prone to hysterical behaviour
- obsessive
- fantasists

- pathological and so unable to distinguish reality from non-reality, fixated on death, possibly even violent or murderous

- vulnerable because of childish, adolescent or immature states of mind

- psychologically inadequate

- deviant and anti-social, maybe leading to harmful behaviour – first, affecting the individual concerned and, perhaps later, the object of his/her obsession

- contagional so that fans are prone to get out of control when they are in groups

- sexually yearning

- gendered feminine when seen as hysterical and inadequately male when seen as dangerous loners.

(Derived from essays by Cheryl Cline, Barbara Ehrenreich, Joli Jensen and Lisa A. Lewis, collected in Lewis 1992)

Keith Negus has suggested that the approaches of intellectuals to popular music culture have changed significantly through the twentieth century. The characteristics identified by Jensen have increasingly been critiqued, he argues, so that the audience is now seen as more active (Negus 1996, 8). It is certainly the case that from the 1950s there was an important shift in sociology towards an interest in studying the culture of working-class adolescents, and in the 1960s the counter-culture of young middle-class Americans. These studies were stimulated by the increasing affluence among young people in post-Second World War America (see, for instance, Abrams 1959), the influence of functionalist sociology, which sought to explain the social function of youth culture as an arena where young people learnt to take on adult responsibilities (see, for instance, Eisenstadt 1956), and a focus on the question of youth deviancy (see, for instance, Becker 1966). All of these studies gave some recognition to the consumption of music.

However, as well as noting these changes, it is also important to identify the continuity in these studies. By keeping an emphasis on music consumption as one part of a whole way of life from the earlier mass-culture studies, later studies of people's involvement in popular music-culture have been able to avoid some of the problems prominent in other media audience studies where consumption is cut off from other social practices. In achieving this integration of music and lifestyle, though, these later studies of cultural consumption have usually neglected the detail of how music is consumed, and on occasions have misunderstood it. So while academics working in the 1970s and 1980s revolutionised thinking about youth as culture – by pluralising the culture of youth into a set of *sub*cultures, by emphasising social class and by giving a greater prominence to music – they kept the emphasis on the interrelationship of music with a whole way of life, although their approaches lacked detail about how exactly popular music is consumed.

Subcultural theory

These subcultural approaches constituted the second strand of approaches to the consumption of popular music. In perhaps the founding book of subculture theory, the authors set out their aims as follows:

> We have tried to dismantle the terms in which this subject is usually discussed – 'Youth Culture' – and reconstruct in its place a more careful picture of the kinds of youth subcultures, their relation to class cultures and to the way cultural hegemony (domination) is maintained structurally and historically.

(Hall and Jefferson, 1975/1991)

The primary motivation in this work by academics at Birmingham University's Centre for Contemporary Cultural Studies (CCCS) was to recast the analysis of what sociologists – along with mainstream society – had seen as 'the problem of deviant youth'. Rather than seeing non-conformist groups of young people as a problem that required a social solution, this group of researchers argued that the cultural activities of these groups represented a form of 'resistance through rituals' (Hall and Jefferson 1975/1991). They looked at a range of 1960s and 1970s subcultures, including teds, mods, skinheads, rastas and rudies, which were distinguished in significant ways by certain forms of popular music. This work in subcultural theory, then, offers some important insights for our study about the 'consumption end' of popular music culture, and was developed by one of the collection's contributors, Dick Hebdige, into what was to become probably the most influential book in the area. The title of his book, *Subculture: The Meaning of Style* (Hebdige, 1979), gives some clues to the approach he took. He argued that subcultural groups like teds or mods or punks (and by extension all musical subcultures) construct a style – of dress, music, forms of transport, and forms of dancing or listening or buying – that is meaningful to them and others. To do this, subcultural groups take products that are available in mainstream society and transform their meanings through 'bricolage': a process of improvisation where conspicuous consumption is organised in distinctive ways to transform the meanings of the objects. Through this transformation of meanings, these styles begin to reinforce each other to create a coherent whole, which Hebdige, following Barthes, calls a 'homology'.

Although his book is driven by an interest in semiological theory, which has become less fashionable today, and is focused on the punk subculture of the late 1970s, it is required reading for anyone interested in the way music is integrated into popular music culture. However, it is also important to be aware of the limitations of the key works of subcultural theory and analysis. Angela McRobbie has consistently raised the issue of the marginalisation of women within the literature on subcultures (McRobbie 1980). Just as the subcultural theorists had recovered the detailed cultural practices of some youth from the simplifying certainties of theories of deviance, and brought the inequalities of class into studies of youth culture, McRobbie attempted to recover the marginalised roles of women in culture, and to bring inequalities of gender into these studies (McRobbie 1984; 1989; 1999).

The number of critiques or reappraisals of the key subculturalist publications provides a clear indication of the influence of the CCCS. Some writers have questioned the claim that there is a direct linkage of types of music and other subcultural practices (Middleton 1990), others that ideas of homology are at best overstated (Toynbee 2000, 110–15), while others have raised doubts about the concept of subculture itself (Redhead 1990). Gary Clarke has investigated the selection process of the subcultural studies arguing that they have privileged certain spectacular groups at the expense of 'ordinary youth' who consume mainstream music and wear chain store clothes (Clarke 1990). For Clarke the meanings of youth cultures are not reducible to a series of separate and homogeneous groups displaying their style in coherent and spectacular form. The approach of starting with distinctive groups inherited from theories of youth deviance did not reveal the complexity of youth culture. Instead, Clarke argues, we should 'start with an analysis beginning with the social relations based around class, gender, and race (and age), rather than their stylistic products' (Clarke 1990). This, he believed, would allow us to examine the sorts of options that are available to different young people, and would avoid viewing the spectacular subculture as some sort of original, which is then watered down for exploitation and mass consumption.

However, for all its limitations, Hebdige's approach provides us with a very useful set of ideas beyond its specific focus that can become tools for our own analyses. By tying the consumption of certain types of music to certain sets of values articulated by a subcultural group he highlights three main characteristics of music consumption.

1. First, that taste and choice in music is not arbitrary or haphazard, nor simply a matter of subjective choice. Rather, it is culturally generated. We do not choose the music we consume in isolation. Our choices of music and the ways we consume them are meaningful to us and those around us.

2. Second, the way in which music is meaningful is not simply reducible to 'the music', but is produced in the particular ways that we consume it. Hebdige shows us that the 'sense of style' generated by the way we consume music transforms its meanings. This was how Hebdige utilised the notion of bricolage. While his examples are most often about clothing, the same idea can be applied to other forms of consumption. For instance, acquiring our music as a vinyl LP from a second-hand stall on a market, as a CD single from a high-street store, as a 12-inch vinyl single from a specialist dance music shop, or as an MP3 file over the internet, are all meaningful choices.

3. Finally, the meaningfulness of one act of consumption relates to other acts of consumption (or other social practice) to form a whole style. This was how Hebdige used the notion of homology. So, the vinyl LP is usually collected, categorised, organised on shelves, listened to in relation to other collected records and the sense of popular music history produced by the collector. The CD single is bought on a Saturday-morning shopping trip, which also includes buying clothes from certain shops, and is undertaken with friends as a social occasion. The 12-inch single is tucked into a record bag to be mixed on a set of home record decks as practice for its use at a club night. The MP3 file is added to a hard disk in a bedroom to be discussed over the internet late into the night. Each of these constitutes a particular and coherent set of ways to consume music, and each is distinctive in its meanings and related associations.

Subcultural theory is useful, then, for developing our thinking about specific subcultures that are covered in the available literature, but they do tend to marginalise women's roles and ignore the way popular music consumption takes place outside of specified subcultures. Behind the analyses, though, are some very useful concepts about taste and meaning in popular music culture, which can be used as a basis to investigate other audiences and consumption practices. The most notable attempts to rethink popular music and everyday life have been in the renewed interest in the idea of the fan.

Fan culture

The idea of fan culture is the third, and most recent, approach to studying the consumption of popular music. This academic work has developed out of the critiques of earlier approaches. Theories of mass culture saw music consumption as a fanaticism associated with individual psychological weakness or crowd hysteria. Subcultural theory understood music production to be one element of a particular cultural group's homology through which it resisted the domination of the powerful elites of modern society. Some more recent theories have rethought the cultural practices of fandom using ideas of active participation derived from subcultural theory. Others have tried to keep the ideas of the 'subcultural' – aligning its sense with that of 'the underground' used by music fans themselves – and so highlighting cultural discursive practices, rather than emphasising academic interpretations of resistance.

These shifts in understanding fan culture from the inside were signalled by the publication of Judy and Fred Vermorel's collection of interviews with fans (Vermorel and Vermorel 1985). While it would be easy to read these fans' accounts of obsession as proof for the mass culture theories, by providing extended space to fans' own ways of articulating their fandom the book signalled a new way to approach fan activity. In an alternative reading of the interviews fandom is revealed as an active process with its own forms of consumption and meaning-making. The accounts are full of references to the texts of fandom – records, pictures, memorabilia, fanzines, fan meetings – activities of listening, watching and discussion, as well as indications of the individual and collective pleasures of fandom. This sort of recognition has been the basis for more developed theories of fandom as more active and contradictory (see, for instance, Hills 2002), and for approaches to understanding 'the cultural economy of fandom' (Fiske 1992).

A number of theorists of fan culture have drawn upon the concept of 'cultural capital' (Bourdieu 1984). This refers to those forms of cultural knowledge that allow intellectuals to create and circulate distinctions between 'good' culture (the high arts, which they like and consume) and 'bad' culture (popular culture that subordinate groups consume). For the French sociologist Pierre Bourdieu the intellectuals who run the education and legal systems, the media and other cultural industries construct hierarchies of what is good and what is bad in culture. This power to make distinctions is a source of social power that he sees as a corollary to the Marxist idea of 'economic capital', the power derived from the ownership of the means of production. By analogy, just as capitalist factory owners invest in more capital to increase production, wealth and ultimately power for themselves, intellectuals invest in forms of restricted education that give them more cultural capital and so more cultural power. Interesting though these ideas are, what is missing from Bourdieu's analysis is any sense of what constitutes popular culture beyond it being '*not* high art'.

Fiske suggests that popular culture is actually another form of cultural capital accumulation, discrimination and meaning production (Fiske 1992). Music fans usually know an enormous amount of detail about their favourite groups or artists. They distinguish 'their' artist from others, and often distinguish between different records produced by that artist, and give significance to the artists and music in their lives. Fiske's approach is useful to our study in so far as we can look at fan activity in a new light in which fandom becomes a set of creative, productive and empowering practices. However, it does treat Bourdieu's idea of cultural capital as a simple metaphorical take on Marx's idea of economic capital. In Bourdieu's own work the idea of cultural capital is a means to explain how certain forms of knowledge and practice *make* groups of individuals powerful. In Fiske's version, education in the high arts is simply an investment in something that *already* assigns power in society. Further, fan self-education is simply a way of achieving prestige within a peer group. In treating the idea of cultural capital simply as a metaphor, Fiske fails to investigate the power relationships between the fan/popular culture and what he calls official culture. Fans just become elites within a distinct sphere of popular culture that is defined by official culture. If we want to understand the social role of fandom we need a far more sophisticated handle on the relationship of fan knowledge to power, and to the economic processes that produce high art and media artefacts, than Fiske can provide.

One approach has been to treat the activities of fan cultural capital accumulation as a contradictory activity. In this sense Henry Jenkins has called fans *powerless elites* (Jenkins 1992; see also Hills 2002). A second approach has been to take a step back from fan activity and attempt to rethink that activity within a wider context of the relationship between production, texts and consumption practices. Some interesting ways into thinking about these issues are to be found in work by Lawrence Grossberg, who argues that 'even if it is true that audiences are always active, it does not follow that they are ever in control' (Grossberg 1992b, 53–4). While he would no doubt agree with Fiske that, 'in capitalist societies popular culture is necessarily produced from the products of capitalism, for that is all the people have to work with' (Fiske 1992, 47), Grossberg wants to explore in more detail what is actually achieved through fan activity, and how is it achieved. Rather than defining the meaning of fan behaviour from a theorist's social position, as the mass culturalists did, Grossberg attempts to understand fans' feelings from a fan's position. First, he suggests that fans operate in 'the domain of affect' those psychological states of feeling and mood that 'give "color", "tone" or "texture" to our experiences' (1992, 57). Second, he suggests that these affects are created through a particular sensibility that defines the possible relationship between texts and audiences, and sets the terms in which texts are experienced (1992, 54). The sensibility of a particular type of fandom, then, will establish the sorts of affective responses that can be experienced. In an echo of Bourdieu, Grossberg contends that affects relate to our practices of making differences matter, but now primarily as a means of defining our identity. Fans are active in the sense that they invest affective states into their consumption of different texts of popular music, and they work within a sensibility that they share with other fans of a particular music or star.

FIGURE 11.1 The practices of popular music fans can be interpreted from a number of different perspectives
Photo: Stefan Klenke

Bourdieu has also been influential in Sarah Thornton's studies of dance music cultures, in her use of this idea of distinction. In Thornton's work, though, Bourdieu's 'cultural capital' is reconstituted as 'subcultural capital'. These are practices and forms of knowledge that confer status on the individual within the club and its associated subcultural spaces. She combines these concepts with an approach based on a critique of subcultural theories, contending that such studies overemphasise the political implications of cultural practices and yet underplay more subtle power relationships at work. Instead she focuses on the subcultural ideologies 'by which youth imagine their own and other social groups assert their distinctive character and affirm that they are not anonymous members of an undifferentiated mass' (Thornton 1995, 10). Thornton's analysis, then, like Grossberg's, suggests that processes defining individual and group identity are central to the operation of these cultures. They also share an emphasis on the idea of 'authenticity'. For Grossberg it is an ideology understood as the articulation of real emotions on behalf of a community, or as the physicality of dancing that transcends the everyday, or the knowing artifice of postmodern rock (Grossberg 1992, 61–3). Thornton uses the same sense of binary opposites, but she suggests that in dance music there has been a transformation of the concept of authenticity from Grossberg's rock sensibility to a new one formed in a new subcultural space of dance music. This transformation is characterised by the shifting of authenticity from the domain of the live performance to the record, from listening to dancing, and from the rock *auteur* to the DJ (Thornton 1995, 26–86).

As significantly, Thornton examines the way that subcultural ideologies construct a sense of difference through the caricaturing of people and practices outside the subculture. In doing so they construct a sense of elitism, achieved in the discourse of clubbers by disparaging dancers, music and dance halls that do not share their particular clique. She shows how particular feminised depictions of homogeneous 'Sharon and Tracy' characters in Mecca ballrooms dancing round their handbags become 'the Other' by which elite clubbers' senses of individual originality and group heterogeneity are constructed (Thornton 1995, 87–115). As Thornton notes, these constructions of the subculture and the mainstream are not substantially different to those deployed by the academics who developed the subcultural studies. Summarising Thornton's conclusions Gilbert and Pearson have noted 'the naiveté and insupportability of the rigid distinction between "underground" and "mainstream" cultures … [through which club subcultures produce] not oppositionality, but elitism and exclusivity' (Gilbert and Pearson 1999, 159). Grossberg has similarly pointed to the way that rock culture has constructed a distinction between authentic and co-opted rock, which is 'often interpreted as rock's inextricable tie to resistance, refusal, alienation, marginality, and so on' (Grossberg 1992, 62).

The distinctiveness of each of the approaches to audiences discussed here becomes most apparent when applied to a particular case. Select two contrasting groups of music audiences – perhaps fans of manufactured bands and nu metal bands, or trance and garage dancers – and then write a paragraph on each group of fans using the analytical methods and concepts of each approach. Is one approach more readily applicable to one group of fans than the others? Do they reveal different facets of those fans? How useful do you find each approach in revealing the social significance of the group of fans?

SUMMARY

In this chapter we have identified the three main approaches that have been used to understand the sociology of music consumption. The mass cultural, subcultural and fan culture theories offer very different views of the role and implication of music in people's lives, but they are important in setting the terms for how we should theorise consumption of popular music. The first swamped an attempt to understand music consumption under an enveloping fear that modern society produced alienated individuals or hysterical crowds. The second offered significant theoretical insights into the way that groups articulate their cultural position and values through their consumption but tended to ignore women, or anyone outside of a clear subcultural group. More recent theories have kept the idea of the fan and culturally located consumption, but attempted to explore the discursive practices of consumption, rather than overwhelm its complex meanings with singular ideas of resistance.

Nevertheless all these approaches remain at a level of abstraction which means that the detailed activities of consumption – the way we listen, watch, dance, buy and collect – have been lost in the drive to theorise their significance. What we need is a dual approach where we examine the detail of these consumption activities and use this detail to test and evaluate these wider debates. Hence the following three chapters will each take an area of consumption in turn, while keeping the questions of culture squarely in view.

Further reading

Grossberg, Lawrence 1992: 'The Affective Sensibility of Fandom', in Lisa A. Lewis, *The Adoring Audience: Fan Culture and Popular Media*. **Routledge.**

Hebdige, Dick 1979: *Subculture: The Meaning of Style*. **Methuen.**

Hills, Matt 2002: *Fan Cultures*. **Routledge.**

CHAPTER TWELVE

Listening and Looking

Listening to, and watching, popular music seem such obvious activities of popular music culture that we can easily take them for granted. However, these two central activities have not been widely and deeply studied. There are some fragmented pieces of work we can draw upon to study these activities, but a systematic and holistic approach to listening has yet to be established. Key questions about how, why and with what implications we listen to and watch popular music are still open to debate, and are ripe for study and analysis. Interestingly, watching popular music has been given relatively more attention than listening to it. Perhaps this is because there has been a more recent shift towards the visual side of music consumption since popular music took a prominent place in developments in television and video, and in this situation listening seems even more 'natural' and not in need of research. It, of course, may also represent a bias towards the visual in critical and social theory.

To grapple with these issues, this chapter starts with an examination of two early studies of listening, compares these with some more recent work that use an ethnographic approach, and then turns attention to the work on watching pop to see what that tells us about both the visual and aural consumption of popular music.

Learning from Adorno and Riesman

It is informative to start with two fairly early attempts to understand the way music is listened to in popular music culture, to assess their methods of research and analysis, and their conclusions, to see how useful they are for our attempts to study listening and watching. I have selected work originally published in the 1940s in books and articles by Theodor Adorno (1941/1990; 1991), and one from David Riesman originally published a few years later in 1950 (Riesman 1950/1990).

Adorno variously characterises popular music listening as passive and 'deconcentrated', 'regressive' in its child-like comprehension (1991, 26–52), and creating responses of authoritarian conformity and romantic longing (1941/1990, 309–14). His aim is wider than merely to denigrate popular music and its listeners; it is to critique their place in modern society. He attempts to explicitly answer our key questions about how, why and with what implications we listen. Central to his explanation is the notion that our listening, and its motivation and results are caught in a series of paradoxes that are born of the contradictions of living in a mass culture. Listening to popular music, Adorno asserts, is 'quotation listening', where the melodic hooks of pieces of music are the focus (1941/1990, 211–14). Furthermore, listening is an activity of both 'distraction and inattention', which must offer some stimulation – usually through the use of novelty – to escape the boredom of mechanised labour, but not too much so that listening becomes intellectually taxing and so fails to offer relaxation. Through these processes, music becomes 'social cement' and these forms of listening lead to an acceptance of the status quo of inequality and exploitation (1941/1990, 310–11).

Riesman's shorter analysis makes a distinction between two kinds of listener – one forming a majority, the other a minority – and two associated types of listening. He defines the majority as having 'an undiscriminating taste … [and they] form the audience for the larger radio stations, the "name" bands, the star singers, the hit parade and so forth' (Riesman 1950/1990, 8), and the minority group that 'comprises more active listeners, who are less interested in melody or tune than in arrangement or technical virtuosity … The group tends to dislike name bands, most vocalists (except Negro blues singers), and radio commercials' (Riesman 1950/1990, 9). He further speculates that, for the majority of listeners, the disconnected presentation of music over the radio, the consumption of music through stars and sales charts, and the emphasis on dancing, reinforce a disconnected way of experiencing cultural life, a conformity to the status quo, and a particular orientation to relationships and sexuality. For the minority group, he suggests that their listening practices are linked to attitudes of rebelliousness and dissent from mainstream values. He speculatively links the actual forms of music listened to by this minority group – mostly small band and trad(itional) forms of jazz – to their social outlook (Riesman 1950/1990, 10). He also notes in a few places that there is a process of minority ideas passing into the majority field, but the potential for rebellion is restricted by 'partial incorporation' into the practices of the cultural mainstream, and at which point the minority lose interest in these aspects of their popular music culture (Riesman 1950/1990, 9).

**X
2.1**It is really worth reading the originals to get a stronger sense of the authors' scholarly and research styles, and this will allow you to understand better the points made below. Adorno's 'On Popular Music' article, written in 1941, and Riesman's 'Listening to Popular Music' piece, written in 1950, are collected in Frith and Goodwin 1990. For each article, try to answer the following questions. How did each author research listening? What are their central propositions about listening? How do they present their ideas (as assertions or questions)? How does the form of research, and the research actually conducted, relate to the conclusions they draw? To what extent do you feel that their conclusions can be supported by their own research and by your knowledge of contemporary listening and watching. It would be very worthwhile to do this activity before you read on.

A direct comparison of the two authors' approaches is revealing. While Adorno *asserts* the nature and implications of listening, Riesman's ideas are put forward as *tentative questions* for further research. In fact Riesman's article is about how research into popular music could be conducted in the context of previous US research, and reports into fieldwork he conducted in Chicago. By contrast, Adorno's work is philosophical in nature, reflecting his contention that the sorts of empirical work suggested by Riesman would not lead to increased insight into the subject. Adorno's writing comes across as opinionated (rather than well researched), damning (rather than illuminating) and partial (rather than rich and diverse). It has even been suggested by one of his colleagues that when Adorno did conduct interview-based research he argued he should replace one set of answers to a question with another set in his transcripts to better represent the 'truth' of what he was investigating (see Morrison 1998, 103–20). Closer reading of Riesman's discussion, though, reveals that his propositions about music listening are not necessarily supported by interview research. He only interviewed 15 'young people', just one of whom he characterised as a member of the minority group he constructs. There is evidence to suggest that his approach shares much with Adorno's speculative philosophy, although it lacks Adorno's rigour and depth of thought (or possibly simply his density of proposition). Perhaps it is because Adorno is producing his analysis from outside popular music culture, and is highly critical of that culture, that he is, first, too rigid in the way he characterises listening, and then over-evaluative in the way he interprets the significance of those listening practices. He wanted to prove that some forms of listening – concentrated, attentive and holistic listening – are superior to others. Riesman shares a similar view, but it is developed so that some forms of listening, by some listeners, to some popular music, conform to these preferred listening practices. And, of course, he expresses his points very differently.

So, what can we learn from these analyses produced over half a century ago? One of the key strengths of these approaches to understanding listening within popular music culture is that they attempt to link listening to the texts and production of popular music and the wider culture in which the activities take place. Both Adorno and Riesman indicate how intimately listening is linked to the social order and to cultural values. Riesman's finessing of this point is to indicate differences of listening within popular music culture. Examining scholarly work produced since Adorno's and

Riesman's articles shows how little of their suggestive ideas have been followed up. It is true that Riesman's notion of the minority group has been shared by the counter-culture analysts of American scholarship, and the British subcultural theorists and sociologists, and his idea of incorporation can be seen to have been explored in some detail especially in the work of Hebdige (1979). As we saw above, this work places a strong emphasis on the relationship of popular music to a range of cultural practices. Both Riesman and Hebdige focus on minority groups because they assume they are politically and culturally oppositional and therefore important. However, the ideas and questions produced by Adorno and Riesman about mainstream popular music listening have been either just assumed, or completely neglected, for 50 years. The assumption that being able to categorise different groups of listeners does not mean that they have fundamentally different ways of listening, even if they have different skills of verbal expression, and articulate different values. Difference is clearly important in understanding listening practices, but what is required is a wider and richer sense of these differences.

If we strip Riesman's questions of some of their more obvious cultural assumptions about listening they can become relevant for today. How does the presentation of music – within the radio text, on a compilation album, in a film or on MTV, for instance – order our listening? How does identification with artists and their celebrity success lead us to think about the wider society in particular ways? How do some individuals come to reject such artists, and are their processes of listening any different? Does popular music present answers to implied questions about our culture and society? Do different listeners ask different questions to which different answers are available through different forms of music? How important is the way we relate to the music through our bodies, for instance as dancers, seated listeners or train riding Walkman wearers? How do these activities construct roles for us?

We need to understand Adorno's and Riesman's arguments within their historical and social location as a product of their time and place (see Middleton 1990, 61–3). However, we also need to recognise that the basic proposition that popular music listening is superficial and stupefying is still widely expressed today. It is a proposition that needs investigating. On the one hand, inside all these evaluative statements about popular music listening there does seem to be some descriptive veracity. In some contexts at least, we do sing along to a song's hook line, play music on the radio to alleviate the boredom of the office or shop floor, immerse ourselves in our current favourite track in order to forget (or remember) our current (or past) circumstances. But on the other hand, these are just some of the ways in which we, individually and as a culture, listen.

Finally we need to be aware of the ways in which we research and theorise listening and watching. It is important to investigate actual listening practices, not simply make hypotheses about them, but while we research we also need to be aware that we construct what we observe through the ideas and assumptions we bring to the research. We need to be careful, when analysing how people listen and watch popular music, to avoid the temptation to prove our own listening practices are superior.

X 2.2

To take you a step further in investigating listening practices, plan out how you would undertake some research into the sorts of questions that Riesman outlined. Many of the considerations about researching listening are the same as those for any audience research within media studies, and so a general discussion on researching audiences would be helpful here. You may find a chapter like Jensen's 'Media Reception: Qualitative Traditions' (in Jensen 2002) useful in assisting your thinking.

Select a research question from the list below and plan out a research approach that you think would allow you to find out more about the issue.

- How do radio, film or TV organise music? In what way does this organisation determine the way we listen to the music?

- How important is a sense of identification with an artist in determining the way we listen to popular music?

- How many different ways, and in what proportions, does an individual listen to popular music?

- How do practices of listening differ between individuals in different social groups?

- Do popular music listeners understand popular music to present a particular perspective on a part of our cultural life?

- How do the different physical activities we undertake while listening to music, like sitting, walking, riding in transport, dancing, produce different listening experiences?

Surveys and ethnographies of listening

The consumption of popular music has been most systematically surveyed by Keith Roe and his various collaborators in a series of research projects in Sweden (Roe 1985; 1990; Roe and von Feilitzen 1992). The findings portray music consumption as a diverse field of culture in which patterns of consumption relate to geography, age, class, gender, ethnicity and education, and they provide empirical support for the idea that music consumption is used as a sign of belonging to particular cultural group and for marking out distinctions from others. The challenge with such empirical work lies in making an assessment of the significance of the data. For instance, Roe and von Feilitzen's findings that up to 90 per cent of listening is linked to other social activities could be interpreted in a number of different ways. Within the mass cultural framework of Adorno it would show that popular music listening is not concentrated, attentive, nor holistic. Alternatively, within the subcultural framework it would suggest that music is actively connected with other cultural practices. Wider-scale studies like Crafts, Cavicchi and Keil's (1993) ambitious Music in Daily Life project, also reveals that music consumption is far from homogeneous, displaying a rich diversity of music, modes of listening and social contexts, the integration of music into daily life is also signalled. However, either because of the diversity and scale of data, or as a result of an attempt to avoid the kind of determinism found in subcultural studies, the authors resist looking for modes of listening that we could understand as culturally significant. Any potential sense of the way that music may operate to construct an identity is limited to the notion that each person's consumption is unique, which then means that opportunities to see consumption in relation to wider groups in society are lost.

It is perhaps better to see the abstract theories of music cultures as attempts to understand the 'big picture' of the relationship between music and culture, and to remain conscious that they rely on quite fundamental assumptions about the nature of music and culture. As interpretative frameworks, they tend to be overwhelming, so that any primary research always seems to support their predictions. On the other hand, survey work provides a useful way to grasp the basics of listening practices; although the significance of these practices is hard to ascertain simply from the data that is generated. What is needed is an approach that adds to the insights of abstract theory and empirical surveys by providing an attempt to understand the fine details of listening in the cultural terms of the listeners themselves. Such an approach is usually associated with ethnographic analysis, which seeks to produce 'thick descriptions' of culture (Geertz 1993) through participation observation (as it is sometimes termed in sociology) combined with unstructured interviewing.

Jo Tacchi's (1998) ethnographic work on the detail and richness of everyday listening practices, and Tia DeNora's (2000) investigation of the way music affects mood and sense of self, are good examples. They both explore the connection between listening practices and emotional states – between sound and sentiment – in what Tacchi calls 'the affective dimension of everyday lives and relationships' (Tacchi 1998, 1). Tacchi showed how those individuals who took part in her research shifted their listening habits as their lives and their emotional states changed. These shifts operated on a series of axes including the medium through which they listened – radio, tapes or records – different versions of a particular medium – different radio stations or tapes bought, compiled or given by others – and the type of music – defined by genre, era or sentiment. Much of the listening of her subjects was ordered by the forms of their relationship with others, including children, lovers or friends. Listening often followed patterns of common listening as a basis for conversation, or as the result of reciprocal activities like tape-swapping. The most prominent factors in listening, she found, were in the affective meanings that music took on in different situations. These meanings were complex and could easily include the lyrics of a song, but also the way that the sound was used to link to 'intangible and non-visible or non-speakable aspects of the world: to feelings, moods, connections through time and space, and fantasy and imagination' (Tacchi 1998, 5). DeNora's more sociological investigation explores the empirical relationship of music to the everyday. That is to say, she seeks to understand how music consumption is ordinary and found in almost all corners of our lives.

The echoes of Grossberg's more theorised work on the 'the domain of affect' (discussed in Chapter 10) is quite striking in both Tacchi and DeNora's work, even though the latter two work up to a theory from their research. All three, though, are working with a notion that Michael Bull has termed 'an aestheticisation of urban life' (Bull 2000): a process by which we deal with the experiences of everyday life by turning them into one mediated through our use of music. It is work like this that suggests music listening is a far more complex practice than that outlined by Adorno or Riesman. At the micro level, listening is infused with patterns of consumption that relate to the shifting routines of our daily lives, and the developing relationships and their associated emotional states. Of course, these micro aspects of music listening do not exclude the wider patterns and the social and political implications of listening suggested by Adorno and Riesman, but they show that a fuller understanding of listening has to work at number of different levels. However, David Hesmondhalgh has pointed to a lack of 'engagement with issues of value, meaning and taste in music' in studies like these (Hesmondhalgh 2002, 124). What is lost in the examination of specific experiences of music, is the wider networks of music that bind us as groups, and which the theories of culture and subculture attempted to theorise.

12.1 Listening to music takes place in so many contexts it is possible to understand each as a different way of listening
Photo: Stefan Klenke

Ethnography does provide us with the potential to reframe how we think about activities like music listening – what Willis has termed 'the possibility of being surprised' (Willis 1976, 141) – however, it is still not entirely free of the possibility of prejudgement. It is easy for us to make interpretations solely from our own position, rather than attempt to understand the cultural meanings given to activities by the participants. It is not that our own position is unimportant, rather we need to recognise that it is just that: a position; and one of no more importance for understanding than that of the participants involved in the cultural practices we are seeking to comprehend.

X 12.3   An interesting and straightforward way to investigate listening and the issue of interpretation is through an auto ethnography. This is an ethnography of your own listening activities. This would involve some form of basic survey activity. It is useful to work in terms of the different ways of listening signalled by Tacchi and DeNora, asking how your listening is organised around different media, variants of those media, and type of music. You can also see if it changes over time, and from place to place.

Ask yourself how far the patterns you identify would be similar to those of someone of a similar cultural position in terms of geography, age, class, gender, ethnicity and education. Judge the degree to which your listening is combined with other activities. Finally try to assess whether these differences of listening relate to your own sense of identity, to changing moods and feelings, and to different ways you relate to others.

Looking at pop

Popular music culture has always been about looking as well as listening. The experience of a performer is as dependent upon their visual image as their musical sound. Of course, the visuals of popular music have often been presented as an inferior part of the experience. It is no coincidence that much of the criticism of fandom as fanaticism focuses on the visual. Judy and Fred Vermorel's exploration of fandom and the critical reaction to it as a social phenomenon is presented through the juxtaposition of images of the objects of fandom and the media's presentation of the fans themselves (Vermorel and Vermorel 1989). Likewise, John Mundy's investigation of the continuities and discontinuities of the relationship between popular music and the various screen media of film, television and video over the last century indicates how vital the visual text has been in the formation and experience of popular music culture (Mundy 1999). There is also a range of excellent resources for studying a wider sense of visuals to be found in publications that draw together the imagery of performers (see Stewart 1981) or album covers (see Thorgerson and Powell 1999).

Equally, though, it is important to note that the role and function of the visual has changed throughout the history of popular music. The music halls, in which popular music was first established in the late nineteenth century, produced popular entertainment for the eyes as well as the ears. Later, music became a significant way in which film was experienced, from the way it supported early film, ushered in sound films, and was a key means of structuring the narratives of the classic Hollywood musical of the 1930s, 1940s and 1950s (Mundy 1999). It would also be reasonable to argue that it was cinema and TV, rather than radio or records, that first spread youth music like rock & roll in the 1950s. However, while visual media have always constituted important parts of the metatext of popular music, the primary means of distributing and experiencing popular music over the twentieth century were the radio and the record. The record certainly became the centre of the youth culture that became the dominant feature of popular music in the 1960s and 1970s. The pre-eminence of sound in the experiences of consuming music through radio and records made the development of music videos in the late 1970s and early 1980s a phenomenon that caught the imagination of many academics, and most studies of the visuals of popular music relate to the pop video and its associated form: music television. Jody Berland, for instance, argues that pop videos of the 1980s reunited the visual and aural of popular music, which had been largely separated because of the dominance of the record and radio after the 1920s (Berland 1993b).

Interestingly most of the analyses of the music videos have focused upon texts (rather than consumption), and have tended to privilege the visuals at the expense of the sound. Nevertheless they do have interesting things to say about the way pop is watched. E. Ann Kaplan's study of MTV (1987) as a postmodern phenomenon laid the foundation for most later debates about analysing pop videos. Underlying her approach are a series of assumptions that share some interesting commonality with those of Adorno. First, she understands the videos as merely adverts for songs, in the same way that Adorno felt that popular songs advertised themselves through their repeated hooks. Second, she assumes that the audience is positioned by five different narrative categories constructed by the visuals of the videos. Again this has some parallels with Adorno's idea that the romantic or rhythmic structure of songs positioned the listener (Kaplan 1987, 55; Adorno 1991, 33). Subsequent critiques highlight limitations in her analysis: the failure to treat videos as texts of popular music (rather than extensions of film), and her neglect of the songs themselves and their relationship to the visuals (see in particular Goodwin 1992). As far as it goes, her work has some very interesting things to say about visual narratives within pop videos, and their differences to other forms of narrative that have developed in cinema and television. Attempts to overcome the limitations of Kaplan's work by Goodwin, and later Negus (1996, 88–93) have added further insights about the textual structure of videos and their combinations of the visual and the aural. (This work was explored in greater depth in Chapter 8). However, the continued emphasis on the text in all these accounts either ignores the actual practices of looking at popular music, or implies a position for the consumer from the text.

Other work has attempted to provide an analogy to recast our understanding of the music video more clearly in the context of its consumption. Keith Roe's work with Lofgren on the way audiences actually watch music videos is most interesting in this regard. They suggest that the audiences they studied related to music videos as a sort of 'visual radio', with an associated set of consumption practices similar to those found with music radio (Roe and Lofgren 1988). By this, they mean the music is experienced as a form of secondary consumption combined with other activities in which the individual videos are part of a flow of visual and aural material. Of course, the analogy only works when we consider the videos screened on music television stations like MTV or VH1, in the context of some morning television shows aimed at children, or on chart rundown shows. Negus has argued that we should go further, and in a suggestive, but undeveloped, series of comments, he combines insights about the creative potential of video production with an awareness of the consumption contexts, to propose that videos are constructed and understood as a series of 'semiotic particles' (Negus 1996, 93–5). First, he notes that videos are consumed in a number of ways beyond the assumptions of the flow model of MTV video plays or the sharp-eyed deconstructions suggested by textual studies. As a secondary activity, in domestic or public places like bars, clubs or shops, music videos are consumed through the relatively poor quality of the television screen. Second, he suggests that video-makers have used their increasing understanding of music video, its role as a promotional tool for itself and the record it relates to, and the way videos are consumed to produce the equivalent of the lyrical hook. He defines these as 'repeated semiotic particles [which] combine music, image and words in [a] particular manner that allows for various accompanying activities' (Negus 1996, 94).

Ethnography is going to be the key methodology for studying looking. This could take the form of a small-scale initial study or a more developed inquiry for a dissertation. Choose a location like a domestic setting, a club or a bar, and observe how other people relate to the television screen and the music. How much awareness of these textual elements do they show? Does attention increase or decrease as the videos change or the social situations alter? Can you identify something in the videos that could be an example of Negus's repeated semiotic particles? If so, do these seem to relate to different levels of attention to the music and the visuals?

SUMMARY

Looking and listening to popular music have been the main ways in which theorists of popular music culture have thought about the consumption of popular music. Strangely, then, these activities have not been the subject of any developed analysis. There is, though, plenty of existing work to suggest ways that such a study could be produced, and the area certainly offers the potential for original and interesting research for students, even those relatively new to the field.

Looking and listening, though, remain quite limited ways of understanding the range of ways we consume popular music. As work like that of Bull (2000) and DeNora (2000) shows, music acts on our bodies, not just our minds, and we experience it as more than a process of perception. This is best exemplified by the role that music has in dancing, and the way that dancing fits with wider concerns about the role and cultural significance of music. This is the subject of Chapter 12.

Further reading

Hesmondhalgh, David 2002: 'Popular Music Audiences and Everyday Life', in D. Hesmondhalgh and K. Negus, *Popular Music Studies.* Arnold.

Goodwin, Andrew 1992: *Dancing in the Distraction Factory: Music Television and Popular Culture.* University of Minnesota Press.

CHAPTER THIRTEEN

Dancing

Given that clubbing is a major social activity for a large proportion of those under 25, dance records are a notable genre in the pop charts, and there is a prosperous dance music industry, it may come as a surprise to find out that scholarship has only recently reflected the role dancing has within music culture. This marginalisation can be seen in a simple piece of content analysis. Frith and Goodwin's (1990) anthology of 50 years of the major writing on popular music culture features only one article out of 35 on dancing, and the author of that 1979 article felt that he had to write 'in defence of disco' (Dyer 1979/1990). As late as the mid-1990s Sarah Thornton made a similar point:

> For many years, discotheques and dance music have been excluded from popular music's own canons. Rock criticism and much pop scholarship have tended to privilege 'listening' over dance musics, visibly performing musicians over behind-the-scenes producers, the rhetorically 'live' over the 'recorded' and hence guitars over synthesisers and samplers.
>
> (Thornton 1995, 1–2)

When approaching dancing as a form of music consumption and cultural practice, then, we need not only to investigate what dance means in its many social contexts, but how academics have approached its study, and why in many cases they have marginalised or ignored it completely. This chapter therefore first explores the politics of dancing in a series of cultural contexts at different points in history.

The politics of dancing

The politics of dancing? The physical pleasures of dancing seem to be so far away from politics that it may seem a strange study to embark on. When recording artists Re-flex used the phrase for the title of a record in 1983, and Paul van Dyk reused it in 2001, they were perhaps being ironic about the juxtaposition of the two ideas, but they were also indexing the increased focus within cultural studies on the political implications of our everyday practices and pleasures. Whether we dance (or do not dance), how, where, and to what music we dance, are all very meaningful acts within popular music culture. They relate to broader issues of class, nationality, ethnicity, gender and sexuality, and their politics have both a history and a contemporary resonance that we need to analyse and understand. It is often hard to immediately see the political significance of our own social lives, but some reflection on the historical position of dance in popular music culture reveals much about today's 'club cultures'.

The cultural practices of 'Saturday night' in the early 2000s, and the attitudes that go with them, can be traced back over the last century and beyond. Two ideas come quickly to the fore in this history: the importance of what it is to be 'modern'; and what it means to dance, or not to dance (for both are equally important and equally articulated). Behind these primary ideas are a more complex set of repertoires: cultural notions and practices that are drawn upon and articulated in each successive juke joint, nightclub, dance hall, go-go, disco, street corner, (ware)house, rave and club, or whatever we call the space we dance in. To demonstrate how the notion of 'the modern' and the meaning of dancing have operated it is useful to examine two historical moments: the one where dancing entered popular music culture, and the one where it became marginalised.

Dancing in New York in the 1920s

The Charleston-dancing 'flapper' is iconic of 'the jazz age' of 1920s New York (Fitzgerald 1922/2000). The so-called dance-crazy 1920s brought together the social dances of white Americans with the hot sounds of jazz, and the vernacular dances of African-Americans filtered through the racist caricatures of vaudeville music halls. At the turn of the twentieth century, the range of white American social dance represented the mixture of European folk dances and the more recent military and waltz dances of 'polite society'. By contrast, African-American dance forms had been forged out of the oppression of slavery, which forbade African dance and music, and while based upon European forms subtly parodied their enslavers. These 'cake walks' became a central part of the minstrel shows that entertained white Americans with a stereotyped view of black culture and commodified popular dance. Outside the music hall, African-American dance forms evolved into a range of fast, frenetic participation dances, and these became the raw material for the 'new' and 'modern' dances adopted by young white Americans and then popularised by Irene and Vernon Castle (Thorpe 1990; Sanjek 1996, 25–30). For their white audiences, the Castles' interpretation of the steps and postures of the African-American dances balanced the exoticism of black dance with a veneer of European-derived, class-based 'sophistication', and an American idea of democracy, and Irene came to represent a new sort of woman: liberated, vibrant and, most of all, modern.

The dance craze was quickly commodified in new Tin Pan Alley songs, and the recording of black-styled music (Shaw 1987). Dance became a key style of commercial music and the new recordings allowed white listeners to hear 'hot' playing – a style of instrumental virtuosity nurtured predominantly in New Orleans – which was then incorporated into the New York dance bands (Stearns 1970). These elements were distilled with prohibition drinking into the mythology of the urban nightclub portrayed in the gangster film. The most famous of all was the Cotton Club in New York where Duke Ellington's 'jungle music' was the soundtrack to affluent whites 'slumming it' in black Harlem (Tucker 1993). Ellington, as musician, songwriter and band leader, remade Irene and Vernon Castle's fusion of black 'primitivism', European 'sophistication' and American 'democracy' from the perspective of an African-American. So successful was he in articulating a moment of modern America that the Ellington band's nightly performances were almost the only black music heard on radio at that time (Barlow 1995). However, just as Ellington was personifying the dance craze within mainstream American culture he was also becoming the symbol for a new way of thinking about popular music and dancing.

X 13.1 This new way of thinking about a popular musician can be found in a contemporary account of one of Ellington's Cotton Club appearances written by the English band leader and critic Spike Hughes. Read through the account below and then, using the questions that follow it, try to identify the different ideas of Ellington the writer criticises and celebrates.

> Most of the time was taken up by a very professional floorshow which is, I suppose, three times too long ... I was more than infuriated at having to pay an immense sum for the privilege of hearing Duke play chords of G, to introduce the spotlight celebrities that were present ... And the Cotton Club is New York's conception of Harlem! A place where no negroes are admitted ... Why they do not move the club ... I cannot imagine. On the other hand, the unimaginative American businessman and his peroxide stenographer might not have felt they were being 'wicked'.
>
> What most outrages me is that Duke Ellington is playing at the Cotton Club ... The Ellington band is all, and more, than I expected. Each individual member of the orchestra is completely and utterly a mouthpiece for Duke's own ideas. There is not a note that comes from that remarkable brass section, or from the rich tone of the saxes, that is not directly an expression of Duke's genius ... Even when an Ellington radio programme includes one or two of the more trashy current popular songs, these are treated with so much contempt as to be most pleasantly unrecognisable.
>
> (Hughes 1993, 69–70)

What is Hughes' attitude to the floorshow and Ellington's role? How does Hughes understand the band's performance? How prominent is participatory dancing within the account?

Not Dancing in London and Paris in the 1950s

Duke Ellington and Spike Hughes are centrally important in understanding the change from hot dance music, which dominated dance culture up to the late 1940s, to a new attitude that became established in Europe in the 1950s. Ellington was caught in a paradox of popular music. On the one hand he aspired to create music that would be accepted as the equal of European music, rejected the term jazz (associating it with 'primitive'), and was enthralled with the European upper classes – he named his band the Orchestra, performed in full evening dress, appointed himself a duke, and composed symphonies. Yet at the same time he played 'jungle music' at the Cotton Club for stage dancers in grass skirts, and employed 'hot players' to make the sounds of wild animals. Hughes' writing is an attempt to resolve this paradox, and he became highly influential in the way jazz was perceived in Britain (Godbolt 1986). While European critics of the 1920s and 1930s tended to dismiss Ellington's music for its African-American 'primitiveness' or American 'commerciality', Hughes championed its sophistication, and argued that such music had rhythmic subtlety and improvisation (Frith 1988d, 56).

European intellectuals, like the African-Americans of the Harlem renaissance (Floyd 1990; Vincent 1995) increasingly distinguished jazz from 'commercial' dance band music, and black musicians were venerated for their musical 'genius', 'modernity' and 'authenticity', separating them from the entertainment context in which they worked. Hot jazz became associated with a commercial and cultural exploitation, and street-smart and intellectual African-Americans alike increasingly took a more reticent disposition, to become 'cool' and 'hep'. The 'hep' of black culture was translated to the 'hip' of white American and European intellectuals, who found in this new black discourse a revolutionary alternative to western culture (Ross 1989). At the centre of hip culture were the jazz records that were listened to in British 'rhythm clubs' or French 'discotheques' (Godbolt 1986; Gourse 2000). Jazz became strongly associated with art-school students, who interpreted it through an aesthetic that derived from the European art tradition. These self-styled 'beatniks' followed musicians who experimented (rather than entertained), who played solo (rather than as part of the ensemble), who played for listening (rather than dancing) (Frith 1987, 71–9; Frith 1988d; Godbolt 1989). Some fans looked backwards from Ellington to the 'authentic' roots of hot playing, while a younger generation turned to the bebop music of young New York players. Bebop was an onomatopoeiac description of the short riffs of sound favoured by the soloists of this small-group jazz. The iconic figure of bebop was Charlie Parker, whose playing and life teetered on the edge of disaster, and who symbolised and mythologised the jazz life for hip fans (Priestley 1984; Townsend 2000). For Francis Newton,

> the quintessential location of the fan is not the dance hall, the night club, or even the jazz concert or club, but the private room in which a group of young men play one another records, repeating crucial passages until they are worn out, and then endlessly discussing their comparative merits.

(Newton 1961, 224)

In the 1960s hip-ness became hippie-ness, but the ideas remained broadly the same even though the musical object now shifted from jazz via blues – celebrated as authentic and free of commercial taint – to rock and folk. Such ideas coalesced in the ideas of the youth counter-culture, FM radio and the concept LP (see Garofalo 1997, 217–38; Keith 1997). These ideas and cultural practices became the basis for the division between 'serious' popular music on the one hand and dance music on the other, which dominated popular music culture until the mid-1980s: there was no dancing if you were hip.

X 13.2 These ideas are still used today by people in their everyday talk about popular music, and by journalists and commentators when they write about music. Start a collection of comments or arguments that you feel show a similar set of ideas as the ones we have termed the idea of 'hot' and the idea of 'cool/hip'. Are these ideas associated with dancing or dance music? If they were we might find dance records being dismissed as commercial or uninteresting musically, or non-dance records being praised for the skill of the musicians. You might ask yourself how often musical skill is associated with dance music-makers. How important are concepts of emotional involvement or transcendence associated with dancing and dance music, and how often with other musics? How important is the idea of diffidence or detachment associated with different types of music-making or consumption?

These two historical moments – one when dancing became dominant and one when not dancing took this cultural role – indicate how the practices of dancing and listening are polarised in the discourse of popular music culture. Judith Hanna has traced the ways that, through the eighteenth and nineteenth centuries, listening and associated musical forms became increasingly associated with masculinity, and dancing with the feminine, spectacle and entertainment (Hanna 1988). Simon Reynolds has suggested a similar polarisation can be found in the binary opposition of handbag with techno, ambient and electronica (Reynolds 1998, 85). Dancing is not simply an innocent pleasure, then, but a cultural practice that becomes bound up with significant political issues, and we could expect that this would also be the case within contemporary social dancing as well. It is to the specifics of the contemporary dancefloor that we now need to turn.

The modern dancefloor

It was because most popular music scholarship up to the 1990s grew out of the rock sensibility, that dancing was relegated to a lower form of culture than that of listening, and that very little was written on social dance within popular music culture. However, in the last few years it has become a major area for research and comment. This does mean that there is now quite a range of secondary sources we can use to develop our thinking and as a basis for the study of dancing. There is a problem, though, because these existing accounts are characterised by two qualities that limit their usefulness. First, most of this work tends to see contemporary dance music as a startlingly new phenomenon (for instance, Toynbee 2000, 131–3). This notion of a disruption is also to be found in the narrative used to discuss post-1980s dance culture in Britain: started in Chicago; culture of drug-assisted transcendence of the mundane; subsequently splintering into a multitude of genres and subcultures (for instance, Gore 1997, 56–61; Reynolds 1998). However, recent histories of dancing suggest that there are continuities as well as disruptions in the development of the practices of dance in popular music culture. For instance, what is so striking about reading Brewster and Broughton's (1999) study of the history of 1970s disco is how, with some substitution of names, places and dates, it could easily be the story of house, which they outline in later pages. Second, there is almost nothing in these accounts about dancing! There are significant discussions of the production and textual qualities of dance music records (which are covered in earlier chapters of this book) and some very interesting ideas about the social contexts of music cultures based upon dancing, but hardly anything about the practices of dancing. Partly this is likely to be a reflection of the difficulty of creating verbal descriptions of an activity that seems to be so non-verbal. Andrew Ward has taken this point a step further and suggests that part of the problem is that while academic study is perceived to be a rational pursuit, dancing has historically been seen as non-rational (Ward 1997, 8; see also Gilbert and Pearson 1999, 38–53).

The good news (again) is that this leaves the field open for original studies that you could undertake. To do so you need to combine the information from recent scholarship with the insights developed from the study of the historically located senses of cultural identity and modernity that relate to practices of dancing/not dancing. Accounts of contemporary dance culture have raised issues about three interconnected areas: the physical experience and meaning of dancing; the way that the dancefloor operates as a cultural space in which certain senses of identity are forged; and finally the way that dancefloors are organised around the playing of records.

The Experience and Meaning of Dancing

Andrew Ward has argued for an approach to understanding dancing as an 'embodied' experience with inherent meaning, and so emphasises the practices of dancing, rather than the structure of dances as non-verbal messages, and the experience of dancers rather than the readings of non-dancers (Ward 1997, 17). In similar fashion, Paul Willis presents dancing as

> the principal way in which musical pleasures become realized in physical movement and grounded aesthetics. The sensual appeal of popular music is at its greatest in dance music, where its direct courting of sexuality generates a heightened sense of self and body.

(Willis 1990, 66)

The importance of dancing as sexual experience was previously proposed by Richard Dyer, who argued that 1970s disco was characterised by a whole-body eroticism that distinguished it from rock's thrusting, grinding, phallic focus (Dyer 1979/1990, 152–4). For Gilbert and Pearson, the experience of dancing is linked to the way we 'feel' music as sound that vibrates through the body (Gilbert and Pearson 1999, 44–7).

They tend to view dancing as an exemplar case of the *jouissance* pleasures of music, which, along with other writers (notably Gill 1995; Reynolds 1998), and following Roland Barthes, they define as rapture, bliss or transcendence. In this context they understand the experience of dance to be

> organised around the pursuit of a certain kind of ecstasy: waves of undifferentiated physical and emotional pleasure; a sense of immersion in a communal moment, wherein the parameters of one's individuality are broken down by the shared throbbing of the bass drum; an acute experience of music in all its sensuality – its shimmering arpeggios, soaring string-washes, abrasive squelches, crackles and pops; an incessant movement forward, in all directions, nowhere; the bodily irresistibility of funk; the inspirational smiles of strangers, the awesome familiarity of friends; the child-like feeling of perfect safety at the edge of oblivion; a delicious surrender to cliché.

> (Gilbert and Pearson 1999, 64)

However, we need to be aware that this ecstatic moment is located in a drug-altered perception of music and social relations, not primarily in the physicality of dancing. Drugs have a long association with popular music (see Shapiro 1999) and particularly with recent dance cultures, but it is not possible to generalise about the relationship of drugs to dance and music. The mods and soul dancers of the 1970s took amphetamines ('speed') to sustain their dancing, but the primary focus was (and still remains) the ritualised dancing styles and interest in small-label soul records (Cosgrove 1982; Milestone 1997; Brewster and Broughton 1999, 83–116). By contrast, LSD ('acid') trips were central to the 1960s hippie happenings in which the experimental nature of the music was far more important than the lightly coded 'freaking out' of freeform dancing (Gore 1997; Brewster and Broughton 1999, 72–9). Reynolds suggests that contemporary dance music forms are created to enhance the intransitive and asexual experience (Reynolds 1998, 86–90) produced by MDMA/Ecstasy, which combines the properties of amphetamines with psychedelic drugs and a 'loved-up' feeling of its own (Saunders 1995). Further, Reynolds also explains the changing and splintering of dance music as mainly the result of the declining efficacy of Ecstasy in clubs and the use of other drugs. So he contrasts Ecstasy-orientated house music – 'song-full, hands-in-the-air' – with techno, ambient and electronica – rave without its 'raveyness, to fit a white studenty sensibility' – and cocaine and marijuana-orientated jungle – 'masked self-containment and controlled dance moves, that shed rave's abandonment and demonstrativeness' (Reynolds 1998, 85).

While these accounts provide us with many useful ideas about the way dancing relates to music and cultural meaning, and the important role of drugs within dance cultures, they only give fleeting glimpses of how we dance. More useful here is Ben Malbon's formulation of dancing as 'a conceptual language with intrinsic and extrinsic meanings, premised upon physical movement, and with interrelated rules and notions of technique and competency guiding performance across and within different situations' (Malbon 1999, 86). This approach allows us to extend our study beyond Ward's concern with the experience of dancers, and the primacy given to the politics of sound in Gilbert and Pearson's work, and avoids Reynolds' tendency to see music, drugs and culture as determinants of dancing. Malbon's focus on different senses of space within the practices of dance is particularly enlightening. He outlines a number of factors to examine including: the physical geography of the club; the environment created by the music that is played, the lights and other effects, and the density of the crowd; the competency of the dancers, their spacing and orientation; and the emotional spacings (what it feels like) produced by the others (Malbon 1999, 90–101). This is an excellent checklist for ethnographies of dancing, but needs extending to include how dancing relates to cultural identity and to the manipulation of records.

FIGURE 13.1 Dancing is one of the main ways that music is embodied as a sensual experience
Photo: Pru Fiddy

The Dancefloor and Cultural Identity

This second area for investigation of the practices of the modern dancefloor is concerned with the dancefloor itself as a physical and cultural space. Dancing has often been interpreted as a form of cultural democracy through which you could 'find yourself'. There are number of interesting articles and books that investigate how the space of the dancefloor has been used to assert black, feminised and gay identities. Particularly interesting in this regard is Paul Gilroy's notion of the dancefloor as a cultural space where the usual hierarchies of society are inverted, and where competences in dance are more important than skills that prevail outside (Gilroy 1991). He assigns a central role to dancing in the development of a black British identity and affiliated identities for white working-class men and women. Gilroy argues that while white men initially reacted negatively to these assertions of a new identity for black migrants and the white women who danced with them, the music and dance forms of black Britons were quickly absorbed into the cultures of white working-class men. The 1970s alone saw the adoption of Jamaican reggae by white skinheads (Chambers 1985, 161–4), the rare soul scene (Hollows and Milestone 1998) and white rastas (Jones 1988).

Now that dancing has such a key part to play in contemporary popular music culture, it is hard to appreciate how marginalised dancing was up until the late 1970s. Although a number of records crossed over into the pop charts, a separate set of institutions catered for the small market for soul, funk and reggae in the UK, and in America these were seen as specialist musics for a black market. There was a mainstream of dancing in popular music culture before 1985, and the disco phenomena of the late 1970s thrust dance music forcibly into discussions of popular music, but dancing was most often portrayed negatively as a feminised (or demasculinised) activity associated with women and heterosexual courtship rituals, or homosexual display. There are examples of academic work that attempts to offer more sophisticated readings of dance culture. Angela McRobbie's discussion of the role of dancing for women in the late 1970s and 1980s constructs the dancefloor as a positive arena for escape, where fantasy was set against the need to maintain respectability and avoid the dangers for women out at night (McRobbie 1984). Northern soul has remained one of the most intriguing underground scenes, and it has been argued that it can be understood as the assertion of a 'northern' working-class identity and a refusal of the south's claim to legitimacy and distinction (Hollows and Milestone 1998).

Identity has become the central theme of recent analyses of 1970s disco. In the USA, before the middle of the decade, different ethnic communities had quite distinct musical and dance cultures, although cross-fertilisations were increasingly taking place. Dancing had remained an important part of black and Hispanic cultures, and the fusion of soul with rock in funk, the evolution of studio soul into the Philadelphia (Philly) sound, and the development of a mixture of Latin musics into salsa, resulted in a profusion of dance records, which were increasingly played in discos across America, Europe and beyond (Cummings 1975; Boggs 1992; Vincent 1996). In the late 1970s the dancefloor became an important space for the increasingly assertive identity of gay culture in the USA (Brewster and Broughton 1999, 135–80). The combinations of highly rhythmic musics, assertive cultural identities and non-stop partying were the primary ingredients of the disco boom of the 1970s. What we now call disco was the result of a series of transformations: first, a modernised term for a dance hall, which made the nightclub mainstream; second, the cross-fertilisation of funk, Philly and salsa into a dance music genre, and a blurring of the boundaries between their respective different musical scenes, largely through the cross-ethnicity of the gay community; and, finally, the perception by the record industry that this was a new market for records. Dancing had finally come out of the margins allocated to it by rock ideology and the practices of the record industry. However, although dance records now became economically significant, the rock view that 'Disco sucks!' prevailed.

Most histories of contemporary club culture place a significant emphasis on Chicago and Detroit (and sometimes New York) in the 1980s (see Reynolds 1998; Rietveld 1998; Sicko 1999). Records from these scenes were clearly important in the foundation of the British house scene, and the analyses of these scenes portray a rich musical influence and the importance of gay, black, or/and Hispanic identities. However, because the dance scene in Britain is perceived to be a significant departure from previous music cultures, there is a danger of reducing the diversity of recorded music played in the 1980s club scene to imported Chicago records, the production of dance records to the influence of a small number of DJs and producers, and the subcultural alternativeness of the British scene to the black or gay origins of these musics (see Hesmondhalgh 1997b). Likewise, Sarah Thornton has shown how the ideology of clubbers often constructs a suitably postmodern sense of their scene as a polyglot of difference set against the monoglot of the mainstream, while even the most basic study of different club nights will show that most attract different cultural groups along lines of sexuality, gender, ethnicity and class (Thornton 1995). In relation to this, Will Straw's observation that 'discussions of dance are often able to privilege its engrossing qualities through an implicit sliding from the subjectivity and corporal sense of release to a notion of collective transcendence' (Straw 1997a, 500) is apposite.

Equally striking has been the attempt to attach spiritual significance to dancing. Georgiana Gore has used the analogy of tribes, deity worship and shaman priests to discuss trance (Gore 1997). While this imagery is itself drawn from the language of the subculture (and originally from anthropology) we should be very cautious about using these ideas as a means to understand the subculture, as superficial similarities do not constitute sharp analysis (see Hesmondhalgh 1997b, 177). However, such arguments do make us aware of the close relationship of some parts of the discourse of contemporary dance culture to the ideas of the hippie movement of the 1960s. Key moments and practices in club cultures have often been expressed in terms that parallel the 1960s counter-culture – 'the summer of love', 'festivals', 'happenings', 'acid' – and certainly trance clubs and events have drawn heavily upon hippie mysticism for their atmosphere.

However, the meanings and practices of dance in the twenty-first century are significantly different from those of the 1960s. The imagery of trance is, of course, just that: imagery. The actual discursive practices have significantly shifted. On the other hand other dance subcultures offer up a discourse of futurology and stark modernism. Jason Toynbee, for instance, has mapped out the argument that the manipulations of recorded sound, the importance of the DJ, and innovative forms of music-making produce a significantly new music culture. In fact, there is stronger evidence to the contrary. Recorded music and dancing have a central, but marginalised, place in popular music culture that continues to today. What has changed is the dominant discourse about the link between recorded music, dancing and cultural value. This constitutes the third set of issues, to which we must now turn.

Manipulating Records and the Dancefloor

Records have always had a connection to dancing and to alternative cultural identities. In the USA the 'bright young things' of the jazz age danced to records at private parties, coin-operated record players provided inexpensive music in clubs and bars from the 1930s (these jukeboxes derived their name from the African-American 'juke joint' clubs), and by the 1950s record hops allowed young white Americans and Europeans to dance to black music (Thornton 1990). In Europe, record clubs established to listen to jazz in the 1950s were adapted in the 1960s for dancing to more contemporary R&B, then soul and ska music, and became particularly associated with the mod movement. In turn, these sorts of spaces became the soul and funk clubs of the 1970s (Chambers 1985, 69–75). Such spaces were increasingly described using the French term 'discotheque' (Thornton 1990, 89–90). In the late 1960s the new discotheques became increasingly allied with the nightclub tradition and with elitist door policies and clientele from the creative industries, while in contrast lunchtime record sessions at the local dance halls remained the preserve of working-class dancers (Melly 1970). At the same time, in the USA, the west coast 'acid tests' – which combined psychedelic rock with state-of-the-art audio and lighting equipment, drug-taking and freeform dancing – spread first to the east coast and then over to Europe (Brewster and Broughton 1999, 72–9).

The rise of the DJ as a key player within contemporary popular music has been widely noted in scholarship, but it remains a complex area. Many contemporary DJ practices have been inherited from previous generations, while others are radical departures. The term disc jockey was first coined to describe the presenter in black American radio after the Second World War (Barlow 1999), and between the 1950s and 1970s the term transferred from the radio to the dancefloor, and DJs turned their attention to using records to keep the floor full of dancers. Ideas of music programming were also adapted from radio, and subsequently the manipulation of the records themselves became a key skill of the DJ. The qualities now associated with contemporary dance DJs have their origins in a diverse range of disc cultures from the Jamaican reggae sound system, the set-ups of the hippie US west coast, the Hispanic and black clubs of eastern US cities, the British rare soul scene and the hip-hop street culture of New York (Brewster and Broughton 1999). Ways of manipulating records on the turntable and producing records for dance parties or clubs spread through migration within the USA, and from the Caribbean to the USA and the UK. Hip-hop, US house and subsequent European dance scenes illustrate the integration of these DJ and production techniques into distinct dance genres.

Although there are many references to the way that DJs select, mix and manipulate records in order to create a particular atmosphere and a changing dance environment, there are no detailed studies of what is done and with what effect and affect. Tony Langlois identified 1980s Chicago as the place that records started being synchronised to produce a continuous flow of music (Langlois 1992), but as Brewster and Broughton more accurately show, this was a technique with a much longer tradition in disco and hip-hop. Central to both these traditions was 'the break', the extended bridges in the song structure, often highlighting percussion, or novel instrumental hooks. To lengthen the few short bars of music on the 7-inch single DJs used the two-deck segue technique they had developed to move from one record to another to repeat the break two or more times. These techniques were aided by the introduction of DJ-only 12-inch singles, which had greater inter-groove spacing, direct-drive turntables with speed manipulation, and rhythm boxes used to keep the beat while the DJ manipulated other sonic properties of the record. These live club techniques were carried over to DJ mix tapes, club-only acetate records and, ultimately, to commercially available discs.

Langlois suggests that we can understand DJing as a musical practice with limits set by technology, aesthetic expectations and performance, but that have led to a change in music aesthetics (Langlois 1992, 235–7). It is certainly the case that modes of dancing in contemporary clubs are distinctly different from those you would have found at other points in dance culture's history. This is obviously related to the music created for dancing, with its characteristic lack of a traditional song structure and musical resolution, which Langlois argues leads to a temporal distortion overlaid with random snatches of sampled sound. What is missing in such accounts of club cultures is the way that different genres organise DJ performance and dancing in different ways. The difference between, say, house and jungle is not simply a sonic one, or to do with the differences of musical form, or production technology or music-making techniques, although all these are distinct; it is in the sensibilities that are created in different clubs.

The contemporary dancefloor and its reliance on DJ manipulations of records is part of a wider and long-term shift in the way records are understood within popular music culture. Thornton has argued that the playing of records, the greater validity given to dancing, and the increasingly important role of the DJ are all part of a process through which the record has become 'encultured'. That is, records are no longer understood as mere artefacts carrying music (and poor records of the authentic live activity of music performance), but as 'authentic' texts of contemporary culture. By this, she means that records have a status of meaning in themselves. This is particularly apparent in the way that vinyl records are considered more authentic within the dance scene than CDs or MP3 files. This is an important shift in sensibility that has ultimately displaced the dominance of rock ideology in music journalism and scholarship (Thornton 1990).

These observations should lead us to a set of conclusions about contemporary dancing that differ from those usually drawn. There have clearly been some shifts in dancing and DJ techniques since the 1980s, but there are far more continuities of practice. The major shift brought about by rave culture is to be found in the way that *thinking* about record-based dancing as an authentic cultural experience has become the dominant discourse of contemporary popular music culture. This discourse gives an important role to the forms of pleasures and identity-affirming cultural practices that are to be found in dance music.

There is clearly a need for some basic research into dancing in all its contemporary manifestations. Even single analyses of dancing in a single club will provide some interesting insights. A combination of ethnographic observation and auto-ethnographic reporting would be useful techniques to examine the physical experience, special dimensions of dancing, and their relationship to the way that DJs use records over a single set and the longer night. Interviews would provide a useful way to examine meanings and senses of cultural identity related to that club night. A larger project, perhaps using research from a number of students, would make for interesting comparisons.

SUMMARY

Dancing has always been a central part of popular music culture, but until recently it has been neglected in the scholarship. This is because dancing (or not dancing) has always been an act with political significance. This chapter has shown how the ideas of 'hot' and 'cool' developed within popular music culture and became part of a discourse on dancing that related to ideas of masculinity and femininity, modernity, class and ethnicity. These discursive positions have had significant implications for the way we experience and understand dancing, the way dancing and the cultural space of the dancefloor is linked to cultural identity, and the role that recorded music has had within these practices. The role of dancing within popular culture has shifted over time, as has the way that it is understood. Today it remains one of the most important ways in which we consume popular music.

Further reading

Langlois, Tony 1992: 'Can You Feel It? DJs and House Music Culture in the UK', in *Popular Music* 11(2).

Thornton, Sarah 1995: *Club Cultures: Music, Media and Subcultural Capital.* Polity Press.

Ward, Andrew 1997: 'Dancing around Meaning (and the Meaning around Dance)', in H. Thomas, *Dance in the City.* St Martin's Press.

CHAPTER FOURTEEN

Consuming Records

Although we consume popular music through a wide range of media – listening on radio, watching on video, television and film, swapping tapes with friends, downloading MP3 files, dancing at clubs and attending concerts – the primary text of popular music remains the recording. Records are also the central commodities of the music industry, where most other activities are thought of as promotional tactics for selling records. The importance of the CD as a commodity can be seen from the response of the industry to the Napster MP3 file-sharing system that was operating in the late 1990s. For the record industry, file-sharing attacked the central economics of its production and distribution system (see the case study in Chapter 15). When we buy a record we gain access to a text of popular music, but we also exchange money for a commodity. Nevertheless there is more to consuming records that simply a financial exchange. The experience of buying the commodity is a meaningful one for audiences, and we not only make choices about what record format and what genre of music we will acquire, we also make decisions about where we will get it. Once we own music we do more than listen to it, and collecting records is also a prominent part of music consumer culture. This chapter looks at each of these areas of consumption, outlining how we could study what we buy, how retailing attempts to order that consumption, and how and why we order our own collecting.

Buying records

Over the century the 'record' has taken various artefactual forms starting with metal or wax cylinders, then shellac 10-inch disks, vinyl 7-inch and 12-inch discs, cassettes and open reel tapes, CDs and mini discs and, most recently, MP3 files. It is interesting to see how the popularity of these formats has changed over time along with the changing patterns of consumption by music genre. An examination of changing buying habits also reveals major shifts in who buys records. Here we will examine some basic statistics of record consumption, and draw some basic conclusions before looking at the record shop and alternative channels of record consumption.

Changing Patterns of Artefact Sales

All the main record markets of the world – the USA, Europe and Japan – have seen a similar pattern of sales. We can see this pattern quite clearly in the trade delivery statistics for the UK. The term 'trade deliveries' merely indicates that these are statistics issued by record companies of the records they have sent out for sale, rather than statistics from retail outlets. Most notable is that while album sales have more than doubled since 1973, sales of singles have fluctuated around the same level, with two peaks in the late 1970s and 1990s. Over the same period, vinyl LPs have declined steadily up to 1988 from whence they collapsed with an almost 50 per cent annual fall in sales recorded in successive years of the late 1980s and early 1990s. Declining vinyl sales in the 1980s were matched by the increasing prominence of the cassette, which was the main medium for album sales after 1985, until CD sales grew and by 1992 the format had taken over as the primary medium for purchasing recorded music. From that point onwards, both vinyl and cassette formats declined as CD sales rose.

This pattern suggests that the new formats of first cassette and then CD were seen as more convenient, and possibly in the case of the CD more desirable. In the 1980s and early 1990s cassettes retailed for a similar price as vinyl LPs while CDs had a premium of up to 50 per cent on their price. The increase in sales of the CD format was also paralleled by a massive increase in catalogue material. Record companies increasingly saw that the establishment of the CD stimulated sales of older material – first, as some buyers replaced vinyl copies of records with CD versions, and then thanks to a general interest in older material. A general rise in the number of compilation albums released in the 1990s was stimulated by CD sales, and a number of small record labels increasingly looked to exploit the master tape banks of long defunct record companies which had back catalogues of genre-specific music now in demand. As we saw in Chapter 5 the rights to produce music for record release now became important properties in themselves. The availability of recorded music over the internet as MP3 files has posed a challenge to the whole organisation of record consumption. The significance of these changes is likely to be as profound as the original development of recorded sound, although like that invention will take some time to become fully apparent. The challenge of internet technologies is the subject of a case study in Chapter 15, but there are some interesting shifts in recent consumption that can be used to inform these debates.

Changing Patterns of Genre Form

There have also been quite dramatic changes in the sales of recordings by genre. This is possibly most dramatic in the USA where genre markets are the strongest. An interesting study of the record-buying habits of US buyers gives some indication of these changes (RIAA 2000). The survey suggests that the proportion of record sales in the rock category declined over a ten-year period to the end of the 1990s when it made up 25 per cent of records sold. A similar, if less dramatic, decline is apparent in sales of music categorised by its purchasers as pop, which fell to 10 per cent or less during the decade. Country music rose steadily before reaching a plateau at about 14 per cent of records sold. Black-influenced forms fluctuated, but showed a general pattern of growth, with joint figures for rap/hip-hop and R&B/urban consistently exceeding 20 per cent. Religious music increased dramatically, but along with other genres like jazz, soundtracks and oldies, it remained a small percentage of the overall market.

These shifts in rock's dominance as a genre of record sales in the USA seem to support those academics who have argued that the ideology of rock has similarly lost its hegemonic position within popular music culture. Equally, those musics associated with contemporary African-American forms like rap and dance genres now attract about 20 per cent of record sales, double that of country or pop and not far off rock sales with a quarter of the market.

Changing Patterns of Who Buys and Where

The same RIAA survey also suggests some interesting changes in who was buying records. Over the decade, buyers in the 45+ age group moved from one of the smallest groupings to become the largest, accounting for nearly 25 per cent of music sales in 1999. That dramatic change should not, however, distract us from the observation that this is much the same proportion as teenagers and young adults, although these categories do show a decline from about 35 per cent to just over 25 per cent in the decade. In part this can be explained in the changing demographics of American society, where those adults who were born in the baby boom of the mid-1950s to the mid-1960s are now in their forties and fifties. So although, as we have seen from other parts of our audience study, popular music culture is still heavily associated with youth, increasingly – for sales of records at least – popular music should be associated with a much wider age range than that suggested by scholarship.

The distribution of sales by format suggested by the US survey follows exactly the same pattern shown by the British trade statistics (BPI 2003). What the British statistics do show, though, is dramatic changes in where records are bought. Over the ten-year period, shoppers switched from traditional record shops (whose share of sales fell from nearly 70 per cent to less that 45 per cent) to general stores (whose share rose from nearly 19 per cent to just over 38 per cent) and the internet (which came from virtually no sales to a small but significant 2.5 per cent in 1999).

Buying records in record shops

The way we buy records is another area that is relatively unresearched by academics. The record retail industry produces a large number of surveys and this market research has been used as the basis of many of the changes in record retailing that have taken place in the last 30 years. However, this work is largely unpublished. We only have two main pieces of writing to build on when we study record buying as a form of consumption, and these both focus on the changes in the structure and philosophy of the retail sector, rather than the practices of record buyers. They do, however, give us a useful basis for such research.

In overviews of record retailing, both Straw (1997b) and du Gay and Negus (1994) have signalled the increasingly plural market for records. They identify a number of trends including: the increased prominence of casual buyers; the decline in the importance of sales charts and radio as a determinant of purchasing; the growth in back catalogue; the segmenting of music within broad genres; and the higher age of buyers, which has led to changing buyer behaviour and the restructuring of the retail environment. The statistical surveys we have already looked at indicated that sales by specialist retailers are in decline and that more people are now buying records from general merchandisers like supermarkets or high-street stores, examples of which would include WH Smith or Woolworths. Changes have been just as dramatic within specialist record retailing where small independent shops have slowly diminished, and multiples and megastores like Virgin, HMV and Tower have replaced them. These larger outlets have also expanded their activities beyond records to general entertainment media like games and DVDs.

Straw has indicated how in recent decades record retailers have attempted to encourage new consumers into shops whom they hoped would buy in a fashion ordered more by the shop, rather than by external motivations. Reissues, classical and easy listening genres have been particularly targeted at these markets. He suggests that this has been accompanied by a redesign of record shops to cater for this new market – which, it is felt, is often put off by record shops' usual organisation – without alienating the traditional record buyer. Du Gay and Negus have suggested we should view the organisation of the record shop as an attempt to create a particular 'reality' around taste formations/genre categories associated with different lifestyles, and set this against the actual behaviour of record buyers (1994, 405–10). The reality is created by the way 'a commercial cultural geography is inscribed in shops' (1994, 405) including high-volume sellers at the entrance, separate – often partitioned – sections for music like classical, jazz and country/folk/world music, and general closer groupings of rock/pop/soul. Considerable attention is played to environment, with thought given to the spacing of racks to allow selection and movement, and height to avoid bending over. An emphasis is placed upon giving buyers information to guide purchases, including listening posts, recommended purchases, special offers and in-house magazines. These shops now increasingly present themselves as a cultural experience in themselves, featuring cybercafés, a full range of entertainment software, and secondary merchandise like blank tapes, T-shirts, videos and DVDs; this is sometimes extended to include music, video and games hardware.

Changes to the categories in which records are ordered within the shop certainly affect how we perceive that music. My local record shop recently reordered its stock, separating out its pop section, the rump of which was integrated with rock. A new easy listening category was created to sit next to the classical and jazz sections, which had previously been separated out at the back of the shop, and these three sections were placed after the chart and special offer sections near the entrance. Part of the soul section was relabelled 'classic soul' and the remaining recent dance records were integrated with the hip-hop sections to form a new 'urban' category. Reggae records were moved from their previous position next to the soul section to form a subsection of a reordered world music section, which was repositioned between the classical/jazz and easy listening sections and the rock and pop, classic soul and urban sections. I read this as an attempt to attract more mature customers by presenting a new series of interconnected sections of mellow 'adult' musics nearer the entrance, and to reorganise the rear of the shop around a new series of sections of general rock/pop (as 'just another genre') and 'specialist' black-originated music for young (urban) and more mature customers (classic soul).

Of course there are gaps in both the academic studies, and my anecdotal evidence may not represent the practices of other retailers. Very little attention has been given to the way that music is integrated into the selling strategies of more general retailers, who account for an increasing proportion of record sales. In these contexts record buying is just part of the weekly shop. Equally, there is no work on how different internet sites present CDs for purchase, and how this organisation relates to buying behaviour or the perception of the customers they serve. Finally, music is increasingly purchased as MP3 files downloaded from a range of sites where the experience of buying music is dramatically different. These are, of course, opportunities for research.

4.1 Compare and contrast the layout of three different types of record shop. Perhaps choose a record chain store (like Virgin or HMV), a general multiple or supermarket (like Woolworths or Tesco), and a specialist record shop. What sorts of pleasures are to be found browsing and buying in each of them? Using the information in this chapter can you suggest the assumptions they make about their customers from the layout of the shop?

This analysis of core record retailing can be compared with other forms of record retailing where other formats and other means of distribution are used. Extend your analysis to shops that deal with vinyl, perhaps second-hand record shops, or specialist dance music retailers. Then compare a range of CD and MP3 retailers and file-sharing sites on the internet. How do they order consumption? What is their assumption about the customer?

Collecting: It's a man's man's man's world

Buying records is not the only way that this primary commodity form of popular music culture and the audience are related. Records are not only purchased, they are also collected. As Will Straw argues, we limit our insight if we restrict our understanding of record collecting to the 'residue' of record buying (Straw 1997b). His starting point is the widely accepted, but often unexplained, notion of record collecting as a key male activity within popular music culture. He suggests that its 'maleness' is perceived both as a private refuge from the world, as a public display of irrational obsession and as means of rationalising meaning. Here he is pointing to the idea that collecting records not only generates private knowledge about the history, genres, artists, composition, recording and issuing of records, but that the collection (and the knowledge it generates) are forms of display linked to identity. In turn, he argues, these images of collecting are linked to the wider ways that 'private knowledge' and 'public display' are related to mastery in representations of maleness that are found in media texts. These ideas have been eloquently expressed in the film *High Fidelity* – and the book on which it is based (Hornby 1995) – which interrogates issues of mastery and power relationships, and their link to male identity. The story centres on, and is narrated by, a socially inadequate male record collector and record shop owner, who eventually learns to leave behind his hardline views about what is worthy in music, and his obsessive cataloguing and list-making, to move onto a more mature relationship with women, sexuality and the world outside his record shop.

Straw's argument is that these sorts of media representations are built around a series of categories of male identity – the dandy, the nerd, the brute and the cool male – each of which is a permutation of the different ways that 'private knowledge' and 'public display' can be combined. Although record collecting is generally associated with a mastery of detailed private knowledge that is seen as 'nerdy', Straw argues that the notion of 'cool' is a more telling model. In male record collecting, what is important is not just the quantity of knowledge but 'the amount of restraint with which it is deployed or guarded' (Straw 1997c, 9). The hipness of cool comes from an attempt to 'repress any evidence that this knowledge is easily acquired in the mastery of lists or bookish sources' (Straw 1997c, 9). In this respect hipness can be distinguished from dandyism, which is mastery of public display without depth of private knowledge, or brutism which shares the naiveté of the nerd with respect to public display and the dandy's lack of private knowledge. However, Straw is not attempting to raise the 'hipness' of male collecting above other forms of male identity, but to reveal its constructiveness. The qualities assigned to being hip are socially constructed, although the cultural practices associated with hipness constantly deny their own construction. 'Hip knowledge' is presented publicly as effortlessly attained and deployed. While the nerd, the dandy and the brute are all signalled by their own adjectives and nouns, hipness has an adjective, but no noun. Just as the brute is maleness without culture, and so presented as natural, hipness – for the hip at least – is presented as natural and 'acultural'. The central question we have to ask about record collecting, then, is what cultural advantage does it construct for the male record collector.

As Straw points out, in part it assigns prestige to the collector. In addition, though, it represents a particular attempt to master and organise the chaos of popular music culture into one that is knowable and open to differentiation, a set of orderings that are part of men's relationship to other men and to popular music. For Straw, record collections are carriers of the information whose arrangement and interpretation is part of the broader discourse about popular music. In a circular process, record collections provide the raw material around which the rituals of homosocial interaction take shape. Just as ongoing conversation between men shapes the composition and extension of each man's collection, so each man finds, in the similarity of his points of reference to those of his peers, confirmation of a shared universe of critical judgment.

(Straw 1997c, 5)

The protagonist of *High Fidelity*, like many male record collectors, judges mainstream music to be uncollectible. In doing so, collecting is linked, argues Straw, not only with the 'naturalness' of hipness, but also with a development of historical depth and the construction of a canon associated with connoisseurship, the anti-commercial stance of bohemianism, and the narratives of adventure and discovery of the hunter. While much of Straw's discussion centres on the sort of rock music collecting celebrated in *High Fidelity*, it also seems to have explanatory power when considering the collecting of jazz, early blues, soul, reggae, or more contemporary dance music.

The particular practices of acquiring and organising records discussed by Straw have led to what Thornton has identified as the enculturation of the record. The meanings that records accrue through this process are in addition to the meanings of the music encoded on the record. In other words the record itself becomes valued, and in Thornton's account, takes on that central quality assigned to popular music: authenticity (Thornton 1995, 26–86). She suggests that two discursive transformations are at play here, one where authenticity is derived from the sense of the record as an original artwork, and the other where authenticity is understood as a true expression of a community. In her account, Thornton ties these two senses of authenticity together through the role of the DJ as a record collector and a (dance) community leader who acquires and plays specific records, and relates their playing to the community of dancers. A new authenticity for records was achieved, then, first at the point at which they were no longer conceived of as transcriptions of another musical entity but as something to be valued for themselves. Then again, when records were played publicly in specialist venues distinct from those with live music. In this context it is no surprise that the qualities she proposes as the basis for authenticity – newness, exclusivity or rareness – are the same ones most often used as a key criteria for the sort of record collecting that Straw discusses (Thornton 1995, 28).

Thornton's analysis draws our attention to the way that the power to draw distinctions is a central one within popular music culture. This power allows some individuals to construct hierarchies of value through the selection of certain types of records over others, certain criteria for acquisition over others, and certain ways of organising a collection. This is also prima facie evidence for Simon Frith's contention that the distinctions often made between processes of high culture evaluation and popular evaluation have been exaggerated by both the detractors and the advocates of popular culture (Frith 1996b, 3–20). Likewise, the activities of fans and academics often cover the same qualities of obsessiveness, attention to detail, and demonstration of knowledge and distinction (Jensen 1992, 18–23). While many academics still dismiss the study of popular culture (see Grossberg 1992b), the growth in media and cultural studies indicates a recognition of its importance among others.

FIGURE 14.1 Record collecting involves the acquisition of obscure knowledge and its public display, as well as the private pleasures of organising and listening
Photo: Stefan Klenke

These debates do throw up important questions about our role as scholars and fans (see also Hills 2002; Maxwell 2002). Anecdotal evidence suggests that most popular music scholars are themselves avid record collectors, and we all involve ourselves in both the private acquisition of knowledge and its public display, and our own scholarship is often mixed up in our own music consumption. We display our scholarship knowledge often with a style analogous to the 'hipness' of popular culture. Of course, it would be stretching the analogy to claim that popular music scholars are cool, but we do select ways to display our mastery of knowledge, which usually hide the ways it was acquired, and which send signals to those 'in the know'. This may be in some way connected to the observation that most textbooks on popular music are written by men, and the way such books (including this one) display knowledge and hide the process of its acquisition in the conventional 'voice' of academic written style. I show you what I know, but not how I came to know it. I self-consciously chose to title this section with an allusion to a James Brown song in my own record collection with the knowledge that some readers would understand the reference.

Of course, all these theories of collecting as a form of popular music consumption depend upon certain definitions of collecting itself. If as scholars of popular music we approach the study of consumption by separating certain forms of acquisition and ordering of records from others we reproduce the sense of 'naturalness' that male 'collectors' attempt to affect. If collecting is presented as being a male activity it is because 'collecting' is defined as more than the piles of records that the record buyer will acquire, but it relates to the way they are systematically acquired and ordered within a collection. Under this definition other 'collections' of records, and other approaches to acquisition and ordering, are excluded. Perhaps it is the particular way in which collections are collected that is gendered male, rather than the act of collecting itself (see Baekland 1994)? How do we account for women who present themselves as record collectors? Although Straw's article makes a very interesting starting point, our understanding of record acquisition and ordering needs to be extended and deepened, and needs to be itself decoupled from a singular focus on male identity.

There are also important distinctions to be made about the format in which a collection is organised. While in certain collecting circles vinyl discs are still privileged over other formats (see Plasketes 1992), most people now buy (and so collect) music on CDs. These formats are in turn being replaced by digital formats like MP3. The experience of collecting music on a computer hard drive, usually without any artwork, is a significant departure, and the possibility of categorising and reordering music within a database changes the very concept of a collection. This provides another fast-changing shift in the dynamics of record collecting.

You can contribute to extending and deepening the study of collecting by undertaking some primary research of your own.

X.2 Undertake a survey of the way that men and women acquire and order their music collections. You will need to avoid a simple binary distinction between 'collecting' and just buying, though, as this will just repeat the distinctions made by self-styled male collectors. Thinking about the reasons that lie behind buying or acquiring music records or data files will both develop your thinking about a fuller theory about collecting and generate categories for a questionnaire. Likewise, thinking about the ways that people organise the records or data files they own, and the different attitudes to that organisation, will add another dimension to your developing theory and give you another set of categories.

SUMMARY

In the four chapters in this part of the book, concentrating on audiences and consumption, we have seen how the perception of music consumption has shifted from an antagonistic one to a more positive perception of the consumer as active. It is striking how approaches to music consumers have kept music as part of a wider way of life, but in doing so these studies have ignored the detail of how we listen to, watch, dance to and buy popular music. This opens up the possibilities for new detailed studies, guidance for which can be found by engaging with the debates of popular music scholarship. However, this reflection should also draw our attention to the difference between our role as fans and scholars. While our fandom gives us the inside track on the consumption of popular music, we need to avoid trying to prove that our own distinctions, hierarchies and knowledges are the most important. Studying popular music culture means throwing our self open to the possibilities of finding out how and why others do it differently.

Further reading

Du Gay, Paul and Negus, Keith 1994: 'The Changing Sites of Sound: Music Retailing and the Composition of Consumers', in *Media Culture and Society* 16(3).

Straw, Will 1997: 'Sizing up Record Collections', in S. Whiteley *Sexing the Groove: Popular Music and Gender.* Routledge.

Thornton, Sarah 1995: *Club Cultures: Music, Media and Subcultural Capital.* Polity Press.

Part FIVE:

Case Studies and Conclusions

The introduction to this book started with the proposition that popular music *is what it has come to be defined as*. In other words, we need to investigate the cultural processes that produce a range of competing definitions. The central process of definition is the one involved in constructing a history of the music. Histories define not only what has happened in the past, but also how we should make sense of the past in terms of the present. As we saw in Chapter 1, histories bring aspects of the past to the fore to tell stories of how startling individuals from the margins disrupted the mainstream of music, or how the roots of one music can be traced back to others. These are important insights, but they have tended to become part of 'totalising' histories that subordinate the detail and complexity of the past to a simple story based upon judgements about the present. This does not mean that the secondary accounts of the past are not worthy of study. On the contrary, they are rich sources of information and insight. However, they have to be read as attempts to define the past. In place of a chronology of popular music's past, the second and third chapters offered a model for analysis that involves examining secondary material along with primary sources like music and contemporary documents to reveal the historically located attempts to define what was popular and what was worthy as music. The three examples in Chapter 4 demonstrated how this could be done.

It is not only historians who have attempted to define what music is. The record industry and the wider mass media also use their own discourses to construct a sense of popular music. These industry discourses understandably serve their commercial interests and, equally understandably, have been attacked either by critics of all mass culture, or by those who believe some popular music escapes the compromises of commercial imperatives. The analysis in Chapters 5, 6 and 7 attempted to show that it is not possible to think about popular music outside its production within an industry, and instead we need to understand how the imperatives of large and small commercial companies are formed in their attempts to deal with the fundamental characteristics of the production of a cultural product like music. While the economics of production benefit the large-scale producers that control the market, the culture of consumption requires that record companies remain flexible if they are to stay in business. This gives record production a volatility that companies attempt to control through the use of the media as promotional avenues. In doing so they contribute another set of meanings in the sounds, images and consumption practices associated with this music.

Just as attention to the structure of the industry gives us insight into popular music culture, the very form of the music is central to our study. The analysis undertaken in Chapter 8 showed how a single dominant form, the song, had developed within popular music, and had been strongly criticised for being formulaic, serving the interests of a commercialised industry and ultimately leading to a paucity of cultural value. However, the form that music takes and the meanings it generates are two connected, but distinct, areas for analysis. Chapter 9 showed how the meaning of music is located in a wider context, which includes how it is performed, the way the sound relates to other aspects of the media text through which it is consumed, and the way it is coded in a genre. Chapter 10 showed how these insights could be applied to the question of how this wider metatext of music constructs senses of stars and of group identity.

In Part 4 the question of meaning was expanded to include the obvious part played by the audience for popular music as consumers. Most work summarised in Chapter 11 has tended to apply an abstract theory of the cultural role of the consumption of popular music to debates. While these approaches have given important insights they have also failed to engage with the detail of how people actually consume the music. Chapters 12, 13 and 14 made suggestions about how such a study could be developed to cover the activities of looking, listening, dancing, buying and collecting.

In each part of the book I have emphasised the importance of being involved in popular music scholarship yourself. One of the earliest books to attempt to study popular music culture in a rounded fashion was Simon Frith's *The Sociology of Rock* (1978). He starts the book by talking about the difficulty of moving from a fan's knowledge and perspective to that of a popular music scholar; 25 years later it is still as difficult, although we have far more material available to us than Frith had. The preceding parts have summarised this work to make it available to you in an accessible form, but there is no substitute for reading the books and articles for yourself. Hopefully the summaries make it easier for you to contextualise and evaluate the contributions of others. In addition the exercises to be found throughout this book have provided opportunities to apply the discussions that have been outlined, but also to promote research and analysis.

CHAPTER FIFTEEN

Case Studies

The purpose of this final full chapter is to show you how the insights that have been developed in the previous chapters could be all applied to specialist case studies. Three case studies have been chosen that raise interesting questions about developments in popular music culture over the last ten years. The first explores the idea that a particular geographic place can have a distinct musical sound and how this idea is being challenged by the globalisation of the music industry and the promiscuity of fans' musical tastes. The second examines the new technologies of the internet which suggest that the whole of popular music culture is going through a period of profound change. The third investigates the claim that in spite of these radical changes, mainstream pop seems to have reasserted itself in the form of the modern manufactured pop star.

The case studies take the form of short analyses on the lines that you may be asked to undertake as a student. As such, they show how the work on history, institution, text and consumption can be integrated in a short piece of research and writing. They also reveal how different aspects of the study of popular music culture can be important in different cases. So the study of local music brings the relationship of consumption cultures with music-making to the fore, while the study of the internet highlights the importance of the industry to cultural and technological changes, and, finally, the study of manufactured stars connects the textual qualities of pop to the promotional activities of the industry and the pleasures of pop for its fans.

The local and the global: The Bristol Sound

The notion that we can trace a particular sound of popular music to a specific locality has a long history. Memphis is irrevocably linked to rockabilly and Elvis Presley, Liverpool is the home of Merseybeat and the Beatles, and Seattle was host to grunge and Nirvana. Likewise, the Bristol scene of the 1990s is associated with trip-hop and Massive Attack, Portishead, Tricky and Roni Size/Reprazent. Interestingly, then, these Bristol artists have all expressed their distaste for the label trip-hop, viewing it as a media creation and rejecting the idea that their music was part of a wider local scene (Reynolds 1998, 314). In part, this may be understood as the musician's desire not to be seen as working in formulaic categories, but it also points to the complexity of understanding localness in music. There was undoubtedly something distinctive about the music coming out of Bristol in the 1990s, but at the same time it also owed a tremendous debt to other music from the USA and the Caribbean.

There have been several attempts to understand this music, but they each relate it to different contexts. Phil Johnson has argued that the music was part of a worldwide phenomenon stimulated 'by hip hop and parallel innovations in music technology, replacing the traditional figure of the musician with the DJ or mixer and his essential counterpart, the clued up engineer' (Johnson 1996, 45). Hesmondhalgh and Melville (2001) present the sound as part of a British hip-hop movement, while Reynolds suggests it was an 'adjunct to rave' (Reynolds 1998, 35). Paradoxically, then, we need to think about the Bristol sound as being simultaneously the articulation of a local and a global music culture. To understand this paradox we need to get some grip on what we mean by this interaction between the local and the global, before applying these concepts to the music culture of Bristol in the 1980s and 1990s, the texts and music-making of the Bristol artists, and the wider industry structures that disseminated the sound beyond Bristol.

Theorising the Local and the Global in Popular Music Culture

Underlying this case study, then, is a question about the relationship between people, a place and a music. These sorts of relationships have always been important in popular music culture, but as music packaged and sold by the major corporations to an international market became dominant many music critics and fans celebrated the music of localised music-makers. The music is valued for the qualities that mark it out as different; qualities that are usually understood as part of the distinctiveness of people and place.

Sometimes local music is celebrated by activists to promote music-making in their own area as a conscious attempt to decentralise popular music culture. At other times, though, the interest involves collectors buying recordings made in localities that are perceived to articulate an authenticity not found in international repertoire. Ironically (given the reasons for fan interest in the music of other cultures), but possibly inevitably (given the imperative within the music industry to order the chaos of meanings that localised music has for a global industry), the diversity of locally produced music has itself become part of a marketing strategy, and is now sold and consumed as world music (Sweeney 1991).

In a thoughtful analysis of the implications of these characteristics of contemporary music, George Lipsitz has argued that musical hybridity, diasporal identity and multiculturalism has a potential for encouraging greater cultural and economic equality (Lipsitz 1994). He points out that the transportability of recorded sound means that music from identifiable locales now circulates much more widely. In the West the authenticity of such music is often seen through its construction as 'primitive', 'Other' and 'exotic', but music of one locale is often adopted into the music-making of other locales because the interpretations of the meanings of the 'borrowed' music seems to resonate locally. Lipsitz sees this as a circuit of exchange where musics such as reggae, salsa and hip-hop are, and become again, the products of international hybridisation. He is careful to note, though, that this exchange is not always one of inequality, and 'the music retains residual contradictions of centuries of colonisation, class domination and racism' (Lipsitz 1994, 5).

This analysis is particularly pertinent for an understanding of the Bristol sound, even though the success of bands like Massive Attack and Portishead in the 1990s would suggest that theirs was music at the very heart of mainstream music culture in Britain. However, Bristol as a city, the bands, their the approaches to music-making, and the music itself are models of the sorts of issues Lipsitz investigates. The national and international success of recordings from these bands, together with the idea that they were part of the wider musical genre of trip-hop, are another of his 'dangerous crossroads' of popular music culture. A useful way to understand this interconnectedness of the local and the global is through Will Straw's suggestive idea of a 'scene' (Straw 1997a).

Music-making in Bristol

Straw defines a scene as a 'cultural space in which a range of musical practices co-exist, interacting with each other within a variety of processes of differentiation, and according to widely varying trajectories of change and cross fertilisation' (Straw 1997a, 494). This cultural space is one that relates not to the traditions of one locality, but to the whole international music culture, making it possible for the geographically isolated individual to be a member of a wider scene just as easily as a geographic community of music-makers. Bristol in the 1980s and 1990s, of course, is a very good example of the latter. It had a vital, if not particularly extensive, popular music infrastructure built around record stores (Revolver was especially important), music venues (local blues parties, carnival, the Tropic, and most vitally the Dugout club), recording studios (primarily the Coach House and Insects' studio), management and promotion companies (particularly Cameron McVey's Cherry Bear) and, later, pirate radio stations (FTP being the most prominent) (Johnson 1996).

Although the ways of making music established in Bristol were innovative, they were not unique to the city, and they reflected and drew upon those established in New York hip-hop and Kingston dub reggae. Similar approaches were being developed during the 1980s in Chicago, LA, Manchester and London. As such, Bristol music seems to share in the 'spatial diversity' that Straw argues is characteristic of dance-based music scenes (Straw 1997a, 501). Intriguingly, though, many of the characteristics Straw associates with the alternative rock scenes of North America are also apparent. Straw's description of alternative rock scenes also seem to be a definition of Bristol music-making:

> a distinctive density of historical time within the performance styles, … an inflection of older residual styles with contemporary irony which evokes a bohemian heritage in which that combination has its antecedents … [and] a detailed synthesis of styles and form, [that] fill in the range of options between canonical styles, the latter serving as markers of privileged antecedents from which eclectic stylistic exercises develop outwards.
>
> (Straw 1997a, 501)

The Bristol sound of the 1990s grew out of earlier music cultures. Jazz was prominent from the 1960s, and bands mixing punk with funk and jazz like the Pop Group, Pig Bag, and Rip Rig and Panic were prominent in the 1980s, and reggae was thriving well into the 1990s. These musics are apparent in the Bristol sound, as a combination of 'the ideological baggage of punk, along with the rhythmic base of reggae' (Johnson 1996, 46). The 1990s music-makers all shared a background that embraced art-school punk, reggae, soul and funk, while the hip-hop culture of the 1980s became a focus for DIY music-making and all-embracing lifestyle. Collecting hip-hop, soul, reggae and funk, and film soundtrack records was a major activity for members of the Wild Bunch/Massive Attack, Portishead, Smith and Mighty, and Reprazent, and samples of these records became the basis for their music-making.

The Bristol sound, then, drew on a range of music traditions. The African-American tradition, the direct influence of reggae, soul and hip-hop is obviously important, as is the European art tradition of experimentation and modernist miscegenation. Equally prominent, though, is the sense of community and music for a shared culture, here defined by the whole-way-of-life ethos of hip-hop culture. Downplaying the mainstream of Tin Pan Alley, the traditions of star image, performance and commercial success were set in a more complex relation to their music-making.

Phil Johnson's history of the Bristol sound further assigns a central role to the social backgrounds of the participants and the way that these related in the particular socio-geography of Bristol as a city (Johnson 1996). Notably the role of St Paul's black community, and its geographic relationship to the adjoining middle-class and working-class communities, and the more distant commuter suburb of Portishead. Johnson is keen to stress the way that the boho punk funk of middle-class Clifton mixed with the reggae and soul of St Paul's in the city's integrating state school system, which drew kids from all areas, but in a context set by the city's past as a slave trade port, where 'questions of race inevitably carry a strong historical resonance' (Johnson 1996, 33).

The social relationships formed at school and in going out became the basis of a network of individuals and groups who defined the extended musical community of the Bristol sound. Central to this network for the future national success of the sound was emblematic singer Neneh Cherry. Daughter of free-jazz/world musician Don Cherry, Neneh had enjoyed some success in Pig Bag, and Rip Rig and Panic, and was a key member of the widely hyped lifestyle-as-politics Buffalo set. Cherry and her partner/manager Cameron McVey offered a connection to London's music and style scene and to the idea of a world music in which the distinctive local musics integrated at a global level. Of course, these negotiations of the local and the global were the central experiences of living in modern multicultural multimedia Britain and made perfect sense to the hip-hop connoisseurs, sound system mixers and DJs who populated the Bristol scene. But Cherry's Native American/African-American/Scandinavian ancestry, itinerant lifestyle, and her involvement in experimental musical and lifestyle-as-politics movements made her a symbol of what could be made of the cross-cultural, global-as-local experience of Bristolians.

The Trip-hop Text and New Forms of Music-Making

This social network, based upon record collecting and club and party DJing, was extended as music consumption blurred into music-making. The foundation of the Bristol sound was established in the local club the Dugout where the future members of Massive Attack worked as a DJ crew along with Nelle Hooper who later formed Soul II Soul with Jazzy B in London. Known as the Wild Bunch, the members moved from a sound system crew to a music-making collective with ease. When Hooper and Johnson moved to London to release records under the Wild Bunch name, the other members – Grant Marshall, Del Naja and Andrew Vowles – formed Massive Attack. The collective was extended to include at different times UK soul vocalist Shara Nelson, veteran Jamaican reggae vocalist Horace Andy, Adrian Thaws (Tricky) and indie rock vocalists Tracey Thorn and Liz Fraser.

Although the first of the Bristol music-makers to gain widespread recognition, Massive Attack were shadowed by Smith and Mighty, Portishead, and Tricky as a solo artist. The next generation of Bristol music-makers, who built their music from the other reggae/hip-hop hybrid drum & bass (and which included Ronnie Size and DJ Krush), worked in similar collaborative ways. They established their own record label and recording studio, and worked as a collective to produce the widely acclaimed *New Forms* (1997).

These artists had a strikingly different way of organising music-making from the tradition of rock groups or pop artists, and it is even noticeably different from the single music-makers or duo collaborators of the house scene. Their approach grew out of the way that reggae sound systems or hip-hop crews operated as large social networks, rather than focused delineated groups. Such forms of collective organisation suited the way that DJs and MCs made music of this kind with studio recording technology. None of the core Bristol sound music-makers were musicians, and they operated far more as textural *auteurs*, guiding and directing the musical montage rather than producing all its elements themselves. The source material for the music was wide and varied, including soundscapes produced from recorded music, rapped vocals, specially commissioned musical or vocal input, all mixed together using the techniques developed through DJing and, later (with the assistance of others), using samplers, bass and drum machines and music sequencers. Perhaps the core music-makers are better understood through the analogy of the film director or montagist working with collaborators, rather than the rock group. So, through the extending network of collaborators who added layer upon layer to the music, the collective of music-makers was formed and the track itself was created.

Song form is far less common here than in most popular music. Songs are most prevalent in Portishead tracks, which draw on the Tin Pan Alley format and feel, even if this is not rigidly structured in their AABA form, probably as a result of a strong input from vocalist Beth Gibbons. The song form is surprisingly uncommon in Massive Attack tracks in spite of the wide use of vocalists. When song structures are the basis of tracks it is because they are covers of existing studio soul or reggae recordings like 'Light My Fire', or 'Be Thankful for What You Got'. Size and Krust do not use the form at all, and mostly dispense with vocalists altogether.

Far more important to the Bristol sound than the widely noted slow tempo of the tracks is the patina of recorded sound. It is the hiss, the crackle, the distortion, the distance, the disorientation of recorded sound and turntable manipulations that are the basis of all these tracks. Even on tracks like Massive Attack's 'One Love' the vocal has been laid down after the track has been constructed, and is the only melody element, which in turn gives the track a 'stripped-down' feeling. The central motif here is the manipulation of sound on the turntable: scratching rhythmically; or releasing snatches of uncompleted melodic material; or looped in a break beat from a 1970s jazz or funk record. Portishead's tracks are so processed that they sound as 'dirty' as worn-out vinyl even when the sound source is a digitally recorded one. Film and TV soundtracks are a commonly evoked soundscape and the ghostly Theremin is emblematic in Bristol's 'hip-hop noir' (Reynolds 1998, 317). Alternatively, melodic material is so extensively processed that it becomes the basis of the rhythm track. By contrast, tracks from the Reprazent collective utilise what became fairly conventional computer-based composition tools, and the faster tempos of drum & bass. So while Massive Attack and Tricky rely heavily on layers of sound and the symphonic styles of studio soul, and Portishead on digital processing, Roni Size is the master of ProTools computer software with its time- and pitch-switching capabilities. Voices in the Bristol sound are closely mic'ed and the spoken or sung lines are delivered without the attack of rap or soul, and at a volume that sometimes barely reaches a whisper. Portishead's Beth Gibbons' voice, and the singing voices of most Massive Attack singers are distinctly 'cool', and under-emoted, avoiding the rich harmonics and wide range of typical soul singers.

From Bristol Sound to Global Pop

Just as recorded music allowed Bristol-based music-makers to hear music from a range of places and eras that became the basis of their soundscapes, so recorded music was the means by which this sound was distributed to a national and international audience. Early releases from most of the Bristol bands were on small, independent companies, some of these labels – like the Bristol-based Full Circle records – were established by the music-makers themselves. However, as the commercial success of the Bristol sound testifies, to promote and distribute your records on a wider than local scale, and to markets outside the underground, requires the involvement of the major corporations. While there are many interesting singles and vinyl 12-inch releases from Bristol that did not get much further than the small independent shops of the dance music scene, the big-selling CDs like *Protection* (1994), *Dummy* (1994), *Maxinquaye* (1995) and *New Forms* (1997) were all released as parts of complex deals involving major companies. The records were presented as band-based labels like Wild Bunch/Circa, or on small labels associated with alternative rock or dance music scenes, like Go Beat or Talkin' Loud, but they were linked to ownership, distribution or promotional deals with majors like EMI and Mercury/Universal.

As importantly, the releases of these records connected with changes in the operation of the wider media. Massive Attack were picked up by the early 1990s style magazines (through the Neneh Cherry connection), indie *NME*, and muso-collector *Q*, and the dance music press. These underground connections were then extended with mainstream media coverage like Portishead's appearance on *Later with Jools Holland*, and heavy plays on Radio 1 as part of its 'new music first' policy (see Hendy 2000b). These media appearances gave exposure to the major-promoted releases, and the way that the music connected indie rock, song-based sensibilities and vocal styles with the artiness of laid-back, filmic music tracks, and an accessible black diaspora music gave them a wide audience.

The music that came from Bristol in the 1990s was innovative, bringing together rock, reggae, soul and hip-hop styles in an original hybrid. The multicultural nature of the groups that made the music, and their approaches to making music, were characteristic of a wider musical scene that included hip-hop and dance-based musical forms found across the world. Central to these musics was the politics of race, and the sense of diasporal identity that first became part of a style-conscious London-based music scene, and then a wider acceptance and chart success. But this success was not just based on innovations in the musical texts, the DJ basis to sound manipulation, or the way the music drew upon musics from across the world. It owed a considerable debt to radio and press coverage, and to Afro-diasporal images, which also avoided the sorts of black essentialism that dominated hip-hop and reggae, and so often alienated white rock consumers. It is no coincidence that the more song-based tracks gained the wider popularity. At a time when the guitar rock of Britpop was at its height these bands offered a different version of British identity that did not rely on a self-conscious notion of a British pop tradition, but articulated a sense of Britishness rooted in migration, cooperation and sound manipulation.

15.1 Map the distinctive music practices of your own locality. While not every town, city or county has given its name to a style of music, there are some very interesting pieces of research waiting to be done into the distinctive music practices in local areas. This activity involves two interconnected pieces of research. First, investigate what range of music scenes can be found locally. Are certain forms of popular music particularly successful? Can you find local institutions of music culture like specialist record shops, venues, specialist magazines or radio stations that suggest a thriving local scene? Second, by selecting one of these scenes, can you identify a particular sound distinctive to local music-makers? If so, is it possible to identify their influences, and particular local conditions that could be used to explain the sound?

Further reading: the Bristol Sound

Johnson, Phil 1996: *Straight Outta Bristol: Massive Attack, Portishead, Tricky and the Roots of Trip-Hop.* **Hodder & Stoughton.**

The new frontier: music and the Internet

Internet technologies and the development of the World Wide Web have played host to rapid changes in popular music culture. In particular, the establishment of file compression (MP3) and streaming audio technologies has enabled both new forms of music distribution and related changes in the way popular music is consumed. These changes have challenged some of the key practices of the music industry and possibly mark a new era for popular music culture. This subject, therefore, makes a fascinating case study of how popular music changes historically and how industry, form and consumption interact.

At the heart of these changes, and the debates on what the final settlement will be, is a central question of popular music culture: Who owns popular music? The star system constantly makes a connection between a piece of music and the artists who recorded or perform it. However, they are hardly ever the legal owners of that music. As fans, we make psychological links to artists, and our record collections turn their music into ours. The small print of any CD, though, reveals that the company that issued the record asserts its ownership and limits the way we can use 'our' records. The rights to perform, record and copy the music are controlled by a set of laws and international agreements that developed over the twentieth century (see Frith, 1993). When artists sign with a record company they agree to share the ownership of their music with the record company in exchange for royalty payments. When we buy a record produced by a record company they share some of the rights of ownership with us in exchange for our money. We have bought the right to play and listen to the record, but not the right to copy it or play it publicly. It is by carefully controlling and exploiting the value of the ownership rights to popular music that record companies make money.

As we will see, the possibility of using the internet to hear music disrupts the system that generated massive profits for these companies, and so they are taking action to control its development. But these disruptions also fuel the utopian dreams of music fans who believe that music culture could bypass global, multimedia corporations, and that our psychological investments in music could be matched by a new relationship between music-making and consumption.

In this case study, then, we must first be clear what these technologies do, then how their applications have caused so many controversies and finally explore how these applications could converge to change popular music culture significantly.

The Technologies of Internet Music

There are three main technologies that we need to understand when discussing internet music.

1. *File compression* – MP3 is an industry standard of digital compression making a computer file of digitised music smaller without losing the key musical qualities. This allows us to send or retrieve it through the internet far more quickly. As any technical manual will tell you, MP3 is the file extension for MPEG-1 Layer III computer files created by a compression–decompression algorithm that uses psycho-acoustic techniques to reduce the average music file to 10 per cent of its original size (see Hacker 2000, 22–46). Basically it squashes the size of a file using a model of how we hear music to remove elements that we will not notice are missing, and so allows us to store up to ten times the number of files on our computer, or transport them ten times more quickly over the internet.

2. *Streamed audio* – This technology allows music to be sent from one computer and to be listened to on another in real time. It was developed first in the Liquid Audio and Real Audio formats, and more recently in the QuickTime or streaming MP3 alternatives. All these technologies do two main things: they compress the file size and use 'packet switching' to send the data (Priestman 2002, 51–76). While the compression shrinks the size of the file, packet switching breaks the file into smaller packets of data and sends them across the internet by the quickest route, constantly switching direction with each packet. The computer receiving the packets of data then rebuilds the music from the individual packets. This rebuilding requires the computer's music player software to create a buffer of data so that the music is played a few seconds after it was received to make sure all parts are present before the next section of music is played.

3. *Peer-to-peer networking* – The Napster software gave people with access to the internet the ability to find music files on other computers and download copies of them. In technical terms this is a peer-to-peer (p2p) technology that brings together individuals on equal terms and allows them access to files on each other's computer hard disks, rather than being supplied from a massive commercial computer server (see Merriden 2001). While Napster has more recently been effectively part of the Bertelsmann conglomerate, its origins are in the study-bedroom culture of US higher education and then the dotcom start-up companies that inaugurated the widespread recognition of the commercial potential of the internet.

These technologies increase the speed at which music can be sent from place to place, but they have also created two distinct ways in which music can be consumed on the internet. These mimic existing forms of consumption: MP3s are an update of listening to records and streaming is usually presented as internet radio. However, as we will see, they have challenged the way that record companies relate to record retailing and radio broadcasting, and undermine the basis on which record companies have so far made money. At the same time they assert new forms of consumption cultures, many of which offer alternative ways to organise music-making, distribution and consumption. These changes are most apparent in two areas: MP3 sharing systems like Napster, and new forms of internet radio.

MP3, Napster and Alternative Popular Music Culture

Napster and its successor p2p systems have been widely discussed even though they are only one of a number of significant developments (see Alderman 2001). Napster's progress as a business from study bedroom to the holding of a major conglomerate is often seen as a metaphor for the increasing control that large commercial corporations have over fan cyberspace, and the demise of systems that benefit music fans, to be replaced by systems that benefit corporations. The technology of file-sharing was exploited so that music fans could swap MP3 music files, and is now increasingly the basis on which record companies attempt to reassert their ownership of music that had slipped into the hands of music fans.

While MP3 compression had been used since the early 1990s to store and exchange music files, and internet music pioneers Jeff Patterson and Rob Lord had distributed MP3 files through their Internet Underground Music Archive (IUMA) from 1993, it was the establishment of Napster by Shawn Fanning in 1999 that was both the most radical innovation and generated the most media interest (see Alderman 2001). This peer-to-peer technology simultaneously united several alternative discourses prominent in internet and music culture ideology. First, Napster's peer-to-peer relationship reproduces the very structure of the internet as a means of exchange through a network of equals (Hafner and Lyon 1996). Second, such a structure of relationships parallels the forms of relationship detectable in fan cultures (see Hills 2002), and reflects a strong anti-centralising tendency within US thought of both liberal and conservative nature. The internet's greatest advocates and many of its pioneers shared a liberal version of this tendency, which is rooted in the counter-culture of the 1960s (see Roszak 1970; Hoskyns 1997a; Green 1999).

In popular music culture these ideals are exemplified by the relationship of west coast band the Grateful Dead with their committed fans, the self-named 'Deadheads' (Weiner 1999). By the 1990s the band has been together for over 30 years and had toured extensively. Deadhead fan activities included the recording and exchange of tapes of the band's concerts (a practice encouraged by the band). This, of course, is a particularly well-developed form of the tape compilation and swapping activities from which Napster and its successors grew. Grateful Dead member John Perry Barlow has been an active advocate of the use of the internet for counter-cultural purposes through the Electronic Frontier Foundation (Barlow 1994; 1996). Of course, it is not surprising that the developments in internet music should reflect these ideals because pioneers like Patterson, Lord and Fanning shared these values.

However, the running of Napster quickly moved on from an idea in a campus bedroom and became one of the success stories of the dotcom boom. Like most dotcom companies, though, there was no clarity about how it would make a profit, and the participants made their millions from the investment of others. Like most investment bubbles, the appearance of success was more important than the balance sheet. Centrally Napster looked attractive to investors because of its p2p basis. Unlike earlier attempts to distribute digital music files like MP3.com, Napster did not distribute digital music files itself but allowed internet users to make contact with other individuals who had libraries of such files and then exchange files with them. It was therefore viewed as a site that attracted considerable use because it gave access to free music, and yet avoided the restrictions of copyright law.

Napster, therefore, not only reconfigured popular music as a new artefact (the MP3 as a replacement for the disc) but also reconfigured the industrial process of music production and distribution (the download as a replacement for record retailing) (Jones 2002). Record companies could control vinyl, tapes or CDs at the point of reproduction and distribution, but MP3s can be copied through p2p systems at zero cost and without much chance of being tracked. In doing so, MP3 collectors avoid the need to buy the right to listen. Record companies had traditionally allowed other forms of 'free' music distribution – like radio play or TV appearances – because they felt that the economic value gained through promoting record buying was greater than the value lost by people not buying because they could hear the music already.

Because digital music files are perceived to be exact copies of the original recording they do not promote buying. As Napster did not offer a way of utilising MP3s as commodities to be exploited for profit it was not something the industry wanted to replicate, only control. There had been some record company experiments with online music – exemplified by Warner's the Music Group led by Stan Cornyn, and by Jim Griffen's work at Geffen records in the 1990s – but these were not followed through, and the companies had successfully closed MP3.com through litigation (see Alderman, 2001). The majors therefore approached Napster with the same tactics, and an alliance of record companies, the industry body (the RIAA) and leading recording artists presented legal challenges to the file-sharing company (Merriden 2001, 31–61).

It is enlightening to examine the rhetoric and legal arguments made by the industry and Napster. The record companies proposed that the Napster system ripped off artists and would kill music, while they made the legal argument that Napster encouraged the infringement of copyrights they held. Napster countered by arguing that members of Napster were making fair non-commercial use of the rights already assigned with the sale of the original record that was converted into an MP3 (Merriden 2001, 50–7). More generally they presented themselves as liberationists, stating on their website: 'technology is again the means for liberation. Join us in our fight to re-build the music industry' (napster.com, 2000). Ultimately, two courts found in favour of the industry, and found that Napster had helped people infringe copyright and had financial interests in that infringement (Merriden 2001, 59–60).

These, though, were more postures from two sets of commercial interests using music-makers and music fans as the basis of their rhetorical defences. While in practice Napster had asserted that consumers own the music, and the industry that music-makers do, they did so to support their own interests. Eventually Napster was restrained from operating, but a whole line of cloned systems quickly replaced it. Then, in October 2000, to many people's surprise, BMG started a joint venture with Napster to supply the major's catalogue on a subscription version of the Napster system. BMG hoped to use the brand identity of Napster, and of course the Napster principals hoped to make a few million dollars more. Ultimately the record companies formed themselves into a number of joint enterprises to supply music online, but none of them captured the alternative ethos of Napster, nor of course supplied free music.

Internet Radio

The public and legal debate about Napster has focused attention on the distribution of music encoded in MP3 files, rather sidelining developments in the second area of development: streamed music. This latter technology has most often been used for fairly traditional music radio programming, and this seeming lack of innovation has tended to obscure the importance of these developments. Streaming technologies were developed at the same time as file compression and have enabled a massive increase in the number of available radio stations in any one locality. We now have access to a combination of parallel broadcasting of AM and FM stations from around the world, together with a large number of internet-only stations. More recently, the issue of internet radio has been highlighted because of the implications of the US Millennium Copyright Act, which has set very high royalty payments for internet stations playing recorded music.

At the time of writing, though, there are very few analyses of the importance of these technologies for popular music culture. To understand its importance we need to broaden our sense of how audio streaming technology is likely to be used by investigating the reasons behind the new copyright developments and their likely effect.

Like the application of most new technologies streamed music reproduces an existing cultural practice, and so internet radio has most often been based upon traditional music radio formats. Quickly, though, the new medium has started to produce variations in two important areas: radio on demand and niche broadcast formats. In the first it is now possible to listen to a programme originally broadcast at a particular time and place, when and where we want to listen to it. This is most developed in the BBC's radio web presence where most of its specialist and word-based programmes are available on demand after their initial broadcast. In the second variation, specialist music formats – with everything from 1930s big band, through 1950s rock & roll to contemporary musics of every genre – are widely available.

These innovations in radio are not just the result of the scale of internet radio, but an exploitation of the distinct qualities of streamed audio. As Chris Priestman has shown, understanding this distinctiveness allows us to analyse the new ways radio may develop (Priestman 2002, 231–43). Most significant is the way that the technology of streamed audio changes the economics of radio broadcasting. Within its broadcast footprint it does not cost a 'wireless' AM/FM radio station anything to add extra listeners and the cost of extending the footprint remains small (at least in urban areas) compared to the number of additional listeners that could be attracted. In internet radio, because each listener must be simultaneously provided with an individual stream of audio by a computer server, each additional listener costs approximately the same amount. In addition, while the computing power to meet the streaming needs of ten listeners is quite small, serving 10 000 listeners demands a high level of capital and computing skill. There is therefore little economic advantage in providing one stream to 10 000 listeners over 10 000 streams to individual listeners. Of course, there are production costs of producing multiple radio stations, but they are lowered by computerisation of production and could be offset by subscriptions for niche services.

FIGURE 15.1 There are thousands of internet radio stations to listen to online, each offering different styles of music, and links to other websites

This is why most internet radio services are computerised – the records are selected and played by a computer system running 24 hours a day – and why they are based on particular music genres or music cultures. DJs with well-known names also use radio-on-demand services to produce programming that would probably not attract a big enough audience to make it worth producing for a one-off broadcast, but over a month or a year may well do so. It is also technically possible to combine the technology of computer programming with the interactivity of the internet to create bespoke radio programming. Rather than selecting a particular station, it would be possible to indicate what types of music in what sorts of combination, with what proportion of known as against unknown tracks, with what amount of DJ chat and spoken features, you want in your service. Of course, this is marginally more expensive to produce than a non-bespoke service, but many people will be prepared to pay a subscription for this.

However, very few of the computerised and on-demand services are yet based on subscription, and many rely on advertising, either featured within the stream or visually on the web page. In fact it is unlikely that subscription services will form the basis of the majority of future provision, which is more likely to be found in hybrid, multimedia services. Internet users with broadband connection have access to a range of stations with programming to suit their tastes. Increasingly the websites for these stations are more than routes to the music stream, but links to an interactive music service. The site indicates the track that is being listened to, and offers the listener the chance to download an MP3 of the track via a record company pay-download service, or buy the whole CD and have it mailed to their home. In addition, there are links to the home page of the artists, discussion groups, the video that was produced to publicise the track. It is possible to indicate those tracks the listener likes so that they can hear more of the same. It is this combination of media in which music radio would be the key element that is the most interesting, and most revolutionary, for our understanding of what music-based programming is.

However, it is developments such as these that concern record companies, and that led to such companies' campaign to get money back from internet radio stations for playing records. This is understandable. The economic success of internet radio stations is based upon attracting listeners with recorded music that record companies believe they own. As with downloadable MP3s the record companies believe that the availability of music streams decreases the likelihood that people will buy the music in formats (like CDs) that they control. The record companies want to be paid for the economic gain that accrues to the internet radio station from playing music they own. Such arguments were successful in persuading the writers of the US Millennium Digital Copyright Act (MDCA), who – assuming listenerships of many thousand per programme – set high royalty payments for every record played. For stations with far fewer listeners, particularly community or alternative music stations, this increases the costs of production and makes streamed programming uneconomic. While the large record companies may feel pleased that the MDCA restores their control, and rewards their ownership rights, such positions seem to show the same sorts of restricted protectionism that have been applied to all technological innovations, and a misunderstanding of the present and likely future of music consumption culture.

New Technology and Consuming Music

The key to understanding how compression, p2p and streaming technologies will be utilised in the future lies in an appreciation of the culture of music consumption. The logic that people will buy a CD because they have heard a track on the radio or via the internet does not make much sense in its self. Record companies have always asked why would people spend money on CDs when they can hear the music in other ways. The traditional answer has always been that buying and collecting records is a cultural practice with psychological benefits for the collector in owning a particular artefact. This means that, as far as record companies are concerned, the promotional value of exposing potential customers to music you own is greater than the disincentive to buy. The new argument is that this balance of value is transformed by digital artefacts that can be copied and stored, or streamed to exact requirements.

Steve Jones has argued that internet music has led to a reconfiguration of the 'affective realm of popular music fans' (Jones 2002, 224). This works at a basic level where the record collector becomes willing to collect MP3s, and web pages or video replace the record cover as a means of engaging with the visual culture of popular music. But he also believes that the geographical terrain on which fans operate is transformed. Just as records both fixed and transported sound, allowing people from one culture to hear the music of another, the ability of music fans to share music and views across the internet means that they are no longer restricted by locality. Jones' ideas are very interesting, but his point seems to be always just out of reach.

Certainly file-sharing, music streaming and internet chat rooms have changed the geography of my consumption. I listen to radio stations broadcasting from San Francisco, swap MP3s with people I have never met nor know where they are, and discuss the music of another continent with other fans from a third. In important ways, then, the music I consider 'mine' is being transformed. These are profound changes in fan culture, and they are not well served by current record industry policies. However, we can also identify other distinct contemporary practices, like the vinyl purist (Plasketes 1992) and the importance of vinyl in dance music culture, which show that there is not a universal move towards a global/virtual/digital consumption practice. The fan cultures of vinyl collectors or dance DJs probably share more in common with the internet music fan than the mainstream popular music fan, and just as whole infrastructures, which include divisions of major corporations, have developed to support these, it is likely that the same will happen in the new culture of virtual music consumption.

Research how widespread the use of the internet for music listening is among different age groups and musical interests. Produce a questionnaire of record buying and listening that will allow you to, first, compare the relative importance of MP3 files, CDs and vinyl discs in different individuals' music collections and, second, the relative use of internet and mainstream radio. Does the number of different record formats seem to vary with age and musical taste? What could be the reasons for this? Does listening to different forms of radio vary with age and musical taste? What could be the reasons for this?

Popular music culture is not determined solely by technological innovation, but by its interaction with other social and economic factors, and with the discursive practices of music-makers, the industry and music consumers. Nevertheless the ability to produce, store and distribute identical copies of recorded music, and the possibility of access to new ways of interacting with a wider popular music culture will undoubtedly transform popular music culture. How this change will actually work out can only be understood by understanding popular music culture as a whole.

Further reading: music and the internet

Alderman, John 2001: *Sonic Boom: Napster, MP3 and the New Pioneers of Music.* **Fourth Estate.**

Hacker, Scot 2000: *MP3: The Definitive Guide.* **O'Reilly.**

Jones, Steve 2002: 'Music That Moves: Popular Music Distribution and Network Technologies', in *Cultural Studies* **16(2).**

Merriden, Trevor 2001: *Irresistible Forces: The Business Legacy of Napster and the Growth of the Underground Internet.* **Capstone.**

Priestman, Chris 2002: *Web Radio.* **Focal.**

And back to pop: manufactured pop stars

One of the most prominent features of popular music at the start of the twenty-first century has been the renewed importance of music made by artists who have been 'packaged' by a manager for the purpose of making money. These artists are almost always singers, their records rely heavily on the professional skills of songwriters and producers, and a key part of their success is dependent upon large-scale media exposure. This is far from a new phenomenon, however, and these so-called 'manufactured' stars have always been a mainstay of popular music culture. From the origins of the music industry in the late nineteenth century, artists did not usually provide their own repertoire, and it was unusual for an artist to have control over what he or she sang, and how they sang it. Until the 1950s pop was always understood to be manufactured entertainment, and this 'manufactured' characteristic of popular music was the quality that was widely understood to distance it from art and folk musics (Middleton 1990, 3–7).

From the late 1950s onwards some popular music was presented as more 'authentic' culture than the more obviously manufactured products of the entertainment industry. Expanding on the ideas that some musicians produced art – for instance, the veneration of Duke Ellington in Hughes (1993) – or that some music was an organic part of a folk culture – for instance, the celebration of American rural music in Lomax and Lomax (1947), or the evaluation of blues in Oliver (1978) – a dominant idea that popular music could be simultaneously a mass music and a music *of* (rather than *for*) ordinary people became apparent (Garofalo 1997, 93–231). Such approaches marked a significant change in the way popular music was valued. Drawing on discourses of folk and art, rock was seen as expressing an authenticity that earlier pop music did not possess (Pickering 1986). Sarah Thornton argues that these discourses were again transformed from the 1980s when dancing and records themselves came to be understood as authentic (Thornton 1995).

So, although the opposition between 'authenticity' and 'artificiality' in the discourses of popular music culture has gone through a number of transformations since the 1960s, it was until recently a key way in which judgements were made about pop music and the values it represents. However, to understand the importance of contemporary pop stars, boy bands or girl groups, we need to do more than take a position on whether we see them as uncomplicated entertainment or plastic fronts for an exploitative music industry. The distinctiveness of contemporary manufactured stars is to be found in three main areas. First, the textual qualities of the singers' performances as part of multimedia texts and the way they articulate star identities draw upon the musical and cultural repertoires of the past in intriguing ways. Second, the way that these texts are used both by the industry and the audience for commercial and cultural ends is characteristic of major shifts in the market for popular music and in the ways it is consumed. Finally, the way these shifts in consumption are contributing to changes in the economics of the industry has a significant influence on how we understand what pop is. To build a full picture we need to take each in order.

The Texts of Twenty-First Century Pop

While the study of the history of popular music shows that today's manufactured pop bands repeat many of the practices of those of past decades, they also have distinctive qualities. The links with the past are mainly to be found in the way that the texts of such stars draw heavily on the repertoires of the Tin Pan Alley pop tradition, while the distinctiveness of contemporary pop is to be found in the way elements from the African-American tradition have been transformed in this new textual form for commercial ends.

Almost all of the music performed by the manufactured stars takes the dominant form of the song, with its conventional patterns of melodic repetition and variation, melodic and lyrical hooks located in the chorus, and themes of love and sex (see Chapter 8). The recordings sound rich and bright through the use of digital drum machines and synthesisers, combined with extensive use of sequenced multitracking to produce a full sound across all four levels of musical organisation, topped with a prominent vocal (Moore 1993, 31–55). However, the recorded music is only part of a wider metatext of personal performance. The songs are produced in such a way that they can be used as the basis for a synchronised routine that emphasises the singers as personalities (and as stars). Stage choreography and dance are prominent parts of this performance, recalling earlier forms of traditional pop with their roots in the song-and-dance routines of music hall.

This analysis, with its emphasis on the traditions of the Tin Pan Alley repertoire, would suggest that the music is read as traditional and old-fashioned. But on the contrary it is understood as modern and up to date. These meanings of modernity are located in the way that manufactured pop draws upon the musical and cultural repertoires of the African-American tradition. Evidence of this can be seen in three distinct qualities.

First, a significant number of today's manufactured stars are mainly groups. Further, the boy bands and girl groups of the 2000s are based upon a form of organisation that has not been seen before in mainstream pop. There is no pretence that the singers are part of a larger music-making ensemble, and none of the groups is shown to be composed of musicians as well as singers. Even more distinctively, there is an equality between the singers within the group that is unusual. Singing groups from nineteenth-century music hall to 1990s boy bands have been organised around a main lead singer and a harmonising chorus or backing singers. The equality between singers is a characteristic of more recent African-American R&B music.

Second, the influence of R&B can also be seen in the stage presence of these pop groups in the way that their routines are derived from the choreography and dress, with its mixing of the glamour of high fashion with street clothes and postures. The music and its performance owe much to the influence of R&B. Spoken or near-spoken singing styles are mixed with a high-key 'emoted' singing style that draws on older gospel-influenced soul styles.

While emerging from the tradition of Tin Pan Alley pop, then, these bands owe significant debts to the African-American repertoire for their musical, vocal and performance practices, most of which are found in contemporary R&B. These organisational and performance practices of R&B are themselves derived from the structure of and earlier generation of rap collectives, where verse lines are shared and turns are taken at the mic (see Toop 2000). It is these cultural links to hip-hop that give R&B, and girl groups/boy bands, their sense of street style and modernity. At the time of writing, and as if to make the point, one of these manufactured bands (Girls Aloud) even had a single called 'Sound of the Underground'. The title of this piece of music, like the performances of any of the manufactured stars, seems to make a claim to be part of a street-based, authentic culture. Of course, the 'borrowing' of elements from an underground/street musical culture is a tried and tested formula for music industry workers who want to make 'modern' mainstream music, but these texts also relate in significant ways to the audiences that consume them, and an exploration of both consumption and production provides a fuller understanding of the phenomenon of manufactured pop.

Consuming Pop

The preferences, values and attitudes that a group of fans share with like-minded people are the basis of their decisions to consume musical entertainment media from a CD through to concert attendance. Because of this, record industry executives attempt to control and transform these fan practices into senses of a coherent and distinct market in such a way that they increase profits for the record company. Fans of manufactured bands, like all consumers of popular music, are therefore as much a part of the political economy of the music industry as they are part of the cultural economy of fandom.

Using market research, major record companies position manufactured pop stars as central to an early-teen audience that has grown significantly in recent years to the point that it now constitutes about 10 per cent of CD sales. This market is now almost as large as the traditional 15–20-year-old market that, since the 1950s, had been understood as the primary market for popular music. The research also shows that CD buying is far more associated with consumers over 30 who now account for 55 per cent of sales (see RIAA 2000). Young consumers of manufactured pop are therefore set against a much older market, which is understood to buy a combination of music from the back catalogue and new releases of artists seen as 'authentic musicians', and a generation of consumers between 20 and 30 who are understood to buy dance music or indie rock.

Younger audiences find that the high media profile of manufactured stars makes them far more accessible than the artists that produce music for the older markets, which require the sorts of cultural capital associated with record collecting or less mainstream media (see Thornton 1995; Straw 1997c). The emphasis on the personality of the manufactured star within both the record industry and fan practices, repeats that of mainstream music aimed at older audiences, but is quite different from the anonymity of music-makers in dance culture. Most significantly, though, record buying is only a small part of fan activity in the market for manufactured stars. This recognition has allowed some workers within the entertainment industry to identify that this is a practice that extends way beyond the younger age group perceived to be the natural consumers of manufactured stars. So, for instance, while television slots for young people have used manufactured pop stars as a staple of programming for 20 years, the extension of this programming to weekend primetime TV has been a more recent recognition of the significant changes in the relationship of older audiences to popular music.

Sheryl Garratt's arguments about pop fandom in the 1970s and 1980s still seem to explain some aspects of the connection of fandom to the manufactured star (Garratt 1984). She counters the dismissive positions taken on young, particularly young women, fans with an examination of the emotional investments of these fans. She argues that fandom is built more around the relationship between fans themselves, than that with the object of their fandom, and she notes the importance of androgyny and sexual ambivalence in the images of stars that attract large young followings.

However, one of the striking characteristics of more recent manufactured pop stars is how they are located within a wider sense of an entertainment industry, and with a wider audience age range. This has some parallels with pop music stardom that were dominant before the 1950s, when popular music stars were also stars of stage and screen. Of course, this is not an identical parallel as the new stardom relies heavily on primetime television rather than film, and audiences engage with the star image in a way that has little to do with the division between 'authentic music-makers' and 'manufactured pop'. Older audiences treat manufactured pop stars with a knowing irony, which glories in celebrity and spectacle. This sensibility has made Tin Pan Alley pop acceptable to a wide spread of audiences from across all ages and social positions. This postmodern sensibility may not translate into new audiences for singles, but it has led to a willingness to make a phone vote, take the kids to a concert or buy a compilation CD.

By focusing our analysis on the way television has been used in manufactured pop in the last few years we can begin to understand how the industry operates in this arena.

Manufacturing Pop

From the perspective of the global, multimedia corporations that dominate the entertainment industry, contemporary manufactured pop can be understood as a recognition of a new pre-teen pop audience, which exercises significant spending power and a wider acceptance of manufactured pop among older audiences, combined with an appreciation of the potential of cross-media marketing strategies. This can be seen most clearly in the commercial and cultural success of the TV shows that followed *Pop Stars* and *Pop Idol*. Although such programmes seem superficially to be simply an updating of the TV variety favourite the talent show, these programmes do not just discover a talented singer or group, but actually reveal the process through which stars are made.

So beyond the selection of a final winner from a cast of all-comers, such shows detail the way individuals learn the skills of the pop star, and juxtapose the opinions of key music industry staff with the audience-democracy of the phone vote. As audiences, we know it is the manager, the producer and the record company executive who will mould our selection for stardom, but we also invest in that star-making process through our participation in the show. In a very real way, before a CD has been released, we have 'made' these new stars. But as the difficulties of sustaining the careers of these TV-created starlets reveals, while the process of star-making is documented and they become famous for being famous, this does not mean that record buyers will sustain their investment.

In many ways the first series of the British *Pop Idol* revealed the tension between TV participation and CD sales. In record industry terms we picked the 'wrong one', and probably self-consciously so. For the investments made by TV viewers in eventual winner Will Young were not sustained into CD sales, and gay Politics students are not the usual stuff of which pop stars are made. Runner-up Gareth Gates, of course, was much more the traditional pop star and transferred to the world beyond the television programme far more readily.

Pop stardom in a music market based upon early-teens and ironic distance is even harder to sustain than traditional teen-based pop, but the short life of the pop star is more than compensated for by the profits of their short media existence for the record industry. Part of this profit is achieved through the old-fashioned economics that it is far better to sell millions of copies of a single release than hundreds of copies of a thousand releases (see Chapter 5), but the rest comes from a reconfiguration of how profit is made in the music industry. These shows were carefully constructed economic activities, owned and controlled by individuals from a generation of semi-independent music industry executives, working with big corporations to generate profits from all aspects of the show: the production costs of the show are paid for by the income from the phone voting; the format of the show is profitably sold to broadcasters throughout the world; the costs of recording, managing and promotions are held within the enterprise, and so are all the revenue streams. In this process record sales are only one part of the source of profit, and it is possible to sustain the activity without record sales.

What is so interesting about this case study, then, is the way that the three elements of text, industry and audience have been so successfully integrated to maximise profits for the entertainment industry. The meanings of modernity articulated by textual elements taken from the African-American tradition are combined with classic Tin Pan Alley techniques to exploit the commercial potential of changes in the audience and mediation of popular music.

Investigate if the people who watch TV programmes like *Pop Idol* are also active CD buyers. Using a questionnaire, find out how many editions of a series an individual watched, and the degree to which they participated in the programme. (Did they want certain individuals to win? Did they vote? Did they read articles on the show in the press? Did they buy the winner's CD?) Then find out about their CD purchases. How many do they buy in a month? Where do they buy their CDs from? Do they download MP3s? Then analyse the results of your survey. Can any conclusions be drawn about the show, about the show as a promotional vehicle, and about TV viewers and CD consumers?

Conclusions

In his book on the independent record company Atlantic, Charlie Gillett recounts an anecdote about Jerry Wexler one of the label's key white producers. The label had originally recorded rhythm & blues and soul music, and to support the black community that had been the source of its artists and commercial success, Wexler went to talk to a group of black students about record production: 'he had hardly begun when he was interrupted by a student wanting to know "How come you are ripping off our culture" Jerry looked at him "What do you mean your culture? It's *my* culture"' (Gillett 1994, 71).

Now, there are many ways in which this story could be interpreted. Wexler clearly felt that he had been so centrally involved in the process of making R&B and soul records that he was immersed in the culture himself. The student, though, recognised the way that African-American cultural forms had been used by white-owned companies to first make a profit out of the black consumers, and then to sell the music more widely to a mainstream white audience. In the process, company executives like Wexler had become very rich. But popular music never simply rose from a single community, and the artists Wexler recorded had learnt to make music by listening to records produced by an earlier generation. In a sense, recorded music is the culture of the record industry. The final dimension to interpreting the story is to be found in the way that a musical form developed within the African-American communities has become a central part of mainstream American culture, and of course world culture. Popular music is as much the culture of the record listener, as it is the music-maker's or record producer's.

Popular music culture is full of these contradictions, and it belongs to all of us and none of us. It is made for us, but we invest it with such important meanings that it is one of the key ways we define who we are. It is more than sound, more than a commodity, more than a consumption activity, and more than a simple historical story. It is so important it deserves serious study. But as an area of scholarship it is also very new and there are vast areas we know very little about. These areas are ready for your contributions.

Bibliography

Abrahams, Roger David 1976: *Talking Black*. Newbury House.

Abrams, Mark 1959: *The Teenage Consumer*. London Press Exchange.

Adorno, Theodor W. 1941/1990: 'On Popular Music', in S. Frith and A. Goodwin, *On Record: Rock, Pop and the Written Word*. Routledge.

Adorno, Theodor W. 1945: 'A Social Critique of Radio Music', in *Kenyon Review* VII(2).

Adorno, Theodor W. 1991: *In Search of Wagner*. Verso.

Adorno, Theodor W. and Horkheimer, Max 1997: *Dialectic of Enlightenment*. Verso.

Alderman, John 2001: *Sonic Boom: Napster, MP3 and the New Pioneers of Music*. Fourth Estate.

Baekland, Frederick 1994: 'Psychological Aspects of Art Collecting', in S.M. Pearce, *Interpreting Objects and Collections*. Routledge.

Bagguley, Paul 1991: 'Post-Fordism and Enterprise Culture: Flexibility, Autonomy and Changes in Economic Organisations', in R. Keat and N. Abercrombie, *The Enterprise Culture*. Routledge.

Bailey, Peter 1986: *Music Hall: The Business of Pleasure*. Open University Press.

Bannerji, Sabita and Baurman, Gerd 1990: 'Bhangra 1984–8: Fusion and Professionalisation in a Genre of South Asian Dance Music', in P. Oliver, *Black Music in Britain: Essays on the Afro-Asian Contribution to Popular Music*. Open University Press.

Barlow, John Perry 1994: 'The Economy of Ideas', at http://www.wired.com/wired/archive/2.03/economy.ideas.html

Barlow, John Perry 1996: 'A Declaration of the Independence of Cyberspace', at http://www.eff.org/~barlow/Declaration-Final.htm

Barlow, William 1995: 'Black Music on Radio in the Jazz Age', in *African American Review* 29(2).

Barlow, William 1999: *Voice Over: The Making of Black Radio*. Temple University Press.

Barnard, Stephen 1989: *On the Radio: Music Radio in Britain*. Open University Press.

Barnard, Stephen 2000: *Studying Radio*. Arnold.

Barnes, Ken 1988: 'Top 40 Radio: A Fragment of the Imagination', in S. Frith, *Facing the Music*. Pantheon.

Barrow, Steve and Dalton, Peter 1997: *Reggae: The Rough Guide*. Rough Guides.

Barthes, Roland and Heath, Stephen 1977: *Image, Music, Text*. Fontana.

Baudrillard, Jean 1983: *Simulations*. Semiotext(e). Inc.

Bayton, Mavis 1997: 'Women and the Electric Guitar', in S. Whiteley, *Sexing the Groove: Popular Music and Gender*. Routledge.

Becker, Howard Saul 1966: *Outsiders: Studies in the Sociology of Deviance*. Free Press.

Berland, Jody 1993a: 'Radio Space and Industrial Time: The Case of Music Formats', in T. Bennett, S. Frith, L. Grossberg, J. Shepherd and G. Turner, *Rock and Popular Music: Politics, Policies, Institutions*. Routledge.

Berland, Jody 1993b: 'Sound, Image and Social Space: Music Video and Media Reconstruction', in S. Frith, A. Goodwin and L. Grossberg, *Sound and Vision: The Music Video Reader*. Routledge.

Boggs, Vernon 1992: *Salsiology: Afro-Cuban Music and the Evolution of Salsa in New York City*. Greenwood Press.

Bourdieu, Pierre 1984: *Distinction: A Social Critique of the Judgement of Taste*. Harvard University Press.

Bowman, Rob 1997: *Soulsville, USA: The Story of Stax Records*. Prentice Hall International.

BPI 2003: 'Markets Statistics', at www.bpi.co.uk

Brackett, David 1991: *Three Studies in the Analysis of Popular Music*. Cornell University.

Brackett, David 2000a: 'James Brown's "Superbad" and the Double-Voiced Utterance', in R. Middleton, *Reading Pop*. Oxford.

Brackett, David 2000b: *Interpreting Popular Music*. University of California Press.

Bradby, Barbara 1992: 'Sampling Sexuality: Gender, Technology and the Body', in *Popular Music* 12(2).

Bradley, Dick 1992: *Understanding Rock 'N' Roll: Popular Music in Britain, 1955–1964*. Open University Press.

Bradley, Lloyd 2000: *Bass Culture*. Viking.

Bratton, J.S. 1986: *Music Hall: Performance and Style*. Open University Press.

Brewster, Bill and Broughton, Frank 1999: *Last Night a DJ Saved My Life: The History of a Disc Jockey*. Headline.

Broven, John 1974: *Rhythm & Blues in New Orleans*. Pelican Publishing Co.

Bull, M. 2000: *Sounding out the City: Personal Stereos and the Management of Everyday Life*. Berg.

Burchill, Julie and Parsons, Tony 1978: *The Boy Looked at Johnny*. Pluto.

Burn, Gary 1987: 'A Typology of "Hooks" in Popular Records', in *Popular Music* 6.

Burnett, Robert 1996: *The Global Jukebox: The International Music Industry*. Routledge.

Cantor, Louis 1992: *Wheelin' on Beale: How WDIA Memphis Became the Nation's First All-Black Radio Station and Created the Sound That Changed America*. Pharos.

Carr, Ian, Fairweather, Digby and Priestley, Brian 1987: *Jazz: The Essential Companion*. Grafton Books.

Carr, Ian 1999: *Miles Davis: The Definitive Biography*. HarperCollins.

Chambers, Iain 1985: *Urban Rhythms: Pop Music and Popular Culture*. St Martin's Press.

Chanan, Michael 1995: *Repeated Takes: A Short History of Recording and Its Effects on Music*. Verso.

Chapple, Steve and Garofalo, Reebee 1977: *Rock 'N' Roll is Here to Pay: The History and Politics of the Music Industry*. Nelson-Hall.

Charters, Samuel Barclay 1982: *The Roots of the Blues: An African Search*. Quartet Books.

Chester, Andrew 1990: 'Second Thoughts on a Rock Aesthetic: The Band', in S. Frith and A. Goodwin, *On Record: Rock, Pop and the Written Word*. Routledge.

Chilton, John 1979: *Jazz*. Teach Yourself Books.

Clarke, Donald 1995: *The Rise and Fall of Popular Music*. Penguin.

Clarke, Gary 1981/1990: 'Defending Ski Jumpers: A Critique of Theories of Youth Subcultures', in S. Frith and A. Goodwin, *On Record: Rock, Pop and the Written Word*. Routledge.

Clarke, Gary 1990: 'Defending Ski-Jumpers: A Critique of Theories of Youth Subcultures', in S. Frith and A.J. Goodwin *On Record: Rock, Pop and the Written Word*. Routledge.

Clarke, Sebastian 1980: *Jah Music: The Evolution of the Popular Jamaican Song*. Heinemann Educational.

Cohen, Albert 1956: *Delinquent Boys: The Culture of the Gang*. Routledge & Kegan Paul.

Cohen, Sara 1991: *Rock Culture in Liverpool: Popular Music in the Making*. Oxford University Press.

Cohen, Stanley 1972: *Folk Devils and Moral Panics: The Creation of the Mods and Rockers*. MacGibbon and Kee.

Cohn, Nik 1989: *Ball the Wall: Nik Cohn in the Age of Rock*. Picador.

Cohodas, Nadine 2000: *Spinning Blues into Gold: Chess Records: The Label That Launched the Blues*. Aurum.

Collin, Matthew 1997: *Altered State: The Story of Ecstasy Culture and Acid House*. Serpent's Tail.

Cook, Richard 2001: *Blue Note Records: The Biography*. Secker & Warburg.

Cosgrove, Stuart 1982: 'Long after Tonight is all Over', in *Collusion* 2.

Crafts, Susan D., Cavicchi, Daniel and Keil, Charles (and Music in Daily Life Project) 1993: *My Music*. Wesleyan University Press.

Cummings, Tony 1975: *The Sound of Philadelphia*. Methuen.

Davis, Stephen and Simon, Peter 1983: *Reggae International*. Thames & Hudson.

Deacon, David 1999: *Researching Communications: A Practical Guide to Methods in Media and Cultural Analysis*. Arnold.

DeNora, Tia 2000: *Music in Everyday Life*. Cambridge University Press.

Di Maggio, Paul, Peterson, Richard A. and Esco Jr, Jack 1972: 'Country Music: Ballad of the Silent Majority', in R.A. Peterson and R.S. Denisoff, *The Sounds of Social Change: Studies in Popular Culture*. Rand McNally.

Du Gay, Paul and Negus, Keith 1994: 'The Changing Sites of Sound: Music Retailing and the Composition of Consumers', in *Media, Culture and Society* 16(3).

Dyer, Richard 1990: *Stars*. BFI Publishing.

Dyer, Richard 1979/1990: 'In Defence of Disco', in S. Frith and A. Goodwin, *On Record: Rock, Pop and the Written Word*. Routledge.

Dyer, Richard and McDonald, Paul 1997: *Stars*. British Film Institute.

Earl, John 1986: 'Building the Halls', in P. Bailey, *Music Hall: The Business of Pleasure*. Open University Press.

Early, Gerald 1995: *One Nation under a Groove: Motown and American Culture*. Ecco.

Eisenstadt, S.N. 1956: *From Generation to Generation: Age Groups and Social Structure*. Free Press.

Eliot, Marc 1990: *Rockonomics: The Money Behind the Music*. Omnibus.

Ellis, John 1982: 'Star/Industry/Image', in C. Gledhill, *Star Signs: Papers from a Weekend Workshop*. British Film Institute Education.

Eyerman, Ron and Jamison, Andrew 1998: *Music and Social Movements: Mobilizing Traditions in the Twentieth Century*. Cambridge University Press.

Fabbri, Franco 1982: 'A Theory of Musical Genre: Two Applications', in D.a.P.T. Horn, *Popular Music Perspectives*. IASPM.

Fiske, John 1992: 'The Cultural Economy of Fandom', in Lisa A. Lewis, *The Adoring Audience: Fan Culture and Popular Media*. Routledge.

Fitzgerald, F. Scott 1922/2000: *Novels and Stories, 1920–1922*. Library of America.

Floyd, Samuel A. 1990: *Black Music in the Harlem Renaissance: A Collection of Essays*. Greenwood Press.

Foucault, Michel 1972: *The Archaeology of Knowledge*. Tavistock Publications.

Friedlander, Paul 1996: *Rock and Roll: A Social History*. Westview Press.

Frith, Simon 1978: *The Sociology of Rock*. Constable.

Frith, Simon 1983: *Sound Effects: Youth, Leisure and the Politics of Rock*. Constable.

Frith, Simon 1987: 'Copyright and the Music Business', in *Popular Music* 7(1).

Frith, Simon 1988a: *Music for Pleasure: Essays in the Sociology of Pop*. Polity Press.

Frith, Simon 1988b: 'The Real Thing: Bruce Springsteen', in S. Frith, *Music for Pleasure: Essays in the Sociology of Pop*. Polity Press in association with Basil Blackwell, Oxford.

Frith, Simon 1988c: 'Why Do Songs Have Words', in S. Frith, *Music for Pleasure: Essays in the Sociology of Pop*. Polity Press in association with Basil Blackwell, Oxford.

Frith, Simon 1988d: 'Playing with Real Feeling: Jazz and Suburbia', in S. Frith, *Music for Pleasure: Essays in the Sociology of Pop*. Polity Press in association with Basil Blackwell, Oxford.

Frith, Simon 1988e: 'The Pleasures of the Hearth – the Making of BBC Light Entertainment', in *Music for Pleasure: Essays in the Sociology of Pop*. Polity Press in association with Basil Blackwell, Oxford.

Frith, Simon 1990: 'Afterthoughts', in S. Frith and A. Goodwin *On Record: Rock, Pop and the Written Word*. Routledge.

Frith, Simon 1992: 'The Industrialization of Popular Music', in J. Lull, *Popular Music and Communication*. Sage.

Frith, Simon 1993: *Music and Copyright*. Edinburgh University Press.

Frith, Simon 1996a: *Performance Matters*. Lawrence & Wishart.

Frith, Simon 1996b: *Performing Rites: On the Value of Popular Music*. Oxford University Press.

Frith, Simon and Goodwin, Andrew 1990: *On Record: Rock, Pop and the Written Word*. Routledge.

Frith, Simon and Horne, Howard 1987: *Art into Pop*. Methuen.

Frith, Simon and McRobbie, Angela 1978: 'Rock and Sexuality', in *Screen Education* 29.

Garfield, Simon 1998: *The Nation's Favourite: The True Adventures of Radio 1*. Faber.

Garofalo, Reebee 1992: *Rockin' the Boat: Mass Music and Mass Movements*. South End Press.

Garofalo, Reebee 1997: *Rockin' Out: Popular Music in the USA*. Allyn & Bacon.

Garratt, Sheryl 1984: 'Teenage Dreams', in S. Steward and S. Garratt, *Signed, Sealed, and Delivered: True Life Stories of Women in Pop Music*. South End Press.

Gates, Henry Louis 1988: *The Signifying Monkey: A Theory of Afro-American Literary Criticism*. Oxford University Press.

Geertz, Clifford 1993: *The Interpretation of Cultures: Selected Essays*. Fontana Press.

Gelatt, Roland 1977: *The Fabulous Phonograph, 1877–1977*. Cassell.

Gendron, Bernard 1986: 'Theodor Adorno Meets the Cadillacs', in T. Modleski, *Studies in Entertainment*. Indiana University Press.

George, Nelson 1986: *Where Did Our Love Go? The Rise & Fall of the Motown Sound*. Omnibus.

George, Nelson 1988: *The Death of Rhythm & Blues*. Omnibus.

George, Nelson 1994: *Urban Romance*. Sceptre.

George, Nelson 1999: *Hip Hop America*. Penguin Books.

Gilbert, Jeremy and Pearson, Ewan 1999: *Discographies: Dance Music, Culture and the Politics of Sound*. Routledge.

Gill, John 1995: *Queer Noises: Male and Female Homosexuality in Twentieth-Century Music*. Cassell.

Gill, Rosalind 2000: 'Justifying Injustice: Broadcasters' Accounts of Inequality in Radio', in C. Mitchell, *Women and Radio*. Routledge.

Gillett, Charlie 1974: *Making Tracks: Atlantic Records and the Growth of a Multi-Billion-Dollar Industry*. W.H. Allen.

Gillett, Charlie 1971: *The Sound of the City: The Rise of Rock and Roll*. Souvenir Press.

Gillett, Charlie 1983: *The Sound of the City: The Rise of Rock and Roll*. Souvenir Press.

Gillett, Charlie 1988: *Making Tracks: Atlantic Records and the Growth of a Multi-Billion Dollar Industry*. Souvenir Press.

Gilroy, Paul 1991: *'There Ain't No Black in the Union Jack': The Cultural Politics of Race and Nation*. University of Chicago Press.

Gilroy, Paul 1993: *The Black Atlantic: Modernity and Double Consciousness*. Harvard University Press.

Gilroy, Paul 1997: *Between Camps: Race and Culture in Postmodernity*. Goldsmith's College, University of London.

Godbolt, Jim 1986: *A History of Jazz in Britain 1919–50*. Paladin.

Godbolt, Jim 1989: *A History of Jazz in Britain 1950–70*. Quartet Books.

Goodwin, Andrew 1992: *Dancing in the Distraction Factory: Music Television and Popular Culture*. University of Minnesota Press.

Gore, Georgiana 1997: 'The Beat Goes On: Trance, Dance and Tribalism in Rave Culture', in H. Thomas, *Dance in the City*. St Martin's Press.

Gourse, Leslie 2000: *The Golden Age of Jazz in Paris and Other Stories About Jazz*. Xlibris Corporation.

Green, Jonathon 1999: *All Dressed Up: The Sixties and the Counter Culture*. Pimlico.

Gribin, Anthony J. and Schiff, Matthew M. 2000: *The Complete Book of Doo-Wop*. Krause.

Grossberg, Lawrence 1992a: *We Gotta Get out of This Place: Popular Conservatism and Postmodern Culture*. Routledge.

Grossberg, Lawrence 1992b: 'The Affective Sensibility of Fandom', in Lisa A. Lewis, *The Adoring Audience: Fan Culture and Popular Media*. Routledge.

Guralnick, Peter 1991: *Sweet Soul Music: Rhythm and Blues and the Southern Dream of Freedom*. Penguin.

Guralnick, Peter 1994: *Last Train to Memphis: The Rise of Elvis Presley*. Little Brown & Company.

Hacker, Scot 2000: *MP3: The Definitive Guide*. O'Reilly.

Hafner, Katie and Lyon, Matthew 1996: *Where Wizards Stay up Late: The Origins of the Internet*. Simon & Schuster.

Hall, Stuart and Jefferson, Tony 1975/1991: *Resistance through Rituals: Youth Subcultures in Post-War Britain*. HarperCollins Academic.

Hall, Stuart 1992: 'The Question of Cultural Identity', in S. Hall, D. Held and D. McGrew, *Modernity and Its Futures*. Polity Press.

Hamm, Charles 1983: *Yesterdays: Popular Song in America*. Norton.

Hamm, Charles 1995: *Putting Popular Music in its Place*. Cambridge University Press.

Hanna, Judith Lynne 1988: *Dance, Sex and Gender: Signs of Identity, Dominance, Defiance, and Desire*. University of Chicago Press.

Haralambos, Michael 1974: *Right On: From Blues to Soul in Black America*. Eddison Press.

Hare, Geoffrey 1999: *A Cultural Maginot Line: Legal Restrictions on Playing English and American Records on French Radio* (publisher unknown).

Harker, Dave 1980: *One for the Money: Politics and Popular Song*. Hutchinson.

Harker, Dave 1985: *Fakesong: The Manufacture of British Folksong: 1700 to the Present Day*. Open University Press.

Harker, Dave 1992: 'Still Crazy after All These Years: What Was Popular Music in the 1960s', in B.J. Moore-Gilbert and J. Seed, *Cultural Revolution? The Challenge of the Arts in the 1960*. Routledge.

Haskins, Jim 1985: *The Cotton Club*. Robson.

Haslam, Dave 1998: 'DJ Culture', in S. Redhead, J. O'Connor and D. Wynne, *The Club Cultures Reader: Readings in Popular Cultural Studies*. Blackwell.

Hatch, David and Millward, Stephen 1987: *From Blues to Rock: An Analytical History of Pop Music*. Manchester University Press.

Hawkins, Stan 1997: 'The Petshop Boys: Musicology, Masculinity and Banality', in S. Whiteley, *Sexing the Groove: Popular Music and Gender*. Routledge.

Hebdige, Dick 1979: *Subculture: The Meaning of Style*. Methuen.

Hebdige, Dick 1987: *Cut 'N' Mix: Culture, Identity, and Caribbean Music*. Methuen

Hendy, David 2000a: *Radio in the Global Age*. Polity Press.

Hendy, David 2000b: 'Pop Music in the Public Services: BBC Radio One and New Music in the 1990s', in *Media, Culture and Society* 22(6).

Hesmondhalgh, David 1996: 'Flexibility, Post-Fortdism and the Music Industries', in *Media, Culture and Society* 15(3).

Hesmondhalgh, David 1997a: 'Post-Punk's Attempt to Democratise the Music Industry: The Success and Failure of Rough Trade', in *Popular Music* 16(3).

Hesmondhalgh, David 1997b: 'The Cultural Politics of Dance Music', in *Soundings* 5.

Hesmondhalgh, David 1998: 'The British Dance Music Industry: A Case Study in Independent Cultural Production', in *British Journal of Sociology* 49(2).

Hesmondhalgh, David 1999: 'Indie: The Institutional Politics and Aesthetics of a Popular Music Genre', in *Cultural Studies* 13(1).

Hesmondhalgh, David 2002: 'Popular Music Audiences and Everyday Life', in D. Hesmondhalgh and K. Negus, *Popular Music Studies*. Arnold.

Hesmondhalgh, David and Melville, Casper 2001: 'Urban Breakbeat Culture: Repercussions of Hip Hop in the United Kingdom', in T. Mitchell, *Global Noise: Rap and Hip-Hop Outside the USA*. Wesleyan University Press.

Hesmondhalgh, David and Negus, Keith 2002: *Popular Music Studies*. Arnold.

Hilliard, Robert L. 1985: *Radio Broadcasting: An Introduction to the Sound Medium*. Longman.

Hilliard, Robert L. and Michael, Keith C. 1992: *The Broadcast Century: A Biography of American Broadcasting*. Focal Press.

Hills, Matt 2002: *Fan Cultures*. Routledge.

Hind, John and Mosco, Stephen 1985: *Rebel Radio: The Full Story of British Pirate Radio*. Pluto Press.

Hirsch, Paul M. 1972/1990: 'Processing Fads and Fashions: An Organisation-Set Analysis of Cultural Industry Systems', in S. Frith and A. Goodwin, *On Record: Rock, Pop and the Written Word*. Routledge.

Hoare, Ian 1975: *The Soul Book*. Eyre Methuen.

Hoggart, Richard 1958: *The Uses of Literacy*. Penguin Books.

Hollows, Joanne and Milestone, Katie 1998: 'Welcome to Dreamsville: A History and Geography of Northern Soul', in A. Leyshon, D. Matless and G. Revill, *The Place of Music*. Guilford Press.

Hornby, Nick 1995: *High Fidelity*. Indigo.

Hoskyns, Barney 1997a: *Beneath the Diamond Sky: Haight-Ashbury 1965–1970*. Bloomsbury.

Hughes, Spike 1993: 'Impressions of Ellington in New York (1933)', in M. Tucker, *The Duke Ellington Reader*. Oxford University Press.

James, Martin 1997: *State of Bass, Jungle: The Story So Far*. Boxtree.

Jameson, Fredric 1990: *Postmodernism, or the Cultural Logic of Late Capitalism*. Verso.

Jenkins, Henry 1992: *Textual Poachers: Television Fans & Participatory Culture*. Routledge.

Jensen, Joli 1990: *Redeeming Modernity: Contradictions in Media Criticism*. Sage Publications.

Jensen, Joli 1992: 'Fandom as Pathology: The Consequences of Characterization', in Lisa A. Lewis, *The Adoring Audience: Fan Culture and Popular Media*. Routledge.

Jensen, Klaus Bruhn 2002: *A Handbook of Media and Communication Research: Qualitative and Quantitative Methodologies*. Routledge.

Johnson, Phil 1996: *Straight Outta Bristol: Massive Attack, Portishead, Tricky and the Roots of Trip-Hop*. Hodder & Stoughton.

Jones, LeRoi 1966: *Blues People: Negro Music in White America*. Jazz Book Club.

Jones, Simon 1988: *Black Culture, White Youth: The Reggae Tradition from JA to UK*. Macmillan.

Jones, Steve 1992: *Rock Formation: Music, Technology, and Mass Communication*. Sage.

Jones, Steve 2002: 'Music That Moves: Popular Music Distribution and Network Technologies', in *Cultural Studies* 16(2).

Kaplan, E. Ann 1987: *Rocking around the Clock: Music Television, Postmodernism, and Consumer Culture*. Methuen.

Katz, David 2000: *People Funny Boy: The Genius of Lee 'Scratch' Perry*. Payback Press.

Kearney, Mary Celeste 1997: 'The Missing Links: Riot Grrrl – Feminism – Lesbian Culture', in S. Whiteley, *Sexing the Groove: Popular Music and Gender*. Routledge.

Keil, Charles 1970: *Urban Blues*. University of Chicago Press.

Keil, Charles and Feld, Steven 1994: *Music Grooves: Essays and Dialogues*. University of Chicago Press.

Keith, Michael C. 1997: *Voices in the Purple Haze: Underground Radio and the Sixties*. Praeger.

Kennedy, Rick 1994: *Jelly Roll, Bix, and Hoagy: Gennett Studios and the Birth of Recorded Jazz*. Indiana University Press.

Kofsky, Frank 1998: *John Coltrane and the Jazz Revolution of the 1960s: Black Nationalism and the Revolution in Music*. Pathfinder Press.

Laing, Dave 1985: *One Chord Wonders: Power and Meaning in Punk Rock*. Open University Press.

Laing, Dave and Tyler, Bob 1998: *The European Radio Industry: Markets and Players*. FT Media & Telecoms.

Langlois, Tony 1992: 'Can You Feel It? DJs and House Music Culture in the UK', in *Popular Music* 11(2).

Larkin, Colin (and Muze UK Ltd) 1998: *The Virgin Encyclopedia of R&B and Soul*. Virgin in association with Muze UK Ltd.

Lee, Stephen 1995: 'Re-examining the Concept of the "Independent" Record Company: The Case of "Wax Trax!" Records', in *Popular Music* 14(1).

Leonard, Marion 1997: 'Rebel Girl, You Are the Queen of My World: Feminism, "Subculture" and Grrrl Power', in S. Whiteley, *Sexing the Groove: Popular Music and Gender*. Routledge.

Lewis, Lisa A. 1992: *The Adoring Audience: Fan Culture and Popular Media*. Routledge.

Lipsitz, George 1994: *Dangerous Crossroads: Popular Music, Postmodernism and the Poetics of Place*. Verso.

Litweiler, John 1990: *The Freedom Principle: Jazz after 1958*. Da Capo Press.

Lomax, Alan (and Stephan Grossman's Guitar Workshop) 1998: *The Land Where the Blues Began: Songs and Stories of America*. Vestapol.

Lomax, John A. and Lomax, Alan 1947: *Folk Song U.S.A.* Duell Sloan and Pearce.

Longhurst, Brian 1995: *Popular Music and Society*. Polity Press.

Lott, Eric 1993: *Love and Theft: Blackface Minstrelsy and the American Working Class*. Oxford University Press.

MacDougald, D. 1941: 'The Popular Music Industry', in P.F. Lazarsfeld and F.F. Stanton, *Radio Research 1941*. Duell, Sloan & Pearce.

Malbon, Ben 1999: *Clubbing: Dancing, Ecstasy and Vitality*. Routledge 1999.

Malone, Bill C. 1985: *Country Music, USA*. University of Texas Press.

Marcus, Greil 1975: *Mystery Train: Images of America in Rock 'N' Roll Music*. E.P. Dutton.

Marks, Anthony 1990: 'Young, Gifted and Black: Afro-American and Afro-Caribbean Music in Britain 1963–88', in P. Oliver, *Black Music in Britain: Essays on the Afro-Asian Contribution to Popular Music*. Open University Press.

Martin, Linda and Segrave, Kerry 1993: *Anti-Rock: The Opposition to Rock 'N' Roll*. Da Capo Press.

Maxwell, Ian 2002: 'The Curse of Fandom: Insiders, Outsiders and Ethnography', in D. Hesmondhalgh and K. Negus, *Popular Music Studies*. Arnold.

McClary, Susan and Walser, Robert 1990: 'Start Making Sense! Musicology Wrestles with Rock', in S. Frith and A. Goodwin, *On Record: Rock, Pop and the Written Word*. Routledge.

McRobbie, Angela 1980: 'Settling Accounts with Subcultures: A Feminist Critique', in S. Frith and A. Goodwin, *On Record: Rock, Pop and the Written Word*. Routledge.

McRobbie, Angela 1984: 'Dance and Social Fantasy', in A. McRobbie and M. Nava, *Gender and Generation*. Macmillan.

McRobbie, Angela 1989: *Zoot Suits and Second-Hand Dresses: An Anthology of Fashion and Music*. Macmillan Education.

McRobbie, Angela 1999: *In the Culture Society: Art, Fashion and Popular Music*. Routledge.

Melly, George 1970: *Revolt into Style: The Pop Arts in Britain*. Allen Lane.

Merriden, Trevor 2001: *Irresistible Forces: The Business Legacy of Napster and the Growth of the Underground Internet*. Capstone.

Middleton, Richard 1990: *Studying Popular Music*. Open University Press.

Middleton, Richard 2000: *Reading Pop: Approaches to Textual Analysis in Popular Music*. Oxford University Press.

Milestone, Katie 1997: 'Love Factory: The Sites, Practices and Media Relationships of Northern Soul', in S. Redhead, J. O'Connor and D. Wynne, *The Clubcultures Reader*. Blackwell Publishers.

Mills, Sara 1997: *Discourse*. Routledge.

Mitchell, Tony 1996: *Popular Music and Local Identity: Rock, Pop and Rap in Europe and Oceania*. Leicester University Press.

MMC (Monopolies and Mergers Commission) 1994: *The Supply of Recorded Music*. HMSO/Department of Trade and Industry.

Mooney, Hughson F. 1954: 'Song, Singers and Society 1890–1954', in *American Quarterly*.

Mooney, Hughson F. 1968: 'Popular Music since the 1920s', in *American Quarterly* 20.

Moore, Allan F. 1993: *Rock: The Primary Text: Developing a Musicology of Rock*. Open University Press.

Morrison, David, E. 1998: *The Search for a Method: Focus Groups and the Development of Mass Communication Research*. University of Luton Press.

Morton, David 2000: *Off the Record: The Technology and Culture of Sound Recording in America*. Rutgers University Press.

Muirhead, Bert 1983: *Stiff: The Story of a Record Label, 1976–1982*. Blandford Press.

Mundy, John 1999: *Popular Music on Screen: From Hollywood Musical to Music Video*. Manchester University Press.

Neale, Stephen 1980: *Genre*. BFI.

Negus, Keith 1992: *Producing Pop: Culture and Conflict in the Popular Music Industry*. Arnold.

Negus, Keith 1996: *Popular Music in Theory: An Introduction*. Polity Press.

Negus, Keith 1999: *Music Genres and Corporate Cultures*. Routledge.

Newton, Francis 1961: *The Jazz Scene*. Penguin.

O'Brien, Lucy 1995: *She Bop: The Definitive History of Women in Rock, Pop and Soul*. Penguin Books.

Oliver, Paul 1963: *The Meaning of the Blues*. Collier Books.

Oliver, Paul 1978: *The Story of the Blues*. Penguin.

Osborne, Ben 1999: *The A-Z of Club Culture*. Hodder & Stoughton.

Paddison, Max 1996: *Adorno, Modernism and Mass Culture: Essays on Critical Theory and Music*. Kahn & Averill.

Palmer, Gareth 1997: 'Bruce Springsteen and Masculinity', in S. Whiteley, *Sexing the Groove: Popular Music and Gender*. Routledge.

Peatman, John G. 1944: 'Radio and Popular Music', in P.F. Lazarsfeld and F.F. Stanton, *Radio Research 1942–1943*. Duell, Sloan & Pearce.

Perry, Steve 1988: 'Ain't No Mountain High Enough: The Politics of Crossover', in S. Frith, *Facing the Music*. Pantheon.

Peterson, Richard A. 1976: *The Production of Culture*. Sage.

Peterson, Richard A. 1990: 'Why 1955? Explaining the Advent of Rock Music', in *Popular Music* 9(1).

Peterson, Richard A. 1997: *Creating Country Music: Fabricating Authenticity*. University of Chicago Press.

Peterson, Richard, A. and Berger, David G. 1975/1990: 'Cycles in Symbol Production: The Case of Popular Music', in S. Frith and A. Goodwin, *On Record: Rock, Pop and the Written Word*. Routledge.

Pickering, Michael 1986: 'The Dogma of Authenticity in the Experience of Popular Music', in G. McGregor and R. White, *The Art of Listening*. Croom Helm.

Plasketes, George 1992: 'Romancing the Record: The Vinyl De-Evolution and Sub-Cultral Evolution', in *Journal of Popular Culture* 26(1).

Porter, Lewis 1998: *John Coltrane: His Life and Music*. University of Michigan Press.

Potter, Russell A. 1995: *Spectacular Vernaculars: Hip-Hop and the Politics of Postmodernism*. State University of New York Press.

Priestley, Brian 1984: *Charlie Parker*. Spellmount: Hippocrene Books.

Priestman, Chris 2002: *Web Radio*. Focal.

Pruter, Robert 1991: *Chicago Soul*. University of Illinois Press.

Raphael, Amy 1995: *Never Mind the Bollocks: Women Rewrite Rock*. Virago.

Redhead, Steve 1990: *The End-of-the-Century Party: Youth and Pop Towards 2000*. Manchester University Press.

Rees, Dafydd, Lazell, Barry and Osborne, Roger 1995: *40 Years of NME [New Musical Express] Charts*. Boxtree.

Regev, Motti 2002: 'The "Pop-Rockization" of Popular Music', in D. Hesmondhalgh and K. Negus, *Popular Music Studies*. Arnold.

Reynolds, Simon 1985: 'New Pop and Its Aftermath', in *Monitor* 4.

Reynolds, Simon 1998: *Energy Flash: A Journey through Rave Music and Dance Culture*. Picador.

RIAA (Recording Industry Association of America) 2000: 'Consumer Profile'.

Richards, Jeffrey 1973: *Visions of Yesterday*. Routledge & Kegan Paul.

Riesman, David 1950/1990: 'Listening to Popular Music', in S. Frith and A. Goodwin, *On Record: Rock, Pop and the Written Word*. Routledge.

Rietveld, Hillegonda C. 1998: *This Is Our House: House Music, Cultural Spaces and Technologies*. Ashgate.

Roe, Keith, E. 1985: 'Swedish Youth and Music: Listening Patterns and Motivations', in *Communication Research* 12(3).

Roe, Keith E. and Lofgren, M. 1988: 'Music Video Use and Educational Achievement: A Swedish Study', in *Popular Music* 7(3).

Roe, Keith, E. 1990: 'Adolescents' Music Use', in K. Roe, U. Carlsson and N. Sverige, *Popular Music Research: An Anthology from Nordicom-Sweden*. Nordicom-Sweden.

Roe, Keith, E. and von Feilitzen, C. 1992: 'Eavesdropping on Adolescence: An Exploratory Study of Listening among Children', in *Communications* 17(2).

Rose, Tricia 1994: *Black Noise: Rap Music and Black Culture in Contemporary America*. Wesleyan University Press.

Ross, Andrew 1989: *No Respect: Intellectuals and Popular Culture*. Routledge.

Roszak, Theodore 1970: *The Making of a Counter Culture: Reflections on the Technocratic Society and Its Youthful Opposition*. Faber.

Rothenbuhler, Eric W. and McCourt, Tom 1992: 'Commercial Radio and Popular Music: Processes of Selection and Factors of Influence', in J. Lull, *Popular Music and Communication*. Sage.

Rothenbuhler, Eric and McCourt, Tom 2002: 'Radio Redefines Itself, 1947–1962', in M. Hilmes and J. Loviglio, *Radio Reader: Essays in the Cultural History of Radio*. Routledge.

Russell, Dave 1997: *Popular Music in England, 1840–1914: A Social History.* Manchester University Press.

Ryan, John 1985: *The Production of Culture in the Music Industry.* New York University Press.

Ryan, John and Peterson, Richard A. 1982: 'The Product Image: The Fate of Creativity in Country Music', in *Sage Annual Review of Communication Research* 10.

Said, Edward W., Jameson, Fredric, Eagleton, Terry and Field Day Theatre Company 1990: *Nationalism, Colonialism, and Literature.* University of Minnesota Press.

Sanchez-Tabernero, Alfonso and Denton, Alison 1993: *Media Concentration in Europe: Commercial Enterprise and the Public Interest.* Europaisches Medieninstitut.

Sanjek, Russell 1988: *American Popular Music and Its Business: The First Four Hundred Years.* Oxford University Press.

Sanjek, Russell and David Sanjek 1996: *American Popular Music Business in the 20th Century.* De Capo.

Sarup, Madan 1993: *An Introductory Guide to Post-Structuralism and Post-Modernism.* Harvester Wheatsheaf.

Saunders, Nicholas 1995: *Ecstasy and the Dance Culture.* Nicholas Saunders.

Savage, Jon 1991: *England's Dreaming: Sex Pistols and Punk Rock.* Faber & Faber.

Scannell, Paddy 1981: 'Music for the Multitude? The Dilemmas of the BBC Music Policy 1923–46', in *Media, Culture and Society* 8(4).

Schiller, Herbert I. 1969: *Mass Communications and American Empire.* A.M. Kelley.

Schwichenberg, C. 1993: *The Madonna Connection.* Westview Press.

Shapiro, Harry Lionel 1999: *Waiting for the Man: The Story of Drugs and Popular Music.* Helter Skelter.

Sharpe, Sue 1976: *'Just Like a Girl': How Girls Learn to Be Women.* Penguin.

Shaw, Arnold 1978: *Honkers and Shouters: The Golden Years of Rhythm and Blues.* Macmillan.

Shaw, Arnold 1987: *The Jazz Age: Popular Music in the 1920s.* Oxford University Press.

Shepherd, John 1980: *Whose Music? A Sociology of Musical Languages.* Transaction Books.

Shepherd, John 1982: *Tin Pan Alley.* Routledge & Kegan Paul.

Shuker, Roy 1994: *Understanding Popular Music.* Routledge.

Shuker, Roy 1998: *Key Concepts in Popular Music.* Routledge.

Sicko, Dan 1999: *Techno Rebels: The Renegades of Electronic Funk.* Billboard Books.

Slutsky, Allan and Silverman, Chuck 1997: *The Funkmasters: The Great James Brown Rhthm Sections 1960 to 1973.* Warner Brothers Publications.

Smith, Chris 1998: *Creative Britain.* Faber & Faber.

Smith, Suzanne E. 1999: *Dancing in the Street: Motown and the Cultural Politics of Detroit.* Harvard University Press.

Southern, Eileen 1983: *The Music of Black Americans: A History.* Norton.

Stearns, Marshall Winslow 1970: *The Story of Jazz.* Oxford University Press.

Stewart, Sue and Sheryl Garratt 1984: *Signed, Sealed, and Delivered: True Life Stories of Women in Pop Music.* South End Press.

Stewart, Tony 1981: *Cool Cats: 25 Years of Rock 'N' Roll Style.* Eel Pie Publishing.

Storey, John 2001: *Cultural Theory and Popular Culture: An Introduction.* Pearson Education.

Straw, Will 1997a: 'Communities and Scenes in Popular Music', in K. Gelder and S. Thornton, *The Subcultures Reader.* Routledge.

Straw, Will 1997b: 'Organized Disorder: The Changing Space of the Record Shop', in S. Redhead, J. O'Connor and D. Wynne, *The Club Cultures Reader: Readings in Popular Cultural Studies.* Blackwell.

Straw, Will 1997c: 'Sizing up Record Collections', in S. Whiteley, *Sexing the Groove: Popular Music and Gender.* Routledge.

Street, John 1992: 'Shock Waves: The Authoritative Response to Popular Music', in D. Strinati and S. Wagg, *Come on Down? The Politics of Popular Media Culture in Post-War Britain.* Routledge.

Street, John 1997: *Politics and Popular Culture.* Polity Press.

Strinati, Dominic 1995: *An Introduction to Theories of Popular Culture.* Routledge.

Sweeney, Philip 1991: *The Virgin Directory of World Music: A Guide to Performers and Their Music.* Virgin.

Tacchi, Jo 1998: *The Consumption of Radio Sound in Domestic Contexts* (publisher unknown).

Tagg, Philip 1987: 'Open Letter: "Black Music", "Afro-American Music" and "European Music"', in *Popular Music* 8(3).

Tagg, Philip 1991: *Fernando the Flute: Analysis of Musical Meaning in an Abba Mega-Hit.* Institute of Popular Music, University of Liverpool.

Taylor, Timothy Dean 1997: *Global Pop: World Music, World Markets.* Routledge.

Thorgerson, Storm and Powell, Aubrey 1999: *100 Best Album Covers.* Dorling Kindersley.

Thornton, Sarah 1990: 'Strategies for Reconstructing the Popular Past', in *Popular Music* 9(1).

Thornton, Sarah 1995: *Club Cultures: Music, Media and Subcultural Capital.* Polity Press.

Thorpe, Edward 1990: *Black Dance.* Overlook Press.

Tomlinson, John 1991: *Cultural Imperialism: A Critical Introduction.* Pinter Publishers.

Toop, David 1995: *Ocean of Sound: Aether Talk, Ambient Sound and Imaginary Worlds.* Serpent's Tail.

Toop, David 2000: *Rap Attack 3: African Rap to Global Hip Hop.* Serpent's Tail.

Townsend, Peter 2000: *Jazz in American Culture.* Edinburgh University Press.

Toynbee, Jason 2000: *Making Popular Music: Musicians, Creativity and Institutions.* Arnold.

Trudgill, Peter 1983: 'Acts of Conflicting Identity: The Sociolinguistics of British Pop Song Pronunciation', in P. Trudgill, *On Dialect: Social and Geographic Perspectives.* Blackwell.

Tucker, Mark 1993: *The Duke Ellington Reader.* Oxford University Press.

Turow, Joseph 1992: *Media Systems in Society: Understanding Industries, Strategies, and Power.* Longman.

van der Merwe, Peter 1989: *Origins of the Popular Style: The Antecedents of Twentieth-Century Popular Music.* Clarendon Press/Oxford University Press.

Vermorel, Fred and Vermorel, Judy 1985: *Starlust: The Secret Life of Fans*. W.H. Allen.

Vermorel, Judy and Vermorel, Fred 1989: *Fandemonium! The Book of Fan Cults and Dance Crazes*. Omnibus.

Vincent, Rickey 1996: *Funk: The Music, the People, and the Rhythm of the One*. St Martin's Griffin.

Vincent, Ted 1995: *Keep Cool: The Black Activists Who Built the Jazz Age*. Pluto Press.

Wale, Michael 1972: *Voxpops: Profiles of the Pop Process*. Harrap.

Wall, Tim 1999: *Constructing Popular Music Radio: Music and Cultural Identity in Radio Station Discourse*. University of Birmingham.

Wall, Tim 2000: 'Policy, Pop and the Public: The Discourse of Regulation in British Commercial Radio', in *Journal of Radio Studies*.

Walser, Robert 1993: *Running with the Devil: Power, Gender and Madness in Heavy Metal Music*. Wesleyn University Press.

Ward, Andrew 1997: 'Dancing around Meaning (and the Meaning around Dance)', in H. Thomas, *Dance in the City*. St Martin's Press.

Ward, Brian 1998: *Just My Soul Responding: Rhythm and Blues, Black Consciousness and Race Relations*. UCL Press.

Weiner, Robert G. 1999: *Perspectives on the Grateful Dead: Critical Writings*. Greenwood Press.

Welch, Walter Leslie and Read, Oliver 1959: *From Tin Foil to Stereo. Evolution of the Phonograph*. Howard W. Sams & Co./Bobbs-Merrill Co.

Werner, Craig Hansen 1999: *A Change is Gonna Come: Music, Race and the Soul of America*. Plume.

Whiteley, Sheila 1992: *The Space between the Notes: Rock and the Counter-Culture*. Routledge.

Whiteley, Sheila 1997a: 'Little Red Rooster vs the Honky Tonk Woman', in S. Whiteley, *Sexing the Groove: Popular Music and Gender*. Routledge.

Whiteley, Sheila 1997b: *Sexing the Groove: Popular Music and Gender*. Routledge.

Williams, Raymond 1963: *Culture and Society 1780–1950*. Penguin Books in association with Chatto & Windus.

Williams, Raymond 1976: *Keywords: A Vocabulary of Culture and Society*. Fontana/Croom Helm.

Willis, Paul 1976: 'The Man in the Iron Cage: Notes on Method', in *Cultural Studies* 9.

Willis, Paul 1990: *Common Culture: Symbolic Work at Play in the Everyday Culture of the Young*. Open University Press.

Wilson, Ollie 1974: 'The Significance of the Relationship between Afro-American Music and West African Music', in *The Black Perspective in Music* 2 (Spring).

Winston, Brian 1998: *Media Technology and Society: A History: From the Telegraph to the Internet*. Routledge 1998.

Wise, Sue 1984: 'Sexing Elvis', in S. Frith and A. Goodwin, *On Record: Rock, Pop and the Written Word*. Routledge.